AN EQUAL START?

Providing quality early education and care for disadvantaged children

Edited by Ludovica Gambaro, Kitty Stewart
and Jane Waldfogel

First published in Great Britain in 2014 by

Policy Press
University of Bristol
6th Floor, Howard House
Queen's Avenue
Clifton
Bristol BS8 1SD
UK
t: +44 (0)117 331 4054
f: +44 (0)117 331 4093
tpp-info@bristol.ac.uk
www.policypress.co.uk

North America office:
Policy Press
c/o The University of Chicago Press
1427 East 60th Street
Chicago, IL 60637, USA
t: +1 773 702 7700
f: +1 773 702 9756
sales@press.uchicago.edu
www.press.uchicago.edu

British Library Cataloguing in Publication Data
A catalogue record for this book is available from the British Library.

Library of Congress Cataloging-in-Publication Data
A catalog record for this book has been requested.

ISBN 978 144731 051 8 (hardcover)

Cover design by Policy Press
Front cover: image kindly supplied by www.istock.com
Printed and bound in Great Britain by CPI Group (UK) Ltd,
Croydon, CR0 4YY
The Policy Press uses environmentally responsible print partners.

Contents

List of figures, tables and appendices

Figures

Tables

Appendices

Acknowledgements

We are very grateful to the Nuffield Foundation for the funding which made this project possible, and in particular to Sharon Witherspoon for her guidance at the outset. We also owe a special thanks to Alison Garnham, who had the initial idea from which the project grew.

We were lucky to have an expert advisory group who were very generous with their time, attending meetings and providing thought-provoking comments and feedback throughout the project: many thanks to Kathy Sylva, Naomi Eisenstadt, Paul Gregg, Bronwen Cohen and Colette Fagan.

We held an authors' conference at the London School of Economics and Political Science (LSE) in September 2012 to discuss the country case studies and to begin to think about common themes and policy lessons. We would like to say a large thank you to the discussants and panellists, all of whom provided invaluable input and insights which made for a very stimulating day and helped shape our conclusions. Alongside our advisory group members, thanks to Eva Lloyd, David Piachaud, Ingela Naumann, Wendy Sigle-Rushton, Heather Joshi, Liz Washbrook, Sandra Mathers and Miho Taguma.

We are grateful to our colleagues at the Centre for Analysis of Social Exclusion (CASE) for feedback at various meetings and seminars and in more informal conversations. We owe a large debt to Jane Dickson for organising the conference, the budget and more or less everything else, to Cheryl Conner for putting the book together and for helping us with the conference, and to Ben Grubb for his help at the very last round. Colleagues in the Department of Social Policy also provided key input and advice at various points: a special thank you to Jane Lewis for very useful early discussions on the value of a comparative project and on countries to consider; to Stephen Jenkins for discussions on data issues; and to Isabel Shutes for putting us in touch with Deb Brennan.

This has been a joint project with Daycare Trust (now Family and Childcare Trust), and we would like to thank Kate Groucutt and Jill Rutter for their input throughout. Finally, we are grateful to all our national case study authors for sharing their knowledge and expertise and for cheerfully meeting all our deadlines and requests. We have learned a huge amount from our collaboration and have enjoyed it immensely too.

Notes on contributors

Yusuf Emre Akgündüz is a PhD student at the Utrecht University School of Economics, the Netherlands. His research field is labour economics with a focus on female labour force participation, childcare and childcare quality.

Deborah Brennan, Professor in the Social Policy Research Centre (SPRC), University of New South Wales, Australia, is one of Australia's leading researchers in gender and social policy. She is the author of *The Politics of Australian Child Care* (Cambridge University Press, 1998) and co-editor with Louise Chappell of *'No Fit Place for Women'. Women in New South Wales Politics, 1856–2006* (UNSW Press, 2006), as well as numerous scholarly articles in the areas of gender, politics and family policy. Together with researchers from SPRC she recently prepared a strategic assessment of the children's services industry for the Community and Disability Services Ministerial Advisory Council. She is a former President of the Australian Political Science Association and a member of the Feminism and Institutionalism International Network.

Anne Lise Ellingsæter is Professor of Sociology at the Department of Sociology and Human Geography, University of Oslo, Norway. Her main fields of research are family policy, work–family relations, gender and work, working time regimes and fertility.

Jeanne Fagnani is Emeritus Senior Research Fellow at CNRS (National Centre for Scientific Research), University of Paris-Sorbonne, France, and Associate Researcher at the Institut de Recherches Economiques et Sociales (Paris). She has written extensively on family policy, work–life balance policies, childcare, mothers' employment and fertility levels in France and Germany. She is Co-editor in Chief of the *Revue française des affaires sociales* (a peer-reviewed journal published by the national Ministère des solidarités et de la cohésion sociale).

Marianne Fenech is a Senior Lecturer at the Institute of Early Childhood, Macquarie University, Australia. She teaches in undergraduate and postgraduate units in early childhood policy, management and leadership. Her research draws on critical approaches to quality early childhood education to promote policy and practice that furthers the rights and interests of young children.

Ludovica Gambaro was Research Officer at the Centre for Analysis of Social Exclusion (CASE) at the time of writing and is now Research Officer at the Centre for Longitudinal Studies, Institute of Education, University of London. Her research interests include early childhood services, family policy and labour market policy.

Katherine Magnuson is an Associate Professor of Social Work at the University of Wisconsin-Madison, USA, and the Associate Director for research and training at the Institute for Poverty Research. Her research focuses on the wellbeing and development of economically disadvantaged children and their families. She examines how disparities in socio-economic status affect children's development, and how these effects may be altered by policies and programmes, especially early childhood education programmes.

Helen May is Professor of Education, and the former Dean of the University of Otago College of Education, Dunedin, New Zealand. She has been involved in advocacy work and advisory roles regarding a range of policy initiatives in both New Zealand and international settings. A key area of work during the 1990s was the development work for the New Zealand early childhood national curriculum, *Te Whāriki*, with Margaret Carr. Her research interests are in early childhood policy, history and curriculum, and she is the author of a number of books on the history and politics of early years education.

Pamela Oberhuemer moved from London to Munich in the mid-1970s and worked for over 30 years at the State Institute of Early Childhood Research (IFP), Germany. She was lead researcher of a study commissioned by the German Federal Ministry for Family and Youth Affairs on the early childhood workforce in the 27 European Union (EU) countries, which was published in 2010 (with Inge Schreyer and Michelle Neuman) in both English and German. In 2011 she conducted a systematic analysis of continuing professional development systems in Denmark, England, Hungary, Italy, Slovenia and Sweden, commissioned by the Deutsches Jugendinstitut for a nation-wide initiative (WiFF) funded by the German Federal Ministry for Education and Research. Pamela is one of three academic editors of the journal *Early Years – An International Research Journal*.

Janneke Plantenga is Professor of Economics at the University of Utrecht, the Netherlands. Her research interest focuses on labour market flexibilisation, the reconciliation of work and family and

(European) social policy. She has written widely on the redistribution of unpaid work, changing working time patterns, childcare issues and modernising social security. She is the Dutch expert and coordinator of the European Network of Experts on Gender Equality (ENEGE).

Jill Rutter is the Research Manager at Family and Childcare Trust where she has worked on a large research study on informal childcare. At present she is working on a study on the early years built environment and a study about consumer rights in the childcare sector. Jill is also an Associate Fellow in migration at the Institute for Public Policy Research (ippr), the UK's leading think tank, where she previously worked as a Senior Research Fellow. Here she undertook work on migrant integration and public service responses. Prior to joining ippr, Jill was Senior Lecturer in Education at London Metropolitan University. From 1988–2001 she was a policy adviser at the Refugee Council, London. She has also worked as a secondary school teacher and on development projects in India. In addition to her work on education and migration, she has a longstanding interest in housing and child poverty issues.

Kitty Stewart is Associate Professor of Social Policy at the London School of Economics and Political Science (LSE) and Research Associate at the Centre for Analysis of Social Exclusion. Her current research focuses on the effect of policy on child poverty and children's life chances, and the relationship between household income and wider outcomes. Recent publications include *Towards a More Equal Society? Poverty, Inequality and Policy Since 1997* (Policy Press, 2009), co-edited with John Hills and Tom Sefton.

Jane Waldfogel is the Compton Foundation Centennial Professor for the Prevention of Children's and Youth Problems at Columbia University School of Social Work, New York, and Visiting Professor at the Centre for Analysis of Social Exclusion (CASE) at the London School of Economics and Political Science (LSE). She has written extensively on the impact of public policies on child and family wellbeing. Her current research includes studies of work–family policies, poverty measurement and inequality and social mobility across countries.

ONE

Introduction

Ludovica Gambaro, Kitty Stewart and Jane Waldfogel

In recent decades, the provision of early childhood education and care (ECEC) has risen up the policy agenda right across the globe. One central driving force has been the increasing labour force participation of women, which has created a growing demand for childcare services for preschool age children. Governments have encouraged and subsidised these services for a number of reasons. Concerns about child poverty have figured prominently in countries such as the UK, while the need to tackle social exclusion among immigrant groups has been a factor in many continental European countries. Demographic change has also been important. Rising rates of lone parenthood have created fiscal pressure in countries where the state has traditionally stepped in in the absence of a male breadwinner. In some countries, for example Germany, the policy goal of facilitating work–family balance has been coupled with that of promoting fertility rates.

At the same time, there has been growing interest in the value of early education from a child development perspective. Research has increasingly underlined the importance of what happens in a child's early years for their later life chances (for a review, see Almond and Currie, 2011). Evidence from a wide range of countries indicates that children who have had exposure to preschool education do better at school, and that the benefits are long lasting (Heckman et al, 2010; Ruhm and Waldfogel, 2012).

Two points in particular emerge clearly from the research into the impact of ECEC. The first is the importance of quality: children stand to gain much more where the quality of provision is higher (Shonkoff and Phillips, 2000; Blau, 2001; Baker and Milligan, 2008; Sylva et al, 2011). What is understood by quality can vary between (and within) countries but broadly, children appear to do best in settings in which adults interact with children in a responsive, sensitive and stimulating way. If care is low quality the expected benefits do not materialise, and some provision may even be damaging to children's prospects. Thus, while at its best childcare is far more than just somewhere to park children while parents are working, not all settings will promote children's cognitive, social and emotional development: *what happens* in a setting is crucial.

The second point is that ECEC appears to make the most difference to children from disadvantaged backgrounds (Ruhm and Waldfogel, 2012). There are a number of possible reasons for this. Children from higher-income backgrounds are more likely to have access to books and educational toys at home, and more likely to be taken on trips to museums and parks which widen their horizons and stimulate their thinking; the added value of attending an early education setting will be greater for children who do not already enjoy these benefits. Many children from immigrant families will speak a different language with their parents, so early education gives them exposure to the national language before they start school. Other children may hear only a limited range of vocabulary at home, may live in cramped conditions with less space to run or play physical games, or may have parents whose attention is distracted by younger siblings or financial pressures.

Thus while childcare provision makes it possible for parents – or more particularly mothers – to go out and work in the paid labour market, children themselves can gain from high-quality early education and care. In principle, this looks like a win-win situation: high-quality care can help tackle income poverty in the short term (and gender inequality in the medium term) while improving children's life chances by preparing them for future learning.

However, *delivering* on this potential 'double dividend' poses clear challenges. Most significantly, high-quality provision is expensive. In the context of scarce resources, the policy goal of making ECEC more universally available is often prioritised over improving quality (Kamerman and Kahn, 2001; West, 2006). But focusing predominantly on ensuring availability and affordability is not adequate if we are interested in fostering child development.

This book brings together eight country studies and examines the issues governments face when they try to expand early childhood provision and make sure that it is an equitable and high-quality service. Our starting point was the UK, where investment in services for young children over the last 15 years has gone a long way towards improving both the accessibility and the quality of early years provision, but continuing challenges remain. Our idea for this comparative volume grew from a belief that the experience of a diverse set of countries would offer new perspectives on how these challenges might be addressed.

Of course, systems of provision and the policies underpinning them vary substantially across countries. Some countries, for example France, have a strong nursery education tradition and offer a school-based service to all children age three and above, while providing parents with generous and universal childcare subsidies for younger children (Martin, 2010). In the Nordic countries, on the other hand, services for children under school age have developed since the 1960s, albeit at varying speeds, and are rooted in the pedagogical tradition, with hardly any distinction between children of different age groups (Leira, 2002). By contrast, English-speaking countries have been historically characterised by low levels of ECEC and by a more marginal role for the state, with perhaps the exception of Australia (O'Connor et al, 1999; Brennan, 2002).

However, despite different starting points, all governments are confronted with the pressure of providing early education and care and face dilemmas regarding the policy instruments to be used to achieve this goal. This book explores how services are organised and how policies are designed in different countries. The aim is not that of favouring 'fast policy transfer'; rather, the idea underpinning the book can be described as 'contextualised policy learning' (Mahon, 2006), whereby attention is given to how policies work on the ground and to the contexts in which they are embedded. We asked each of our authors to address the same question: How does your country ensure access to high-quality early childhood education and care for disadvantaged children? Their answers are rich in policy detail and empirical evidence, and offer new ideas and insights – although, as often as not, they highlight common policy challenges rather than identifying clear solutions.

The rest of this introductory chapter takes the following structure. We begin by discussing current evidence on the impact of early education and care for children's outcomes. We then turn to explore the purpose of this book in more detail. We discuss our rationale for choosing the eight countries and consider some broad similarities and differences between them, drawing on international data. Finally, we provide a brief overview of each of the country chapters, highlighting the key policy issues that arise in each one.

Why does it matter? What we know about early education and care and children's outcomes

A growing body of evidence points to the importance of ECEC for child development, and hence its potential impact on longer-term educational, employment and wider social outcomes. Initially, such evidence came from US evaluations of small-scale trials, including the

Perry Preschool project, which provided high-quality early childhood education to a randomly selected group of disadvantaged children in Michigan. Studies which have followed the Perry children into their forties have found long-term gains attached to enrolment in the programme, including improvements in educational attainment, employment and earnings, as well as social benefits such as reduced criminal activity (see, for example, Karoly et al, 2005; Heckman et al, 2010). Waldfogel (2006) discusses evaluations of other similar experimental programmes, all of which point to substantial gains in cognitive achievement.

These evaluations have been influential, despite small sample sizes, because the randomised project design allows us to be confident that identified effects are causal and do not simply reflect hidden differences between families, such as differing parental attitudes to education. However, while they offer solid guidance for the impacts of small, high-quality interventions on very disadvantaged children, they are less helpful in relation to universal or large-scale programmes (Baker, 2011). In this respect, evidence from European countries is illuminating. This strand of research has made use of regional variations in service provision, birthday cut-offs or rigorous econometric techniques to get close to identifying causal effects in the absence of randomised design (see Ruhm and Waldfogel, 2012 for a review). For example, studies in France, Norway and Denmark have exploited variation in local provision to examine the effects of the expansion of universal preschool programmes during the 1960s and 1970s, and found positive benefits for attainment and later labour market participation (Havnes and Mogstad, 2011; Bingley and Westergaard-Nielsen, 2012; Dumas and Lefranc, 2012). More recently, universal prekindergarten programmes have been implemented in a number of US states, and the related research points to positive short-term effects on children's literacy and maths scores and on socio-emotional development (Gormley et al, 2005, 2008; Magnuson et al, 2007a, 2007b; Wong et al, 2008).

In England, the best available evidence comes from an observational study, the Effective Provision of Preschool Education (EPPE) project, which observed children in a range of different preschool settings in 1997 and tracked their progress on into compulsory schooling. Children who had attended preschool had higher levels of cognitive and social-behavioural outcomes on entry to primary school than children who had not (Sylva et al, 2004). Follow up studies found that positive effects were still apparent at the end of primary school (Sylva et al, 2008). Higher-quality preschool continued to predict maths, science and social-behavioural outcomes at age 14 (Sylva et al, 2012b).

Analysis of the Organisation for Economic Co-operation and Development's (OECD) education survey, the Programme for International Student Assessment (PISA), also indicates that early education can have lasting effects. In nearly all OECD countries, 15-year-olds who had attended pre-primary education outperformed those who had not: even after controlling for socioeconomic background, a year of preschool was associated with a test score improvement of 33 points, close to the 39 points linked to a year of formal schooling (OECD, 2011a). Using these same data, Mostafa and Green (2012) estimate that if Sweden and the UK had had universal preschool programmes in place in the early 1990s, Sweden would been seven places higher up the OECD league table in PISA 2009, and the UK twelve places higher up.

Aside from the generally positive impact of early education on later outcomes, two further findings emerge clearly from the research in this field. The first is that the quality of provision matters; not all formal provision is alike. Studies that assess both the quality of provision and children's outcomes are relatively rare, and the available evidence is largely observational, but findings are very consistent: children make more progress in settings with high 'process quality', meaning settings where interactions between adults and children are warm and responsive. This is in turn associated with particular structural features, most notably staff qualifications and child-to-staff ratios (see, for example, Ruopp et al, 1979 for a rare example of experimental research in this area, and literature reviews in Shonkoff and Phillips, 2000; Vandell and Wolfe, 2000; Blau, 2001).

The OECD PISA analysis finds the strongest association between preschool education and later test scores in countries that have invested to improve the quality of provision (OECD, 2011a), while in England the EPPE results also underline the importance of quality. The study rated the quality of provision using the Early Childhood Environment Rating Scale (ECERS), which includes observation of classroom practice and interactions between staff and children. Higher quality was found to be strongly associated with more highly qualified staff, and with the presence of trained teachers in particular. The effect of preschool experience on outcomes at entry to school was greater where the quality of early education had been higher. By age 11, attendance at a low-quality preschool setting carried almost no benefits in comparison to non-attendance; and by 14, only the highest quality settings appeared to have left a mark (Sylva et al, 2011, 2012b).

There is also evidence that low-quality provision can have a negative impact. In Canada, studies examining a childcare subsidy programme that led to big increases in the use of non-parental childcare found significant negative effects on socio-emotional outcomes, health, and the vocabulary of young children. Researchers attributed these effects in part to declines in parental health and relationship quality (in turn linked to more hostile, less consistent parenting), and in part to the fact that most of the childcare taken up was informal and of poor quality (Baker and Milligan, 2008; Lefebvre et al, 2011).

The second clear finding is that gains are largest for children from low-income or immigrant households, and for those with less educated parents. Indeed, in many studies the positive effects are confined to these groups (Ruhm and Waldfogel, 2012). In England, the EPPE study finds a stronger effect of high-quality preschool on children from disadvantaged backgrounds (Sylva et al, 2011, 2012a). In the US, studies of prekindergarten and kindergarten expansion find larger effects for families with low levels of education, low-income, immigrant or non-English speaking backgrounds, and families from disadvantaged neighbourhoods (Gormley et al, 2005, 2008; Magnuson et al, 2007a; Figlio and Roth, 2009; Fitzpatrick, 2010; Dhuey, 2011). The studies cited earlier of preschool expansion in Denmark, France and Norway all find stronger effects for disadvantaged children, in particular the children of less educated mothers in both Denmark and Norway (Havnes and Mogstad, 2011; Bingley and Westergaard-Nielsen, 2012; Dumas and Lefranc, 2012). Studies by Spieß et al (2003) for Germany and Fredriksson et al (2010) for Sweden find that preschool attendance closes gaps in attainment at age 12 or 13 between children of immigrants and children with native-born parents.

One question on which research is less clear, however, concerns the benefits of ECEC for *younger* children – those under three years old. Most of the research cited so far focuses on preschool programmes for children aged three, four and five. There is less research into the impact of formal provision for under threes. A wide range of literature looks at the impact of maternal employment during a child's first year and is fairly consistent in identifying negative effects for health, cognitive and socio-behavioural development, especially where mothers work full time, although the effects vary by the quality of alternative care provided, by the quality of maternal care, and also by the extent to which employment leads to increases in income (see the discussion in Waldfogel, 2006).

Studies of maternal employment at ages one and two generally find either positive or neutral effects for children's cognitive outcomes, although long hours of group care have been linked to negative social and behavioural outcomes, particularly for boys, and again the quality of provision seems important (see Langlois and Liben, 2003; Waldfogel, 2006). These findings suggest that some exposure to high-quality group ECEC provision, perhaps part time, might have a positive impact on child development for one- and two-year-olds, as it does for older children, but research that has focused specifically on this question, largely for two-year-olds, has been inconclusive. For France, Goux and Maurin (2010) (making use of regional variation in availability) find that enrolment in nursery school at age two rather than three shows no significant relation to later school achievement, while an observational study by Caille (2001) finds only slightly less likelihood of children being held back a class in their later schooling if they started attending at age two rather than three, although results are larger for children of immigrants. For England, Sylva et al (2012a) find very little medium-term advantage associated with starting preschool at age two rather than three. On the other hand, in Germany, Felfe and Lalive (2011) find that centre-based care for nought- to three-year-olds is associated with small developmental benefits for the average child and larger and lasting benefits for children from lower-income families.

So while there is strong evidence that preschool attendance is beneficial once children reach three, it is less clear that we should worry about access to group settings before that point. On the other hand, just as for older children, there is good evidence that where children do attend, the *quality* of provision makes a significant difference to outcomes. And, in practice, in all the countries in our study, use of formal provision for the under threes is rising as maternal employment increases. So making formal services for babies and infants both accessible and high quality is an increasing priority for policy.

The purpose and scope of this book

The literature reviewed so far offers solid evidence that investing in high-quality ECEC can have positive returns for child development as well as facilitating female labour force participation, but it provides little guidance on *how* to deliver such services. This kind of analysis – focused on the ways government can intervene – has been carried out chiefly by the OECD, particularly an influential review, *Starting Strong*, which offered a detailed analysis of countries' different institutional arrangements and the common policy issues that emerge in relation to early education and care (OECD, 2001, 2006). Our approach in this book is similar to that in *Starting Strong*, providing an updated account for the eight countries we cover. However, we look at policy through a particular lens, focusing specifically on the extent to which policies in different countries enable disadvantaged children to receive high-quality provision.

Our examination of policy distinguishes between three main policy tools: provision (who directly provides early education and care?), regulation and funding. In all the countries included in the book, early education and care is delivered, albeit to a varying extent, by a mixed economy of providers, with providers from the state sector, the voluntary sector and often also the private for-profit sector operating alongside one another. The existence of a mixed economy is important and interesting for a number of reasons. For one thing, who the providers are determines the *nature* of the services available: in several countries staff qualifications, ethos and opening hours vary sharply between sectors. A variety of providers may offer parents the possibility of choosing the service that best fits their needs. But it can also lead to fragmentation, where children are segregated or enjoy little continuity, moving from one provider to another depending on their age, the time of year, or even the time of day.

Second, the presence of a variety of providers makes the state's role more complicated. Where government provides services directly (as in most compulsory education systems), questions of how much to spend, how to spend it, and how to improve and monitor quality remain. But when voluntary or for-profit providers are involved, influencing the cost and quality of services becomes more challenging. The government has two broad policy mechanisms – funding and regulation. How best to deploy them to deliver on the dual goals of child development and adequate childcare for working parents leads to numerous policy dilemmas. For example, should governments focus regulation on quality or should they also attempt to control prices? Are high regulatory standards for all settings necessary or should governments allow the market to operate freely, with parents choosing the standard of care they prefer for their children? If the latter, how can they ensure that children from lower-income families are not priced out of better quality options? Can governments encourage or incentivise quality improvements without mandating them? And if the state is subsidising for-profit providers, how can we be sure the funding goes towards improving quality and not boosting profits?

These are the challenges we set out to examine in this book. Our goal was to learn from the experience of a range of countries grappling with these issues. To achieve this we aimed to bring together detailed discussion of the 'nuts and bolts' of policy with empirical evidence on the extent to which children from disadvantaged families do in fact access early education and care services, and on the quality of the provision they receive. Empirical evidence of this kind is not always easily available. Because governments have turned their attention to the issue relatively recently, and because administrative responsibility has traditionally been split across departments, official statistics are often patchy and rarely contain information specific to disadvantaged children. Better data collection is indeed an OECD recommendation in this field (OECD, 2006, 2011c). Notwithstanding these challenges, the authors of each of our country chapters have managed to shed light on how successfully national policies operate in practice for disadvantaged children, by retrieving information from a variety of sources, including up-to-date government or research reports, and in some cases by carrying out new analysis on recent data.

The advantage of comparative international research is that it enables us to examine a wider variety of policies and systems of provision. But it also poses some formidable challenges. First and foremost, early education and care arrangements are deeply embedded in national socioeconomic systems, cultural values and norms. This is a point that comparative scholars have amply explored, touching on different aspects of service provision (for example, Michel and Mahon, 2002; Cameron and Moss, 2007; Kremer, 2007; Leira and Saraceno, 2008; Scheiwe and Willekens, 2009). Early education and care reflect different responses to the question of how far the state should support families in their dual role of providing for children financially and caring for them (Gornick and Meyers, 2003; Lewis, 2006; Saraceno, 2011). They also reflect national variations in the organisation of the school system (Moss and Penn, 1996; Scheiwe and Willekens, 2009). More generally, countries' different approaches relate to national specific norms and practices concerning the primacy of market forces in the allocation of services and resources (O'Connor et al, 1999). In short, national differences in the organisation of children's care and education are deeply rooted in different historical developments and reflect the wider set of relations between families, the market and the state.

While our focus in this book is firmly on current policy developments, each country case is introduced with reference to its specific historical trajectory. But it should be clear that our objective is not so much to understand the *causes* of national differences. Rather, our interest lies in exploring what *consequences* such different arrangements have for children, and for disadvantaged children in particular. In that respect, the contextual differences across countries become less salient. Furthermore, while we pay attention to different policy levers – provision, funding and regulation – we also consider how the *combination* of policy choices affect disadvantaged children.

Thus, we maintain throughout the book a focus on the possible tensions or synergies across various policies within each country, so that our attention to policy details does not lead to discussing individual features in isolation from the context in which they emerge.

The second challenge of bringing together the experience of different countries relates to the understanding of quality. The problem is twofold – not only does quality mean something different in each country, it is also a broad concept, which encompasses different dimensions. Yet, while we acknowledge that there is no single quality metric, our view is that some features are indispensable for services to be responsive to children's needs and able to foster their development. These features include sufficient resources and standards to ensure that children are safe, that staff are adequately paid and trained, and that the types of practices that take place in settings have high pedagogical value. Although these conditions seem quite obvious they are not achieved in several countries; and where they are, they are greatly facilitated by existing policy arrangements.

Other aspects of quality matter too. For example, in France an important aspect of quality is a sufficient social mix within individual nurseries, which resonates with the idea that early childhood services should contribute to social cohesion. Likewise, continuity of arrangements is relevant in some contexts but not others, and is explored where appropriate.

The final challenge we face relates to the definition of disadvantage. The position and the characteristics of disadvantaged children vary markedly across the countries considered here. For one thing, levels of inequality and poverty vary significantly across the countries considered, as we will illustrate later. Furthermore, not all aspects of disadvantage are salient in each country. Income is an important dimension, and one that most of the authors look at, but other dimensions matter too. Immigration status is a key factor in some of the countries examined, notably in Germany, Norway and the Netherlands. The position of Māori and Aboriginal children is discussed in the chapters on New Zealand and Australia. Thus, disadvantage is defined *within* each chapter in order to be relevant to the specific national context. One gap, however, is the important theme of disability, missing mainly for reasons of space. Disability is far from a homogenous category: children with certain disabilities may be well accommodated by a specific system of services while others may not. A meaningful discussion would have required authors to delve into these issues, and space was simply not adequate. However, the book offers a useful starting point for investigating this theme. Lack of subsidies and weak regulatory systems serve all children poorly, but particularly those with additional needs.

The countries

Our comparative study includes eight countries: Australia, France, Germany, the Netherlands, New Zealand, Norway, the UK and the US. We had three main criteria driving our choice of case studies. First, we restricted ourselves to industrialised countries. While there are interesting developments in the provision of ECEC in many areas of the globe (see, for example, Penn, 2004 for an overview of initiatives in developing countries), we wanted to explore approaches to provision in countries with similar income levels to the UK. Second, we chose countries that rely on a range of providers from different sectors to deliver early education and care, ruling out those where the state directly provides the bulk of services. As noted earlier, the issues that arise in funding and regulating services are much more complex where a range of providers is involved. Third, we sought to capture a variety of different country experiences, and to include countries that had undertaken recent reforms or were actively grappling with the questions raised here.

The countries chosen thus have some commonalities, but are also very different. In particular, the 'mixed economy' of services includes different types of organisations depending on the country. In the UK, early education and care is delivered in part by the state, and in part by both for-profit and non-profit organisations. Among for-profit settings, there is a conspicuous presence of commercial chains, as is the case in Australia, New Zealand and the US. The presence of commercial providers raises important questions, which we explore in the book. In other countries, such as Germany, there is a stronger tradition of collaboration between the state and the third sector: the voluntary sector delivers the majority of early education provision in a wider context in which voluntary sector providers are heavily involved in the delivery of other services, including health and education.

There are also differences in relation to whether early childhood services have been seen traditionally as primarily educational or primarily as childcare, or whether they are fully integrated (Kaga et al, 2010; Moss, 2010). France is notable because it has a strong tradition of a two-tier system, whereby children aged three to five are catered for by the school system (albeit not compulsory), and 'childcare' refers to children under three. Norway and New Zealand have an integrated system: the education and care of children falls under the responsibility of the education ministry and is seen as educational in the broadest sense of the word. The distinction between education and care is also fuzzy in other countries, where there may be an overlap between preschool and day-care services.

This overlap reflects the fact that the expansion of services has blurred the historical distinctions between childcare and education, and providing services that meet both goals is now a widespread ambition, even in countries without a history of integrated provision. Relatedly, the term 'early childhood education and care' has gained widespread acceptance as the most appropriate way to refer collectively to the services discussed in this book. We have encouraged chapter authors to use this term, but in places it has been more natural for them to use the term that is common in a particular country – 'kindergarten' in Norway, for example, is used for services for children aged one to six. Where different terminology is used, chapter authors explain and clarify this as they go.

In the rest of this section we present some background data for the eight countries to provide some context for the case studies that follow.

Table 1.1 presents some immediate similarities and differences between the countries. One obvious source of difference is population size: included are some of the smaller countries in the world (Norway and New Zealand) as well as one of the larger ones, the US. On the other hand, all eight are higher-income countries, although with a per capita income which ranges from $PPP25,000 (Purchasing Power Parity) in New Zealand to nearly twice that in Norway. But while all are rich countries, income is distributed very differently across the eight, with a divide between the four Anglophone countries, where child poverty and income inequality are above the OECD average, and the four more egalitarian European countries. Lone parenthood rates also vary substantially, from a low of 11% in the Netherlands to a high of 26% in the US. These differences are clearly relevant to the provision of ECEC: there may be stronger demand for childcare in one-adult households, while providing high-quality services may be both more important and more challenging and expensive in countries with higher child poverty rates. At the same time, child poverty rates will, to some extent, reflect the availability of affordable and trusted childcare services. A further demographic factor that will affect demand for childcare is the fertility rate, which is above the OECD average in all the countries except Germany.

Table 1.2 shows employment indicators of female and maternal labour market participation. Employment rates for women are at or above the OECD average in all cases, ranging from a low of 70% in

Table 1.1: Background statistics on case study countries

	Popula-tion (million) 2011	GDP per capita ($PPP) 2009	Gini coefficient 2008	Child poverty rate 2008	Lone parent-hood rate 2007	Total fertility rate 2009
Australia	22.6	34,259	0.315	14.0	16.8	1.90
France	63.1	29,578	0.293	9.3	13.5	1.99
Germany	82.2	32,255	0.295	8.3	15.0	1.36
Netherlands	16.7	36,358	0.294	9.6	11.1	1.79
New Zealand	4.4	24,706	0.330	12.2	23.7	2.14
Norway	4.9	47,676	0.250	7.8	25.0	1.98
UK	62.4	32,147	0.342	13.2	21.5	1.94
US	313.1	41,761	0.378	21.6	25.8	2.01
OECD average			0.314	12.3	14.9	1.74

Notes: GDP per capita is given in 2005 $PPP. Gini coefficient for Australia is 2007/08 and for New Zealand and UK 2008/09. Child poverty rate shows percentage of children living in households below 50% equivalised median income; UK figure is 2007. Lone parenthood rate shows percentage of children aged 0–17 living with one parent. Lone parenthood for Norway is 2011.

Sources: Population and GDP from United Nations Development Programme (UNDP) Human Development Database (http://hdr.undp.org/en/statistics/). Child poverty rate from OECD Social Indicators, *Society at a Glance* 2011. Gini coefficient from OECD database on income distribution and poverty (www.oecd.org/els/social/inequality). Lone parenthood rate and total fertility rate from OECD (2011b) except lone parenthood in Norway which is from Statistics Norway (www.ssb.no/barn/)

Table 1.2: Female employment rates in case study countries

	Employment rate for women aged 25–54 (%) 2009	Part-time employment as a share of total, women (%) 2009	Maternal employment, youngest child under 3 (%) 2007	Maternal employment, youngest child 3–5 (%) 2007
Australia	72	34	48	n/a
France	77	21	54	64
Germany	75	39	36	55
Netherlands	80	56	69	68
New Zealand	74	30	45	61
Norway	84	22	81	88
UK	74	35	53	58
US	70	14	54	63
OECD average	71	22	52	61

Notes: Part-time employment data are 2005 for US. Maternal employment data for Australia are 2005 and for Norway 2009.

Source: OECD (2011b) except maternal employment for Norway, which is from Meld St 6 (2010–11) *Likestilling for likelønn* [*Gender equality for equal pay*], Table 6.1

the US to a high of 84% in Norway. However, interesting differences emerge in relation to both part-time work and maternal employment. Part-time work is extremely common in the Netherlands (56%), and also common in Germany, the UK, Australia and New Zealand, where roughly one-third of women work part time. This contrasts with the situation in France, Norway and especially the US, where part-time employment is the exception. In relation to employment in the first few years of a child's life, in six of our countries barely half of women undertake employment in the first three years. The Netherlands (69%) and Norway (81%) stand out here. In the years between three and five the gaps close slightly, but a divide remains between Norway, where 88% of mothers work, and the other countries, in which no more than two-thirds do.

Table 1.3 shows enrolment in ECEC at different ages in 2008. In several countries participation has increased significantly since that date, as discussed in the country chapters, but these are the latest comparable figures published by the OECD. From age three onwards enrolment is at least 80% in all countries except Australia and the US, and from age four effectively universal except in these same two countries. Of course, Table 1.3 does not tell us whether attendance is part time or full time, whether it works effectively as childcare as well as early

Table 1.3: Enrolment rates in childcare and early education services, 2008 (%)

	Under 3 years	3 years	4 years	5 years
Australia	29	12	53	100
France	42	99	100	101
Germany	18	87	95	96
Netherlands	56	n/a	100	99
New Zealand	38	88	95	100
Norway	51	92	95	96
UK	41	82	97	99
US	31	36	58	73
OECD average	30	60	80	92

Notes: Enrolment rates for under three-year-olds concern formal childcare arrangements such as group care in childcare centres, registered childminders based in their own homes looking after one or more children and care provided by a carer at the home of the child. Enrolment rates for three- to five-year-olds concern those enrolled in formal preschool services, and in some countries four- and five-year-olds in primary schools. The reported figure for three-year-olds in the Netherlands was implausible (below 1%) and has not been included. In some countries enrolment has increased significantly since 2008, especially for the under threes.

Source: OECD Family Database (www.oecd.org/els/social/family/database)

education, whether children have access to highly trained staff and in what ratios, and whether children from disadvantaged backgrounds are the children most likely to miss out or least likely to receive the best provision. These questions are explored in the country case studies, and we return to them in our concluding chapter.

Table 1.3 shows much lower, and more varied, enrolment rates in relation to children under three, ranging from 18% of children in Germany to 56% in the Netherlands (although by 2012 enrolment had reached 27% in Germany for this age group). In part, low enrolment rates for young children reflect a growing movement across countries towards helping parents to remain at home with children during their first year of life. Figure 1.1 shows that, with the exception of the US, all our countries provide the right to at least nine months combined maternity and parental leave; and in practice, in all but the US a parent can remain at home for at least a year.[1] Not all of this leave is paid, but Norway, France and Germany provide the *equivalent* of full pay for at least nine months.[2]

For children aged between one and three, variation in enrolment rates is likely to reflect a combination of (related) factors: maternal employment; the cost, accessibility and quality of formal provision; and a certain amount of ambiguity about the value of formal provision for children aged between one and three (which in turn may reflect the mixed evidence discussed earlier in this chapter). As the country chapters will show, there is only one country in our study in which there is no divide in the options available for children under and over three: Norway, in which one- to six-year-olds are all provided for in the same kindergartens as part of a social pedagogical tradition within which kindergarten attendance is largely accepted as positive for the development of one- and two-year-olds as well as older children. In most countries, the provision of places for under threes has been driven by labour market rather than child development demands – providing care where parents need it, but not because children do – although several countries (including the UK, France and Germany) are now making moves to provide some part-time provision for two-year-olds, whether parents are working or not.

Finally, Table 1.4 shows OECD figures for public expenditure on early education, childcare and other 'benefits in kind', which include family services, but not spending on broader social policy domains such as health and housing. These numbers provide a rough guide both to differences in overall spending between countries, and to the way spending is structured across age groups. For instance, in the UK and New Zealand spending is strongly concentrated on children aged

Figure 1.1: Maternity and parental leave policies in case study countries, 2008

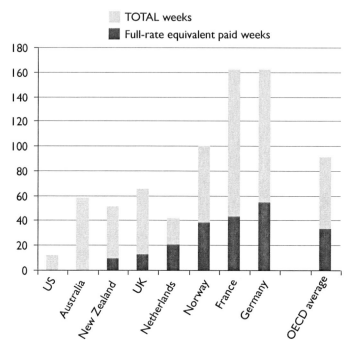

Notes: The figure shows the combined total of maternity and parental leave entitlement. Maternity leave figures alone are misleading because some countries have short maternity leaves plus longer parental leave which parents can share between them. 'Full rate equivalent paid weeks' shows the duration of leave in weeks' payment as a percentage of average earnings received by the claimant over this period. Payments include child rearing benefit (for example, *Complément de libre choix d'activité* in France). In the Netherlands, fathers have a right to 26 weeks' leave that cannot be transferred to mothers; this is not shown in the figure.

Sources: OECD (2011b, Figure 4.1). Data refer to 2008. In 2011 Australia introduced the right to 18 weeks' leave paid at the minimum wage and an additional two weeks for partners. This is not reflected in the figure.

between three and five, while in France it is more evenly spread. These figures provide some interesting context that readers may wish to return to as they read the country chapters, although they should be used with a little caution for a number of reasons. Inevitably, in international comparisons of this kind, there are questions about whether countries have captured precisely the same categories. In addition, the per child numbers are calculated as a share of median income, which varies both because of total national income and because of the income distribution: Norway is both rich and relatively equal, so median income is higher than in the UK. Thus, while average

Table 1.4: Public spending per child on childcare, early education and other benefits in kind as a share of median working-age household income, 2007 (%)

Age of child	Australia	France	Germany	Netherlands	New Zealand	Norway	UK	US
0	4.1	19.3	2.8	11.8	0.7	7.0	2.6	1.7
1	6.0	19.3	3.0	12.0	1.0	10.5	2.6	1.2
2	6.5	25.0	7.5	12.1	1.4	14.1	4.8	1.3
3	11.1	36.5	21.1	12.3	34.4	31.2	41.2	8.2
4	23.5	37.0	23.3	36.7	38.2	32.7	45.3	12.4
5	31.7	37.0	23.5	37.0	24.6	33.0	30.8	15.6
Average per child 0–5	13.8	29.0	13.5	20.3	16.7	21.4	21.2	6.7
Total spending as a share of GDP (%)	0.65	1.66	0.75	1.39	0.79	1.45	1.13	0.55

Notes: Spending per child includes spending on childcare, education and 'other benefits in kind'. The latter covers spending exclusively for families (for example, family outreach). Spending on other social policy areas such as health and housing is not included.

Data presented in the final row differs from the OECD social expenditure database as it takes direct taxes into account.

Source: OECD (2011b, Figures 1.11, 2.4)

spending per child looks similar in the two countries, it will be higher in $PPP terms per child in Norway (as indeed is reflected in the table's bottom line, which shows significantly higher spending in Norway as a share of gross domestic product, GDP). Nevertheless, the figures provide a useful broad tool for thinking about the scale and shape of investment in ECEC in different countries, and we revisit them in the conclusions.

One final general note before we turn to introduce the individual chapters. In discussing charges and subsidies, chapter authors frequently use their own national currency. To aid interpretation, we have included a currency conversion table as an Appendix to this opening chapter.

Overview of the country chapters

The volume begins with the UK. As Ludovica Gambaro, Kitty Stewart and Jane Waldfogel document, ECEC provision in the four nations that make up the UK has come a long way in the past 15 years, but there are still considerable gaps and challenges in the extent to which disadvantaged children access high-quality ECEC. The entitlement to part-time preschool means that nearly all three- and four-year-olds have some exposure to ECEC, but concerns remain about access beyond the entitlement and about the quality of provision. Financial support is only available to those in work, and even then it is only a partial subsidy, with parents having to pay at least 30% of the cost of a place. With regard to quality, staff qualifications in the UK – in particular, in the large private, voluntary and independent sector – are low in comparison to other countries, and there is evidence that low-income children are particularly likely to attend low quality provision in that sector. Although local authorities are encouraged to reward quality using local funding formulae, they receive little or no extra funding for this. Outside the entitlement, settings can only improve quality if they can pass the cost on to parents, and costs are already very high. One positive note is that in England, three- and four-year-olds in more deprived areas are relatively protected by the fact that they are much more likely than children from better-off areas to attend maintained settings, where staff include qualified teachers. While the situation in the UK is challenging, the authors do offer some suggestions for improvements, including expanding maintained nursery classes to deliver the entitlement (including for two-year-olds), raising and equalising qualification levels across all settings, and extending supply-side subsidies to cover younger children, to make care affordable for parents.

The Norwegian case, as described by Anne Lise Ellingsæter, provides an interesting contrast to the UK. Universal access to 'kindergarten' is legislated as a social right for children aged one to six, and indeed the great majority of children in this age group – 90% – are enrolled. Like in the UK, the private sector is quite heavily involved in actual service delivery (with about half of all institutions privately owned), but, unlike in the UK, this has not prevented the system from delivering generally high-quality provision, in large part because of the education levels of ECEC staff, including a high share of graduate pedagogues (teachers specialising in the early years). As the author discusses, recent policy efforts have focused on expanding access to services at a reasonable cost for parents as well as strengthening the quality of services, with positive results in relation to the inclusion of children who come from low-income households or whose parents have lower levels of education.

France, like Norway, is a leader in the ECEC arena. But, as documented in the chapter by Jeanne Fagnani, while France has achieved universal preschool provision for children aged three and up in high-quality écoles maternelles, it faces challenges in the supply of care for children under the age of three. There is a shortfall of places, and participation is strongly graded by social class, with children of non-working, low-income or low-educated parents less likely than their more advantaged peers to participate and, in particular, less likely to attend a *crèche* (childcare centre). To meet the shortfall (and to expand employment opportunities for low-skilled women), the government is taking steps to expand the supply of childminders, even though most parents, given a choice, would prefer a *crèche*, which is seen as a higher-quality form of provision. The supply concerns have meant that the thrust of recent policy efforts has been to expand the number of places available, even if this means potentially reducing quality (by, for example, permitting lower staff qualifications and increased child-to-staff ratios).

The Netherlands system of ECEC also has divisions by social class, as we learn in the chapter by Emre Akgündüz and Janneke Plantenga. Private day-care centres provide care for young children whose parents are employed, often on a part-time basis but with the potential to attend full time and year-round. Publicly funded playgroups, in contrast, are more child-centred, focus only on children aged two to four, and cover only about 10 hours a week and 42 weeks per year. Because of the difference in focus, playgroups tend to serve children from lower-income families and minority backgrounds; they also host special programmes for disadvantaged children. The authors provide new evidence on the relative quality of care children receive in the two types of programmes, using data from the Pre-COOL survey for two-year-olds. Reassuringly, they find that the average quality of care on offer in playgroups is at least as good as that provided by private day-care centres, suggesting that low-income and minority children are not disadvantaged by their disproportionate attendance in that sector. However, they also find that within the private day-care sector, higher-income children tend to receive care of higher quality than their lower-income peers.

The final European case is Germany. As Pamela Oberhuemer documents, Germany is experiencing a rapid expansion of provision in the ECEC sector, motivated by concerns related to gender equity and female labour force participation, educational achievement of children and social inclusion of groups at risk, in particular children from families with a migration background. The change has been particularly dramatic in the Western part of the country, where levels of provision were traditionally very low. Since 1996, all children from the age of three have been entitled to a nursery or family day-care place, and that entitlement is now to be extended downwards to reach children aged one and two. However, thus far, it is mostly the more highly educated and higher-income families who are accessing ECEC for younger children, in part because mothers in these families are most likely to be employed. Young children with a migration background are much less likely than their peers to be enrolled both before and after age three, in spite of the entitlement to provision from three upwards.

The next two chapters turn to New Zealand and Australia. Helen May chronicles the remarkable changes in ECEC policy that have occurred in New Zealand over the past few decades, with the establishment of a universal entitlement to preschool for three- and four-year-olds, subsidies for children under the age of three and a commitment to quality that included the goal of having 100% of staff in the sector be qualified teachers. While New Zealand has now entered a period of retrenchment (with, for example, a freeze in funding for the three- and four-year-old entitlement and a revision of the teacher target to 80% rather than 100%), at least part of the stated purpose for this is to free up funds that can be focused on increasing access and quality for the most vulnerable children. It remains to be seen what the net effect of these reforms will be for disadvantaged children, and for the system as a whole.

ECEC in Australia is also undergoing reform, but in a complex federal landscape. As Deborah Brennan and Marianne Fenech chronicle in their chapter, current national initiatives include an aspiration to provide all children with high-quality preschool, staffed by trained teachers, in the year before school entry. There are also efforts to improve quality through an early years learning framework. However, considerable local and state variation remains, and the chapter points to concerns about whether children from lower-income families will be priced out by quality improvements. The preschool offer is not free, although it is intended that cost should not be a barrier to entry. Enrolment is not universal and children from low-income families are less likely to attend than their higher-income peers. A further complicating factor in the Australian context is the large role that has been played by the private sector, including for-profit providers.

Our final case, the US, is in some ways not dissimilar from Australia. As Katherine Magnuson and Jane Waldfogel discuss, responsibilities are split between federal and state (and local) governments, and as in Australia the private sector (including for-profit providers) plays a large role. And, as in Australia, significant disparities in enrolment are evident, with low-income children and children of immigrants less likely than their peers to be enrolled, and less likely to be in formal school or centre-based care. Low-income children also attend care of lower average quality than that attended by higher-income children. The authors discuss current policy initiatives to reduce disparities, including efforts to expand and improve the federal Head Start programme for low-income children, federal and state quality improvement efforts, and state and local expansions of prekindergarten programmes serving three- and four-year-olds.

Policy implications

The volume concludes with a chapter by Kitty Stewart, Ludovica Gambaro, Jane Waldfogel and Jill Rutter, drawing out the policy implications from the country studies. While the country contexts and particular challenges vary, some common themes emerge. To summarise briefly here, we argue that free and universal provision (as for three- and four-year-olds in the UK, France and New Zealand) is the most effective way to achieve high enrolment rates. Where there are charges, it is important that they are income-related and generous at the bottom of the income distribution, and that subsidies cover the children of non-working as well as working parents. Subsidies should also be transparent and stable, with at least the option that they flow directly from state to provider, without the need for reimbursement. Income-related fees (operated in many countries including France, Norway and Germany), rather than tax credit or reimbursement systems, may be the simplest way of achieving this.

The most effective way to ensure that the settings lower-income children attend are high quality is to raise standards overall. Quality is understood a little differently in different countries, with variations in the emphasis on curriculum and monitoring and structural indicators, but the level of staff qualifications is a constant. All children benefit from access to a graduate teacher or early years professional, but disadvantaged children stand to gain the most.

To ensure that lower-income children are not priced out by quality improvements in services that charge fees, strong minimum regulations are important, and state subsidies should also be linked to the quality of provision (for example, to staff qualification levels), rather than a flat rate to all providers. This allows providers to raise quality without passing the cost on to parents, and lets parents choose higher-quality provision without paying a heavy top-up. Subsidies linked to quality are currently rare, but New Zealand provides an example. Supply-side subsidies to settings in disadvantaged areas (similar to the 'pupil premium' used in compulsory schooling in England in Wales) are another important way of supporting the quality of provision in areas where parents might not be able to afford it.

We also draw out particular lessons for countries operating a 'mixed economy' of provision, including a for-profit sector. There is no evidence in our country studies that competition between providers in a mixed economy itself drives quality improvement. Perhaps because quality is hard for parents to observe, competition seems to be dominated by price, as the Netherlands case illustrates. Several countries, including the UK, US and Australia, are seeking to encourage parents to be more responsive to quality differences by publishing quality ratings, but policy makers should be aware that without the measures described above this is likely to lead to a greater socio-economic gradient in access to quality. The recent expansion of for-profit provision in Norway indicates that a for-profit sector can form a part of a high-quality and equitable system of provision, but this appears to work because of tight regulation, including high minimum standards for staff qualifications and limits on both prices and profits, alongside generous government funding of the sector. Furthermore the sector is still relatively small, and the Australian experience shows how a more substantial for-profit sector, including large corporations, can be powerful enough to resist regulatory reforms.

Finally, we conclude that, while there are certainly ways in which resources can be spent more effectively than at present, and potential gains from trading off different aspects of quality with each other – for example, letting child-to-staff ratios rise slightly to fund higher-qualified staff – many of our suggestions for how to improve both quality and access require increased spending. We argue that most of the countries in this study need to be prepared to invest a greater share of national income in ECEC. This investment will pay off in the short run by making it easier for mothers to choose to work, reducing child poverty and increasing growth, and in the long run by boosting children's long-term life chances. Not least important, it is also in the current interests of the wellbeing of young children of all backgrounds.

Notes

[1] In the Netherlands parental leave is organised as an individual right, rather than a family right: parents cannot transfer their entitlement between them. Fathers are entitled to 26 weeks of parental leave, mostly unpaid, which can be taken up flexibly (for example, part time). If both the father *and* the mother take their respective leave, the cumulative duration is over a year.

[2] Here the total duration of the leave is weighted by the level of compensation. In Germany, for example, payment is 67% of net earnings for 12 months.

References

Almond, D. and Currie, J. (2011) 'Human capital development before age five', in O. Ashenfelter and D. Card (eds) *Handbook of Labor Economics*, Amsterdam: North Holland, Vol 4, Part B, pp 1315–486.

Baker, M. (2011) 'Innis Lecture: Universal early childhood interventions: What is the evidence base?', *Canadian Journal of Economics*, vol 44, no 4, pp 1069-105.

Baker, M. and Milligan, K. (2008) 'Maternal employment, breastfeeding, and health: Evidence from maternity leave mandates', *Journal of Health Economics*, vol 27, no 4, pp 871–87.

Bingley, P. and Westergaard-Nielsen, N. (2012) 'Intergenerational transmission and day care', in J. Ermisch, M. Jantti and T. Smeeding (eds) *From Parents to Children: the Intergenerational Transmission of Advantage*, New York: Russel Sage Foundation, pp 190-203.

Blau, D. (2001) *The Child Care Problem*, New York: Russell Sage Foundation.

Brennan, D. (2002) 'Australia: Child care and state-centered feminism in a liberal welfare regime', in S. Michel and R. Mahon (eds) *Child Care and the Welfare State Restructuring: Gender and Entitlements at the Crossroads*, New York and London: Routledge, pp 95–112.

Caille, J.P. (2001) 'Scolarisation à 2 ans et réussite de la carrière scolaire au début de l'école élémentaire', Éducations and Formations, vol 60, pp 7–18.

Cameron, C. and Moss, P. (2007) *Care Work in Europe: Current Understandings and Future Directions*, London and New York: Routledge.

Dhuey, E. (2011) 'Who benefits from kindergarten? Evidence from the introduction of state subsidization', *Educational Evaluation and Policy Analysis*, vol 33, no 1, pp 3–22.

Dumas, C. and Lefranc, A. (2012) 'Early schooling and later outcomes', in J. Ermisch, M. Jantti and T. Smeeding (eds) *From Parents to Children: the Intergenerational Transmission of Advantage*, New York: Russel Sage Foundation, pp 164-88.

Felfe, C. and Lalive, R. (2011) *How Does Early Childcare Affect Child Development?*, Mimeo, University of St Gallen.

Figlio, D. and Roth, J. (2009) 'The behavioral consequences of pre-kindergarten participation for disadvantaged youth', in J. Gruber (ed) *The Problems of Disadvantaged Youth: An Economic Perspective*, Chicago, IL: University of Chicago Press, pp 15-41.

Fitzpatrick, M.D. (2010) 'Preschoolers enrolled and mothers at work? The effects of universal prekindergarten', *Journal of Labor Economics*, vol 28, no 1, pp 51–85.

Fredriksson, P., Hall, C., Johansson, E.A. and Johansson, P. (2010) 'Do preschool interventions further the integration of immigrants? Evidence from Sweden', in E.A. Johansson (ed) *Essays on Schooling, Gender and Parental Leave*, Economic Studies, 121, Uppsala: Department of Economics, Uppsala University, pp 45-68.

Gormley, J., Gayer, T., Phillips, D. and Dawson, B. (2005) 'The effects of universal pre-K on cognitive development', *Developmental Psychology*, vol 41, no 6, pp 872–84.

Gormley, W.T., Phillips, D. and Gayer, T. (2008) 'Preschool programs can boost school readiness', *Science*, vol 320, no 5884, pp 1723–4.

Gornick, J.C. and Meyers, M. (2003) *Families that Work: Policies for Reconciling Parenthood and Employment*, New York: Russell Sage Foundation.

Goux, D. and Maurin, E. (2010) 'Public school availability for two-year olds and mothers' labour supply', *Labour Economics*, vol 17, no 6, pp 951–62.

Havnes, T. and Mogstad, M. (2011) 'No child left behind: Subsidized child care and children's long-run outcomes', *America Economic Journal – Economic Policy*, vol 3, no 2, pp 97–129.

Heckman, J.J., Moon, S.H., Pinto, R. and Savelyev, P.A. (2010) 'The rate of return to the HighScope Perry Preschool Program', *The Journal of Public Economics*, vol 94, no 1–2, pp 114–28.

Kaga, Y., Bennett, J. and Moss, P. (2010) *Caring and Learning Together*, Paris: UNESCO.

Kamerman, S.B. and Kahn, A.J. (2000) 'Child and family policies in an era of social policy retrenchment and restructuring', in K. Vleminckx and T.M. Smeeding (eds) *Child Well-being, Child Poverty and Child Policy in Modern Nations: What Do We Know?*, Bristol: Policy Press, pp 501–26.

Karoly, L.A., Kilburn, M.R. and Cannon, J.S. (2005) *Early Childhood Interventions: Proven Results, Future Promise*, Santa Monica, CA: RAND Distribution Services.

Kremer, M. (2007) *How Welfare States Care: Culture, Gender and Parenting in Europe*, Amsterdam: Amsterdam University Press.

Langlois, J.H. and Liben, L.S. (2003) 'Child care research: An editorial perspective', *Child Development*, vol 74, no 4, pp 969–75.

Lefebvre, P., Merrigan, P. and Roy-Desrosiers, F. (2011) *Quebec's Childcare Universal Low Fees Policy 10 Years After: Effects, Costs and Benefits*, CIRPEE Working Paper 11-01 (www.cirpee.org/fileadmin/documents/Cahiers_2011/CIRPEE11-01.pdf).

Leira, A. (2002) *Working Parents and the Welfare State: Family Change and Policy Reform in Scandinavia*, Cambridge: Cambridge University Press.

Leira, A. and Saraceno, C. (eds) (2008) *Childhood Changing Contexts*, Bingley: Emerald.

Lewis, J. (2006) 'Introduction: Children in the context of changing families and welfare states', in J. Lewis (ed) *Children, Changing Families and Welfare States*, Cheltenham and Northampton, MA: Edward Elgar, pp 1–24.

Magnuson, K.A., Ruhm, C. and Waldfogel, J. (2007a) 'Does prekindergarten improve school preparation and performance?', *Economics of Education Review*, vol 26, no 1, pp 33–51.

Magnuson, K.A., Ruhm, C. and Waldfogel, J. (2007b) 'The persistence of preschool effects: Do subsequent classroom experiences matter?', *Early Childhood Research Quarterly*, vol 22, no 1, pp 18–38.

Mahon, R. (2006) 'The OECD and the work/family reconciliation agenda: Competing frames', in J. Lewis (ed) *Children, Changing Families and Welfare States*, Cheltenham and Northampton, MA: Edward Elgar, pp 173–97.

Martin, C. (2010) 'The reframing of family policy in France: Actors, ideas and instruments', *Journal of European Social Policy*, vol 20, no 5, pp 410–21.

Michel, S. and Mahon, R. (eds) (2002) *Child Care and the Welfare State Restructuring: Gender and Entitlements at the Crossroads*, New York and London: Routledge.

Moss, P. (2010) 'Early childhood education and care', in S.B. Kamerman, S. Phipps and A. Ben-Arieh (eds) *From Child Welfare to Child Well-Being*, Dordrecht: Springer, pp 371–84.

Moss, P. and Penn, H. (1996) *Transforming Nursery Education*, London: Paul Chapman.

Mostafa, T. and Green, A. (2012) *Measuring the Impact of Universal Preschool Education and Care on Literacy Performance Scores*, LLAKES Research Paper 36, London: Centre for Learning and Life Chances in Knowledge Economies and Societies (www.llakes.org).

O'Connor, J.S., Orloff, A. and Shaver, S. (1999) *States, Markets, Families: Gender, Liberalism, and Social Policy in Australia, Canada, Great Britain, and the United States*, Cambridge: Cambridge University Press.

OECD (Organisation for Economic Co-operation and Development) (2001) *Starting Strong: Early Childhood Education and Care*, Paris: OECD.

OECD (2006) *Starting Strong II: Early Childhood Education and Care*, Paris: OECD.

OECD (2011a) *PISA in Focus: Does Participation in Pre-primary Education Translate into Better Learning Outcomes at School?*, Paris: OECD.

OECD (2011b) *Doing Better for Families*, Paris: OECD.

OECD (2011c) *Starting Strong III: A Quality Toolbox for Early Childhood Education and Care*, Paris: OECD.

Penn, H. (2004) *Childcare and Early Childhood Development Programmes and Policies: Their Relationship to Eradicating Child Poverty*, Childhood Poverty Research and Policy Centre Report No 8, London: CHIP.

Ruhm, C. and Waldfogel, J. (2012) 'Long-term effects of early childhood care and education', *Nordic Economic Policy Review*, no 1, pp 23-51.

Ruopp, R., Travers, J., Glantz, F. and Coelen, C. (1979) *Children at the Center: Summary Findings and their Implications*, Cambridge, MA: Abt Books.

Saraceno, C. (2011) 'Childcare needs and childcare policies: A multidimensional issue', *Current Sociology*, vol 59, no 1, pp 78–96.

Scheiwe, K. and Willekens, H. (eds) (2009) *Childcare and Preschool Development in Europe: Institutional Perspectives*, Basingstoke: Palgrave Macmillan.

Shonkoff, J.P. and Phillips, D. (2000) *From Neurons to Neighborhoods: The Science of Early Childhood Development*, Washington, DC: National Academy Press.

Spieß, C.K., Buchel, F. and Wagner, G.G. (2003) 'Children's school placement in Germany: does kindergarten attendance matter?', *Early Childhood Research Quarterly*, vol 18, no 2, pp 255–70.

Sylva, K., Melhuish, E., Sammons, P. and Siraj-Blatchford, I. (2011) 'Preschool quality and educational outcomes at age 11: Low quality has little benefit', *Journal of Early Childhood Research*, vol 9, no 2, pp 109–24.

Sylva, K., Melhuish, E., Sammons, P., Siraj-Blatchford, I. and Taggart, B. (2004) *The Effective Provision of Preschool Education (EPPE) Project: Final Report*, London: Department for Education and Skills.

Sylva, K., Melhuish, E., Sammons, P., Siraj-Blatchford, I. and Taggart, B. (2008) *Final Report from the Primary Phase: Preschool, School and Family Influences on Children's Development during Key Stage 2 (7–11)*, Research Report DCSF-RR061, London: Department for Children, Schools and Families.

Sylva, K., Melhuish, E., Sammons, P., Siraj-Blatchford, I., Taggart, B., Hunt, S. and Jelicic, H. (2012a) *The Effect of Starting Pre-school at Age 2 on Long Term Academic and Social-behavioural Outcomes in Year 6 for More Deprived Children: Analyses Conducted for the Strategy Unit*, London: Department for Education.

Sylva, K., Melhuish, E.C., Sammons, P., Siraj-Blatchford, I. and Taggart, B. (2012b) *Effective Pre-school, Primary and Secondary Education 3–14 Project (EPPSE 3–14): Final Report from the Key Stage 3 Phase: Influences on Students' Development from Age 11–14*, Research Report DfE-RR202, London: Department for Education.

Vandell, D.L. and Wolfe, B. (2000) *Child Care Quality: Does it Matter and Does it Need to be Improved?*, Washington, DC: Office of the Assistant Secretary for Planning and Evaluation, US Department of Health and Human Services.

Waldfogel, J. (2006) *What Children Need*, Cambridge, MA: Harvard University Press.

West, A. (2006) 'The preschool education market in England from 1997: Quality, availability, affordability and equity', *Oxford Review of Education*, vol 32, no 3, pp 283–301.

Wong, V.C., Cook, T.D., Barnett, W.S. and Jung, K. (2008) 'An effectiveness-based evaluation of five state pre-kindergarten programs', *Journal of Policy Analysis and Management*, vol 27, no 1, pp 122–54.

Appendix 1.1: Currencies exchange rates

	Australian dollar[a]	Euro[b]	New Zealand dollar[c]	US dollar[d]	UK pound sterling[e]
Australian dollar	I	1.24	0.78	0.97	1.53
Euro	0.8	I	0.63	0.78	1.23
New Zealand dollar	1.28	1.59	I	1.23	1.96
Norwegian krone	6.03 [f]	7.48	4.71 [f]	5.82	9.22
US dollar	1.04	1.28	0.81	I	1.59
UK pound sterling	0.65	0.81	0.51	0.63	I

Notes: The exchange rates reported are annual averages of 'spot exchange rates' for 2012 as reported by various central banks. Each column indicates how much the currency reported at the top buys.

Sources:
[a] Reserve Bank of Australia: Statistics, historical exchange rates; [b] European Central Bank: Statistical Warehouse – Exchange rates – Bilateral rates; [c] Reserve Bank of New Zealand: Statistics – Foreign exchange rates – Bilateral rates; [d] Bank of England: Statistical interactive database – Daily spot exchange rates against US dollar; [e] Bank of England: Statistical interactive database – Daily spot exchange rates against sterling; [f] Norges Bank: Exchange rates

TWO

Equal access to early childhood education and care? The case of the UK

Ludovica Gambaro, Kitty Stewart and Jane Waldfogel

Introduction

Early childhood education and care (ECEC) has occupied an important place on the political agenda in the UK since the mid-1990s. Under the Labour government in office from 1997 to 2010, the expansion of childcare was seen as a crucial plank in the campaign against child poverty. At the same time, increasing evidence pointed to the importance of early education in promoting more equal life chances, suggesting the 'double dividend' which could be delivered by high-quality ECEC (DfES et al, 2002: 29). Spending on services for children under five increased threefold in real terms between 1997 and 2007, faster than spending on any other policy area (Sefton, 2009). The Conservative–Liberal Democrat Coalition government, which took office in 2010, has so far reduced support for childcare subsidies, but remains committed to early education, including expansions to disadvantaged two-year-olds, as part of its social mobility agenda.

While provision has come a long way in 15 years, there are still considerable gaps and challenges in the extent to which disadvantaged children access high-quality ECEC. Only a minority of children under three experience any formal childcare, which remains relatively expensive, and the available evidence suggests that more disadvantaged children are less likely to attend. Part-time nursery provision for three- and four-year-olds is free and nearly universal, but still has gaps, especially for three-year-olds. Quality has improved on several different measures, but continues to vary widely.

This chapter sets out the main policies governing ECEC provision for children under five in the UK, and asks how effectively these operate to ensure equality of access to high-quality services. We begin by describing the system of provision in the UK and patterns of usage.

From here we look at the evidence on differences in attendance and quality of provision among children. Finally, we consider the link between these patterns and the policy framework.

The story is complicated by the fact that the UK has four constituent nations – England (where 84% of the UK population live), Scotland (8%), Wales (5%) and Northern Ireland (3%). While control over taxation is retained by the UK Parliament in Westminster, the devolved administrations for Scotland, Wales and Northern Ireland have authority over most domestic policy areas, including education and ECEC policy.[1]

Mixed provision, varied quality

A variety of services provide ECEC to children under five in the UK. Settings can belong to the state (maintained) sector, or to the private, voluntary and independent (PVI) sectors. Maintained services are, in the main, school based, although local authorities also run other types of settings, most notably children's centres. Outside maintained services, the most significant provider is the private for-profit sector.

Sectors vary in terms of workers' qualifications and, in turn, quality. School-based provision is staffed with teachers and nursery nurses, while outside schools the presence of graduate workers is scant, at around 4% of the workforce (Phillips et al, 2010; Brind et al, 2011; Gambaro, 2012). Crucially, observational studies of quality, as measured by the Early Childhood Environment Rating Scale (ECERS), have found that schools offer higher-quality provision than PVI settings, although voluntary settings have made the largest improvements in the most recent years (Sylva et al, 2004, 1999; Mathers et al, 2007).

Education becomes compulsory in the term after a child turns five in England, Scotland and Wales. In Northern Ireland, compulsory schooling starts in September for any child who has turned four before 1 July in a given year. Such a relatively early school starting age across the UK, combined with the right to a year's maternity leave, means that ECEC services cover a maximum of four years of children's lives.

In England, since 1999, children aged four have been entitled to 15 hours a week of free early education for 38 weeks a year; a similar entitlement applies in Scotland and Wales, although the number of hours is somewhat lower, as set out in Table 2.1. Children can access the entitlement in schools or in settings belonging to the PVI sectors. In practice, however, in England and Wales it is the norm for children to begin school the September after they turn four, in 'reception' classes. Once in reception class, children attend for a full school day,

Table 2.1: Early education entitlement in the four UK nations

	England	Wales	Scotland	Northern Ireland
How many hours per week?	15	10	12.5	12.5
When?	Usually term time	Term time	Usually term time	Term time
Starting what age?	First term after third birthday			
Where?	Maintained sector schools, private and voluntary sectors settings, independent schools, childminders			
Organisation	Reception classes + Nursery classes/ schools or PVI provision	Reception classes + Nursery classes/ schools or PVI provision	Preschool (maintained and PVI) + Ante-preschool (maintained and PVI)	Compulsory schooling (from age four) + Nursery classes/schools or reception units

so will be accessing longer hours than are covered by the entitlement. In Scotland, provision the year before compulsory schooling is still part time, and one in five children spend this year in a PVI setting (Gambaro et al, 2013a).

The entitlement to part-time free early education was extended to three-year-olds in 2004.[2] Three-year-olds receive free early education in a variety of settings. In the maintained sector, three-year-olds are catered for in nursery classes or nursery schools, where they attend part time (five mornings or five afternoons). Alternatively, children access the entitlement at one of a range of PVI settings. The choice includes private nursery schools and classes; voluntary or privately run playgroups; and childcare centres offering full day-care. In England, 40% of three-year-olds are in maintained schools, with 60% in PVI settings (Gambaro et al, 2013). In Scotland, maintained provision is slightly more prevalent, with almost 70% of children enrolled in school-based early education two years before compulsory schooling (Gambaro et al, 2014).[3] There are thus differences across nations in the extent of the role played by the PVI sector, as illustrated in Figure 2.1. This in part reflects the actual make-up of services in different parts of the UK, but it also reveals different national policy approaches (see Gambaro et al, 2014 for details).

Figure 2.1: UK: Three- and four-year-olds in early education, by sector

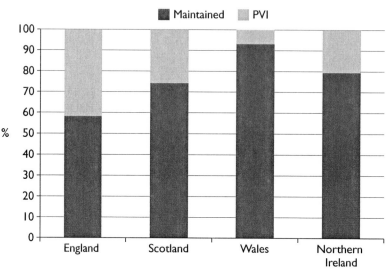

Sources:
England: School Census and Early Years Census 2011
Scotland: Pre-school Census 2011
Wales: School Census 2011 – information from schools only. Total calculated on the basis of Office for National Statistics population estimates. Thus, caution is needed when interpreting Welsh data
Northern Ireland: School Census 2011–12

In theory, registered childminders are also able to offer the entitlement provided they fulfil certain additional requirements related to quality. In practice, however, local authorities have generally been reluctant to deliver the offer through childminders and, in England, fewer than 1% of three-year-olds receive the entitlement in a home-based setting (Gambaro et al, 2013).

For children younger than three, there is very little publicly provided provision. In England there are local authority children's centres which offer childcare alongside other services, but the number is small, with roughly one such centre for every 3,500 children under five.[4] Thus, ECEC for the under threes is largely delivered either in PVI settings or by childminders, and parents have to pay for it. At the time of writing, a small number of disadvantaged two-year-olds are offered a free place for 15 hours a week in settings which are judged as offering good quality provision, and the government plans to extend the offer to 130,000 disadvantaged children in September 2013. Besides this programme, fees generally do not vary according to parents' income, but do vary depending on children's age, with provision becoming less expensive as the child gets older (Brind et al, 2011). Daycare Trust, the national childcare charity (now Family and Childcare Trust), collects information on costs every year, and reports that in 2012 average costs in Britain ranged from £92 a week for 25 hours of childminder care for a child over two, to £102 for 25 hours of centre-based care for a child below two (Daycare Trust, 2012). Evidence from the government-sponsored annual survey of providers offers similar figures, albeit on England only, with settings offering full-time care charging £4.10/hour for children below two, and childminders charging on average £3.60/hour per child (Brind et al, 2011).

An annual survey of parents in England finds that 59% of children under three received some form of non-parental care in 2010: 39% were in formal (paid) care (33% in centre-based care, and 7% with a childminder or nanny), while 33% used informal (unpaid) care (mostly grandparents) (categories sum to more than 100%, since children could use more than one kind of care) (Smith et al, 2012). Data from a similar survey in Wales show similar patterns (Smith et al, 2010).

Policy framework

Besides direct public provision, the British government intervenes in the ECEC services sector in a number of ways. This section reviews the main policy mechanisms in place and focuses in particular on government funding and quality control.

Funding

In the UK, there are two main funding schemes in operation: one related to the free entitlement and one related to provision before and beyond the entitlement. Funding for the entitlement is decided at national level, distributed to local authorities and then channelled directly to providers. In England, local authorities receive the resources from central government as part of a larger grant, which provides per capita funding for education for three- to 16-year-olds, largely based on the previous year's allocation. Funding for the entitlement is not ring-fenced: each local authority decides for itself how much to spend on early education as opposed to primary and secondary schools, although they have a statutory duty under the Childcare Act 2006 to provide a free part-time place for every eligible child who wants it. In practice, a recent report for England by the National Audit Office (NAO) found that spending on the entitlement varied from 3.5% and 9.8% of the grant, with some evidence that more deprived authorities had a higher share of spending on early years than others (NAO, 2012).

Initially, there were very few criteria governing the allocation of funding from local authorities to individual providers (Campbell-Barr, 2007). Since April 2011, however, authorities have been required to use a base rate (funding per child per hour) and to supplement it with additional resources to disadvantaged children. The aim is to create an incentive for providers to enrol more disadvantaged children. However, such deprivation supplements vary widely in magnitude: the NAO sampled 24 local authorities and found that the extra resources provided varied from 3p to 79p per child per hour. Other supplements encouraging providers to increase quality or flexibility are optional. Around half of authorities chose to include quality supplements in 2010–11, based on criteria including a 'good' or 'outstanding' judgement by the education inspectorate, Ofsted, employment of a graduate, or the authority's own assessment of provider quality. (The NAO report found that 78% of authorities make such assessments, but these are not routinely published or made available to parents.)

Overall, payments were slightly higher to maintained providers than to those in the PVI sector, at £3.97 per child per hour for nursery classes and £3.77 for PVI settings (NAO, 2012). As we will see below, staff in the maintained sector have considerably higher qualification levels than in the PVI sector, and as staff costs typically represent over two-thirds of the cost of early education, this difference looks surprisingly small. However, nursery classes benefit from shared overheads with the primary schools they belong to (and there may also be cross-subsidy of nursery classes within a school's budget). Funding for nursery *schools* in the maintained sector – which must employ a headteacher and have no shared overheads – is considerably higher, at £6.83 per child per hour.

The funding of the entitlement in Scotland, Wales and Northern Ireland is broadly similar (see Gambaro et al, 2014 for details). In Scotland, until 2009, the education minister used to issue an 'advisory floor' rate every year, which was the minimum price local authorities had to pay when commissioning preschool education from PVI providers (Scottish Executive, 2003). Local authorities now have complete flexibility in how they use the grant. In Northern Ireland, private and voluntary providers receive an annual grant, which is a flat rate per child. In statutory settings, funding is similarly allocated on the basis of the number of pupils attending each school, but the level of funding is higher, and statutory settings are able to access capital grants and other funding streams (Northern Ireland Audit Office,

2009). As for Wales, the number of providers fluctuates depending on 'arrangements to fund the provision locally' (Estyn, 2011).

Two final points are worth drawing out about the early years entitlement. In all four nations, local authorities are not financially rewarded for improvements in the quality of provision among the providers they fund. Second, there is a strong sense among many PVI providers that funding for the entitlement is not sufficient to cover the cost. In 2011, 58% of day nurseries reported that unit funding did not cover the costs of provision, although very few have withdrawn from offering the entitlement (Laing & Buisson, 2011, reported in NAO, 2012).

Outside the entitlement, ECEC services tend to be expensive. The second way the UK government intervenes to fund ECEC is by subsidising working parents directly. At the time of writing, there are two types of subsidies. First, parents can opt to be part-paid in childcare vouchers, reducing income tax liability on the first £2,860 spent on childcare per year. The scheme allows savings of up to around £900 a year per qualifying parent, as long as the employer is signed up to the voucher scheme. Second, and more significant for lower-income households, parents can claim back a portion of registered childcare costs if they qualify for a particular level of tax credits, which means having earnings below a certain threshold (dependent on household size), and if all parents in the household work at least 16 hours a week. This is the childcare element of Working Tax Credit, often referred to as the Childcare Tax Credit. As of April 2011, eligible parents could claim up to 70% of the cost of registered childcare, with a maximum claim of £122.50 a week for one child and £210 a week for two or more children; awards are tapered with household income. The most recent estimate of take-up of the credit put it at 81% of eligible families (HMRC, 2011), but the overall number of eligible families is, in fact, fairly small, either because families do not work enough hours to qualify or because they do not use registered childcare. In April 2012 there were 946,000 families with a child under five in receipt of Working Tax Credit, and just 31% received the childcare element (HMRC, 2012, Tables 3.2 and 4.4).[5]

Qualifying parents can reclaim the costs of any registered provider, including childminders and home childcarers, and reimbursement does not vary depending on the choice made. Importantly, there is no additional payment for higher-quality providers, for example. The intention behind the minimum 30% part payment of costs appears to be to provide parents with an incentive to shop around for good value for money (Waldfogel and Garnham, 2008), but it also means that lower-income parents may be priced out of higher-quality provision, or, indeed, discouraged from choosing formal care at all.

In March 2013, the government announced reforms to such funding schemes, which should come into force between Autumn 2015 and April 2016. In relation to tax-free vouchers, the proposal is to increase the cap: parents would enjoy 20% tax relief on childcare spending up to £6,000 a year, which could be worth up to £1,200 per child as long as both parents are in work. The new scheme is overall more generous, and does not rely on employers' involvement. But it favours, in particular, dual-earner couples with high childcare expenses. As for the tax credit, it will cover up to 85% of childcare costs. This change benefits low-income working families, but fails to reach those out of work who are on the lowest incomes.

Quality: qualifications, curriculum and inspection

The quality of ECEC settings in the UK is supported and monitored in three main ways. First, there are minimum requirements governing structural features including staff qualifications and staff-to-child ratios. These requirements vary substantially across different settings, as discussed below. Second, all nations have a national curriculum. For example, the Early Years Foundation Stage (EYFS) curriculum in England covers all providers catering for nought to fives, irrespective of whether they receive public funding. Third, in all nations there is a system of regular government inspection.

Table 2.2 reports statutory requirements regarding group size, staff-to-child ratios, and staff qualification requirements for England. Two things are immediately clear. First, there are effectively no minimum requirements for staff working with very young children. Instead, minimum requirements operate at setting level, requiring that all managerial and supervisory staff have a qualification at Level 3 (equivalent to secondary schooling), and half of remaining staff have qualifications at Level 2 (exams taken at age 16). For childminders, the current minimum requirement is an introductory course.

Not only are these requirements low, but a recent independent review has suggested that the training and courses leading to early years qualifications at Levels 2 and 3 are particularly weak, both because they attract those with the poorest academic records and because they fail to prepare students for the job (Nutbrown, 2012). Indeed, a Level 3 qualification can amount to one year of training on the job, with little exposure to different practice and little college-based learning. The review put forward the proposal of having all centre-based workers

Table 2.2: Statutory requirements for different types of provider in England

Centre-based provision

Type of provider	Age of child	Staff-to-children ratio	Staff qualification requirements
PVI	Under two	1:3	
	Two	1:4	At *individual* level, no requirement
	Three	1:8	At *setting* level, 50% of staff should hold a Level 2 qualification, and all supervisory and management staff should hold a relevant Level 3 qualification
		1:13 *if* qualified teacher or EYP*	
	Four	1:8	
		1:13 *if* qualified teacher or EYP*	
Maintained nursery class	Three	1:13 (max class size 26)	One qualified teacher per class
	Four	1:30 (max class size 30)	One qualified teacher per class
	Five	1:30 (max class size 30)	One qualified teacher per class

Childminders

	Age of child	Group size	Qualification requirements
	Under eight	Max 6 children	Completion of introductory course in home-based childcare
	Of whom:		To offer the free entitlement a childminder must also be a member of a Childminding Network and have (or be working towards) a Level 3 qualification
	Under five	Max 3 children*	
	Under one	Max 1 child	

Notes: EYP – early years professional. *The ratio applies during school hours only (8.00am–4.00pm). Outside these hours, PVI settings need to comply with the 1:8 ratio, while childminders can look after more than three children aged four outside school hours.

and childminders qualified to at least at Level 3. The need for more stringent regulation appears necessary, also because workers have very little financial incentive to improve their qualifications. Not only is the sector characterised by very low pay, but there is also no evidence that workers with higher qualifications are paid more than staff who have received little training (Gambaro, 2012).

Second, three- and four-year-old children will have very different experiences in terms of their interaction with staff depending on whether they attend a setting in the PVI or maintained sector. Most significantly, while schools in England are required to employ a teacher in nursery or reception, PVI settings are not. On the other hand, child-to-staff ratios are higher in schools, with one adult to every 13 children and a maximum class size of 26 in nursery classes, compared to one to eight in PVI settings if no teacher is present. In reception classes, ratios are higher still – one adult to every 30 children (although in practice a 1:30 ratio is uncommon as it is the norm to deploy at least one teaching assistant in a reception class (Tickell, 2012).

Under the Labour government, it was a stated policy intention to have one graduate in every PVI setting by 2010 – either a teacher or an early years professional, a new category introduced in 2005 open to graduates who undergo specialised training in early childhood. But this was never made a requirement and, in practice, only 36% of children accessing the free entitlement in the PVI sector do so in settings that employ a graduate, and this may not mean that all children in those settings have regular exposure to them (Gambaro et al, 2013).

In the other UK nations, the regulation around qualifications has been, until recently, fairly similar (see Gambaro et al, 2014 for details).

The introduction of play-based developmentally appropriate curricula has been the second main way policy makers in the UK have pursued quality. There are, however, important differences across the UK. In England, the EYFS curriculum specifies learning and development objectives for children from birth to five and is compulsory for all providers of ECEC, including childminders. The Welsh Foundation Phase is for children aged three to seven (and thus straddles across compulsory schooling age). Despite being more firmly anchored to the schooling system, the Foundation Phase advocates children's active and experimental learning and places great emphasis on their emotional and social development. A distinctive feature is the importance given to the outdoors. Scotland is very similar to Wales. A national curriculum – the Curriculum for Excellence – covers children from three to 18; its 'early level' covers both preschool and the first year of primary education and is based on the principle that children learn through play and first-hand experiences. In Northern Ireland there is 'curriculum guidance' for preschool education, covering children in all 'preschool settings' defined as all ECEC centres (DENI et al, 2007).

The third mechanism used to ensure quality is inspection. In England, regular inspection of all early years settings is conducted by Ofsted (Office for Standards in Education, Children's Services and Skills). Ofsted has inspected maintained schools in England since the early 1990s, and since the early 2000s has also been responsible for inspecting PVI settings.

In Scotland, Wales and Northern Ireland the respective education inspectorates inspect schools and PVI settings that offer funded places, while all settings serving children aged nought to five are inspected by each nation's care inspectorate.

In principle, the inspection results should make it possible to compare quality across settings offering funded places, regardless of whether they are in the PVI or maintained sector. Perhaps surprisingly, the most recent summary report for England (Ofsted, 2011) suggests that average quality is higher in PVI settings than in the maintained sector: 70% of PVI settings were rated good or outstanding compared to 55% of early years provision in primary schools; and only 2% were rated inadequate, compared to 5% in primary schools.[6] In practice, however, there are differences in the way settings in the two sectors are inspected, which mean comparisons across the two should be treated with caution. Most notably, PVI inspections are shorter and are conducted by staff with lower levels of experience and training than Ofsted school inspectors. By contrast, inspections carried out by the education inspectorates in Scotland and Northern Ireland are comparable across types of settings, because the same group of inspectors assesses provision in PVI settings and schools. In both nations, maintained provision is generally found to be of better quality (Education Scotland, 2012, p 9; NIAO, 2009, Figure 9).

There are also more general questions about the merit of inspectorates' ratings, what aspects of quality they capture, and their use as an official measure of quality by government.

The value of Ofsted ratings of early years settings as a quality measure has been called into some doubt by research which has found that they are poor predictors of children's outcomes at age five (Hopkin et al, 2010), and by a study that finds only a weak correlation between Ofsted ratings and other quality assessments, including the widely respected Infant/Toddler Environment Rating Scale (ITERS) and the Early Childhood Environment Rating Scale (ECERS) (Mathers et al, 2012). Undoubtedly, inspection systems seek to capture a wider range of factors and characteristics of a setting than process quality alone, as they need to ensure compliance to minimum statutory requirements on staffing, ratios and health and safety standards. But there is evidence that Ofsted ratings are also sensitive to settings' intake: settings with high concentrations of poor children are less likely to receive a positive rating, holding other factors including staff qualifications constant (Gambaro et al, 2013). This could be because high numbers of disadvantaged children within settings often make quality more difficult to achieve or because Ofsted judgements of quality also reflect children's levels of development, thus rating settings with a high concentration of disadvantaged children more poorly. There are therefore good reasons to avoid using Ofsted ratings as the *only* indicator of quality, as reliance on one indicator is likely to be misleading and to further penalise settings that cater for the most disadvantaged children. In particular, it would be dangerous if funding to providers became linked to their Ofsted result.

In sum, regulatory systems in the UK tend to impose bare minimum requirements on staff qualifications outside the maintained sector, but through a unified curriculum and inspection framework attempts to ensure a high-quality experience for all children, regardless of which setting they attend (for Northern Ireland, Scotland and Wales the curriculum applies to three- and four-year-olds only). This approach might be seen as trying to ensure high *process* quality – meaning, what goes on inside the classroom, and in particular the nature of interactions between staff and pupils – without worrying unduly about inputs or *structural* quality measures. On the surface this may seem reasonable, given considerable research evidence that process quality is what matters most to children's development (Blau and Currie, 2006; Sylva et al, 2004). But it is odd in light of strong evidence across the UK that structural measures, and particularly staff qualifications, are predictive both of higher process quality and – where evidence exists – of better child outcomes (Sylva et al, 1999; Sylva et al, 2004; Melhuish et al, 2006; Siraj-Blatchford et al, 2006; Mathers et al, 2007; Sylva, 2010; Ranns et al, 2011).

Who goes where? Differences in patterns of usage of ECEC in the UK

We now turn to examine data on whether children from more disadvantaged families differ from their more advantaged peers in their use of ECEC services. In particular, we consider the types of settings attended by children from different backgrounds and – where possible – variation in quality.

We have limited information on the background of children who use formal care before three, although data from the first wave of the Millennium Cohort Study, when children were nine months old, confirms that across the UK children from more advantaged backgrounds are much more likely than their peers to be in formal care at this age. For example, just over one-quarter of children whose parents owned their own home were experiencing some formal childcare at nine months, compared to 10% of the children of non-home owners (Roberts et al, 2010).

As described above, once the free entitlement begins at age three, enrolment at ECEC settings increases sharply, with coverage close to universal by four. However, evidence from England suggests that take-up rates are slightly lower among families with low maternal education or low income, and for children from Pakistani/Bangladeshi or Black African backgrounds (Speight et al, 2010). Take-up also varies by local authority (NAO, 2012, p 17). At the same time, English children from the most deprived areas accessing the entitlement in the maintained sector are more likely to attend full time, as in many authorities priority for this option is given to children perceived to have greater need (Gambaro et al, 2013).

We now turn to examine what we know about whether children from different backgrounds are more or less likely to be accessing particular forms of provision. We have two sources of information here. The first are recent cohort studies in England and Scotland. The Quality of Childcare Settings in the Millennium Cohort Study (QCSMCS) investigated the quality of centre-based provision received by a subsample of 1,217 English children when children were around three years old (Mathers et al, 2007). This study found that children from lone-parent or workless households and those in rented accommodation were much more likely than other children to access provision in the maintained sector. As a result, they were also more likely to be in higher-quality settings, as measured using ECERS scores, as the highest quality was observed in maintained settings. For Scotland, Growing up in Scotland (GUS) follows two cohorts of children born in the first years of the millennium. In 2007, it found that among children just under four it was much more common (85%) to attend a local authority nursery than a private one (15%), but the use of private nurseries remained more common among more affluent families than those living in deprived areas (Bradshaw et al, 2008). Although process quality was not observed directly, both the Scottish Education Inspectorate ratings and the presence of teachers are higher in local authority nurseries.

The second source of information is our own analysis of administrative data on childcare providers and take-up of free early education places for the four UK nations. The advantage of these data are that they have much wider coverage and are also more up to date than the QCSMCS and the GUS; the major disadvantage is that we have little or no information on the children in the settings. In some cases (three- and four-year-olds taking up their free place in England) we do know the area within which a child lives, and we match this to area deprivation data so that we know the probability of a child being income deprived. Where we do not have data on children themselves, we use the same area deprivation indices linked to the address of the setting. More detail on the analysis for England is available in Gambaro et al (2013). We concentrate below on the results for three- and four-year-olds.

For England, our analysis finds (consistent with the QCSMCS) that children from areas with a higher concentration of poverty are much more likely to attend settings in the maintained sector, and hence settings where staff are more highly qualified. Figure 2.2 shows the

Figure 2.2: UK: Type of provision attended by three- and four-year-olds in England, by decile of area deprivation

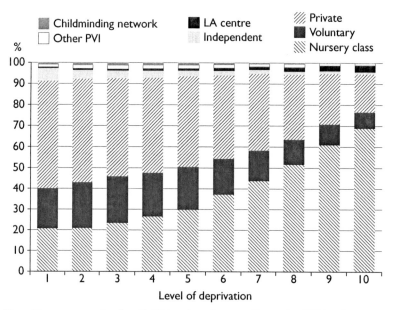

Notes: Figure reports data for all children born between September 2006 and December 2007 receiving the free entitlement In January 2011. Children with special education needs (SEN), those in Reception classes or Year 1, and those who could not be matched to an English Lower Super Output Area are not included.

Source: Early Years Census 2011 and School Census 2011

percentage of children accessing the free entitlement who do so in the PVI or maintained sector, by the level of deprivation in their local area. Among children from the decile of areas with the highest levels of poverty, 69% accessed the entitlement in nursery schools or classes, compared to just 21% of children from the least deprived areas. These differences are reflected in the likelihood of a child being in a setting that employs a graduate – either a teacher, an early years professional, or both. Of the children from the most deprived areas, 80% attend a setting where a graduate is present, compared to 53% of children in the least deprived areas.

Within each sector, however, the picture looks a little different. If we confine our attention to PVI settings, children from richer areas are slightly more likely to have a graduate than children from poorer areas, although differences are not large, and the relationship with area deprivation is slightly U-shaped (Figure 2.3), which may indicate the

Figure 2.3: UK: Percentage of children in England accessing the free entitlement in a setting with a graduate, PVI settings only

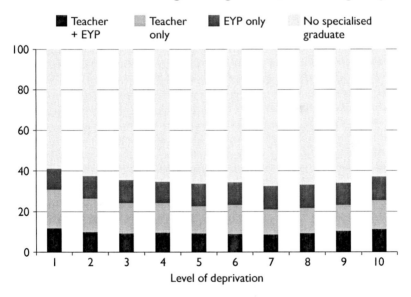

Notes: Figure refers to all children born between September 2006 and December 2007 who were receiving the free entitlement in all types of provision other than maintained schools in January 2011.
Children with SEN and those who could not be matched to an English Lower Super Output Area are not included.
Children receiving the entitlement by a childminder are included; however, information on staff qualification could refer to either the individual minder or the network coordinator.
Source: Early Years Census 2011 and School Census 2011

effect of public subsidies on both the demand and the supply-side in supporting provision in poorer areas. But low qualification levels are the norm in PVI settings: even in the least deprived areas, a clear majority of children who access the entitlement in the PVI sector do so in settings which do not employ a single graduate.

The other quality measure that we have for all settings is the rating given by Ofsted in the most recent inspection. Here we see a clear and consistent gradient within both the maintained sector and the PVI settings (Figure 2.4). Children from less deprived areas are more likely to attend settings rated as 'outstanding', and less likely to attend those rated 'satisfactory' or 'inadequate'. Differences are significant in size: in the PVI sector, children in the least deprived areas are three times as likely to attend an outstanding setting than one that is rated satisfactory or inadequate (27% to 9%), while in the most deprived areas the likelihood of each is the same (16%). Similarly, within the maintained sector (where inadequate settings are almost non-existent), children from the least deprived areas are more likely to attend an outstanding setting (21%) than one that is satisfactory (15%), while the opposite is true for those from the most deprived areas − 12% in outstanding settings and 23% in satisfactory.

We see similar patterns with respect to the concentration of maintained sector providers in disadvantaged areas in Northern Ireland (details in Gambaro et al, 2013a). The same analysis for Scotland, however, tells a rather different story. In contrast to England, we find very little variation by area deprivation level in the share of children attending maintained sector or PVI provision for either preschool (age four) or ante-preschool (age three). (The Welsh government does not collect data on the PVI settings that receive public funding, so it is not possible to examine patterns of provision in relation to varying levels of disadvantage there.)

What can be said about provision for younger children? We can answer this by examining data from England only, where *all* settings catering for children nought to five are inspected by Ofsted against the curriculum. Unlike the results for the entitlement, here figures refer to settings rather than children, and as parents may well travel outside their area for childcare the numbers will not give a fully accurate picture of the provision children receive. Nevertheless, they show us what parents in different areas have available on their doorstep. The bottom line is that there is a higher incidence of settings judged as 'outstanding' or 'good' in the least deprived areas relative to the most deprived ones. The gradient is fairly large and statistically significant. For example, while only 14% of PVI settings in the least deprived areas are rated

Figure 2.4: UK: Ofsted quality ratings for settings in England

(a) Percentage of children in PVI settings with different ratings

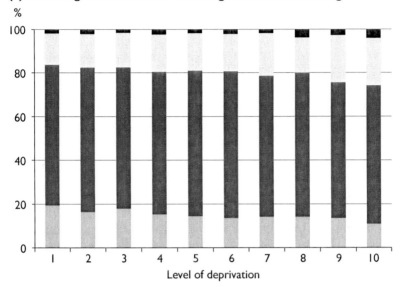

(b) Percentage of children in maintained sector nursery classes and nursery schools with different ratings

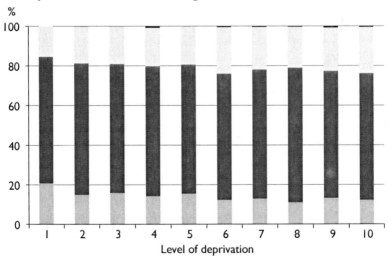

Note: Percentage of children accessing the free entitlement in settings with different ratings, by child's area deprivation level.

Source: Schools Census 2011, Early Years Census 2011 and Ofsted inspection data September 2010–August 2011

'satisfactory', this percentage goes up to 22% in the most deprived areas. A similar picture emerges in relation to childminders. A childminder located in a deprived area is much more likely to be judged by Ofsted as 'satisfactory' or 'inadequate' than other childminders are.

Conclusions

Up to a point, the UK is doing a good job of ensuring that all children aged three and upward have some exposure to ECEC. From the term after a child turns three, he/she is entitled to between 10 and 15 hours of free early education, and more than nine in ten three-year-olds and 98% of four-year-olds take this up. Most children are in school full time (9.00am–3.30pm) from the September after they turn four. For children in nursery classes and schools this means being in the classroom with a qualified teacher, although with fairly high child-to-staff ratios.

However, concerns remain, both about access to ECEC beyond the entitlement and about the quality of provision received by some children within the entitlement. First, financial support for hours beyond the 10 or 15 entitlement hours, and for younger children, is only available to those in work, and even then it is only a partial subsidy: even those receiving the maximum level of support must pay 30% of the cost of a place. This makes formal (paid) ECEC for a child under three unfeasible for families with no member in work, and challenging for many working families too.

Second, requirements for staff qualifications in PVI settings are very different to those in the maintained sector: among children accessing the free entitlement in the PVI sector, just a third of children in England have a graduate in the setting, and shares are likely to be lower for younger children. Likewise, children in Scotland are more likely to be catered for by a teacher if they are enrolled in a local authority nursery school or class. Staff qualifications are an important input into the 'quality production' process, but the evidence suggests that in the PVI staff tend to have low qualifications and low pay.

Despite this, policy has actively encouraged the expansion of places through the PVI sector. In England, PVI settings have been heavily relied upon both to deliver the free entitlement and to provide childcare for working parents. All expansion of ECEC places for three- and four-year-olds in England has come through PVI provision (Stewart, 2013), and indeed the English Childcare Act 2006 stipulates that local authorities can only create new maintained places if no private or voluntary provider is willing to do so. The new part-time offer for disadvantaged two-year-olds will be delivered almost entirely in PVI settings. This is of concern, given that the greatest shortfall in staff qualifications tends to be in the PVI settings serving disadvantaged children. In other UK nations, the balance between PVI and maintained settings is tilted more favourably towards the maintained sector, but there remains the problem of providing high-quality places outside the entitlement.

At the same time, while the EYFS curriculum and other nations' curricula have raised standards by imposing a common framework on the sector (and have been widely welcomed by practitioners), very little has been done to raise qualification levels in the PVI sector. Within the entitlement, local authorities are encouraged to reward quality using local funding formulae, but receive little or no extra funding to make this possible without affecting the rest of the local education budget. Outside the entitlement, settings can only improve quality if they can pass the cost onto parents, and costs are already very high.

The good news from an equity perspective is that in two ways the system turns out to be better for disadvantaged children than might be expected. First, at least in England, three- and four-year-olds in more deprived areas are relatively protected by the fact that they are much more likely than children from better off areas to go to maintained settings. Second, within the PVI sector there appears to be a smaller relationship between quality and deprivation than we might have anticipated.

On the other hand, not all disadvantaged children live in areas where maintained nursery places are available, so many such children will receive the entitlement in PVI settings. Furthermore, while concentrating the highest quality ECEC in part-time settings may be effective at reaching the children of non-working parents, it potentially excludes many equally needy children of working parents. Finally, while the limited disparity in quality between nurseries located in different areas may be encouraging, low quality across the board will affect disadvantaged children the most, as they have most to gain from high-quality provision. High quality for all would be a much more equalising scenario.

Of course higher-quality care would be likely to cost more, as evidenced by the big difference between per capita spending on delivering the entitlement through stand-alone nursery schools as opposed to other PVI settings, although the difference between maintained nursery classes and PVI is fairly small, perhaps because of cross-subsidy from the wider school budget and perhaps because of higher ratios of children to staff. Thus, options worth considering include the wider expansion of maintained nursery classes to deliver the entitlement, along with the equalisation of qualification levels across all settings, with larger group sizes reducing the cost increase, and supply-side subsidies extended to cover younger children, to make care affordable for parents. Some increase in costs overall is inevitable, but is a price worth paying to secure the high-quality provision which research has pointed to as beneficial, and which is currently only on offer at a minority of settings in the UK.

Notes

[1] The Scottish Parliament also has the power to vary the base rate of income taxation by up to three pence in the pound, but has never yet used this power. For a discussion of the different approaches to ECEC in Scotland and England, see Cohen et al (2004).

[2] In Northern Ireland, provision for all three-year-olds is a policy aim but not a statutory guarantee.

[3] Figures for Wales are less reliable because there are no data available on provision outside schools. However, it seems clear that maintained sector provision is prevalent, with between 80% and 90% of children enrolled in nursery classes two years before compulsory schooling (Gambaro et al, 2014). In Northern Ireland, two children out of three receive early education in schools (Gambaro et al, 2014).

[4] This is a very rough 'back of an envelope' calculation, as data on children's centres are patchy. The calculation is based on Lambert et al (2011, p 13), who report that 41% of the children's centres they contacted offered full-day provision. Of these, 60% were run by local authorities (Brind et al, 2011, p 41), which is around 25% of the original sample (Brind et al, 2011). If the same percentage is applied to the total number of children's centres (DfE, 2010) one obtains the estimate of 3,500 children under five for each local authority children's centre offering childcare services.

[5] At the time of writing, Working Tax Credit and its childcare element are due to be eliminated and subsumed into a new Universal Credit system, but the timing of the change is not yet clear.

[6] Since January 2012, changes in the inspection system have meant that Ofsted does not report judgements on the foundation stage in primary schools, thus it is no longer possible to compare provision between nursery classes in the maintained sector and PVI settings.

References

Blau, D. and Currie, J. (2006) 'Pre-school, day care, and after-school care: Who's minding the kids?', in E. Hanushek and F. Welch (eds) *Handbook of the Economics of Education*, Amsterdam: Elsevier, pp 1163–278.

Bradshaw, P., Cunningham-Burley, S., Dobbie, F., MacGregor, A., Marryat, L., Ormston, R. and Wasoff, F. (2008) *Growing Up in Scotland: Year 2*, Edinburgh: Scottish Government.

Brind, R., Norden, O., McGinigal, S., Garnett, E., Oseman, D., La Valle, I. and Jelicic, H. (2011) *Childcare and Early Years Provision: Providers' Survey, 2010*, Nottingham: Department for Education.

Campbell-Barr, V. (2007) 'Contextual issues in assessing value for money in early years education', *National Institute Economic Review*, vol 207, no 1, pp 90–101.

Cohen, B., Moss, P., Petrie, P. and Wallace, J. (2004) *A New Deal for Children? Re-forming Education and Care in England, Scotland and Sweden*, Bristol: Policy Press.

Daycare Trust (2012) *Childcare Costs Survey 2012*, London: Daycare Trust.

DENI (Department of Education Northern Ireland), DHSSPS (Department of Health, Social Services and Public Safety) and CEA (Council for the Curriculum, Examinations and Assessment) (2007) *Curricular Guidance for Pre-School Education*, Belfast: CEA.

DfE (Department for Education) (2010) *Numbers of Sure Start Children's Centres as at 30 April 2010*, ORS 14/2010, London: Department for Education.

DfES (Department for Education and Skills), DWP (Department for Work and Pensions), HM Treasury, Women & Equality Unit, and Strategy Unit (2002) *Delivering for Children and Families: Inter-departmental Childcare Review*, London: Strategy Unit, Cabinet Office.

Education Scotland (2012) *Quality and Improvement in Scottish Education: Trends in Inspection Findings 2008–2011*, Livingston: Education Scotland.

Estyn (2011) *Annual Report 2010–2011*, Cardiff: Estyn (www.estyn. gov.uk/english/annual-report/annual-report-2010-2011).

Gambaro, L. (2012) 'Why are childcare workers low paid? An analysis of pay in the UK childcare sector, 1994–2008', Doctoral thesis, London: London School of Economics and Political Science.

Gambaro, L., Stewart, K. and Waldfogel, J. (2013) *A Question of Quality: Do Children from Disadvantaged Backgrounds Receive Lower Quality Early Years Education and Care in England?*, CASE Working Paper, London: CASE, London School of Economics and Political Science.

Gambaro, L., Stewart, K. and Waldfogel, J. (forthcoming, 2014) *Early Years Services across the UK: Comparing Policy Approaches and Outcomes,* CASE Working Paper, London: CASE, London School of Economics and Political Science.

HMRC (HM Revenue and Customs) (2011) *Working Tax Credit: Take-up of Childcare Element 2008–09,* London: HMRC (www.hmrc.gov.uk/stats/personal-tax-credits/wtc-take-up2008-09.pdf).

HMRC (2012) *Child and Working Tax Credit Statistics: April 2012,* London: HRMC (www.hmrc.gov.uk/stats/personal-tax-credits/cwtc-main-apr12.pdf).

Hopkin, R., Stokes, L. and Wilkinson, D. (2010) *Quality, Outcomes and Costs in Early Years Education,* Report to the Office for National Statistics, London: National Institute of Economic and Social Research (www.niesr.ac.uk/pdf/Quality%20Outcomes%20and%20Costs%20in%20early%20Years%20Education.pdf).

Lambert, H., Norden, O., McGinigal, S., Brind, R., Garnett, E. and Oseman, D. (2011) *Childcare and Early Years Providers Survey 2010: Technical Report,* London: Department for Education.

Mathers, S., Singler, R. and Karemaker, A. (2012) *Improving Quality in the Early Years: A Comparison of Perspectives and Measures,* London: Daycare Trust, A+ Education and University of Oxford (www.education.ox.ac.uk/wordpress/wp-content/uploads/2012/03/Early-Years-Quality-Mathers-et-al-Final-Report-2012.pdf).

Mathers, S., Sylva, K. and Joshi, H. (2007) *Quality of Childcare Settings in the Millennium Cohort Study,* Research Report SSU/2007/FR/025, Nottingham: Department for Education and Skills.

Melhuish, E., Quinn, L., Hanna, K., Sylva, K., Sammons, P., Siraj-Blatchford, I. and Taggart, B. (2006) *Effective Pre-school Provision in Northern Ireland (EPPNI) Summary Report,* Bangor: Department of Education (NI).

NAO (National Audit Office) (2012) *Delivering the Free Entitlement to Education for Three- and Four-Year-Olds,* London: The Stationery Office (www.nao.org.uk/publications/1012/education_for_3-4-year-olds.aspx).

NIAO (Northern Ireland Audit Office) (2009) *The Pre-school Education Expansion Programme,* Belfast: The Stationery Office (www.niauditoffice.gov.uk/a-to-z.htm/report_archive_2009_preschool).

Nutbrown, C. (2012) *Foundations for Quality: The Independent Review of Early Education and Childcare Qualifications: Final Report,* London: Department for Education.

Ofsted (2011) *The Annual Report of Her Majesty's Chief Inspector of Education, Children's Services and Skills 2010/11*, London: The Stationery Office.

Phillips R., Norden, O., McGinigal, S. and Oseman, D. (2010) *Childcare and Early Years Providers Survey 2009*, London: Department for Education.

Ranns, H., Mathers, S., Moody, A., Karemaker, A., Graham, J., Sylva, K. and Siraj-Blatchford, I. (2011) *Evaluation of the Graduate Leader Fund: Evaluation Overview*, DFE-RR144d, London: Department for Education.

Roberts, F., Mathers, S., Joshi, H., Sylva, K. and Jones, E. (2010) 'Childcare in the pre-school years', in K. Hansen, H. Joshi and S. Dex (eds) *Children of the 21st Century: The First Five Years*, Bristol: Policy Press, pp 131-51.

Scottish Executive (2003) *Guidance on Commissioning Pre-school Education Partners*, Edinburgh: Scottish Executive Education Department (www. scotland.gov.uk/Resource/Doc/46930/0023887.pdf).

Sefton, T. (2009) *A Child's Portion: An Analysis of Public Expenditure on Children in the UK*, London: Save the Children and CASE, London School of Economics and Political Science.

Siraj-Blatchford, I., Sylva, K., Laugharne, J., Milton, E. and Charles, F. (2006) *Foundation Phase Pilot: First Year Evaluation Report*, Cardiff: Department for Training and Education, Welsh Assembly Government.

Smith, P., Gilby, N., Dobie, S., Hobden, S., Sulliva, L., Williams, M., Littlewood, M., D'Souza, J. and Flore, G. (2012) *Childcare and Early Years Parents' Survey 2010*, London: Department for Education and Ipsos MORI.

Smith, R., Poole, E., Perry, J., Wollny, I., Reeves, A., Coshall, C. and d'Souza, J. (2010) *Childcare and Early Years Survey Wales 2009*, Cardiff: Welsh Assembly Government.

Speight, S., Smith, R., Coshall, C. and Lloyd, E. (2010) *Towards Universal Early Years Provision: Analysis of Take-up by Disadvantaged Families from Recent Annual Childcare Surveys*, London: National Centre for Social Research and Department of Education (www.education.gov.uk/ publications/eOrderingDownload/DFE-RR066-WEB.pdf).

Stewart, K. (2013) *Labour and the Under Fives: Policy, Spending and Outcomes 1997–2010*, CASE Working Paper, London: CASE, London School of Economics and Political Science.

Sylva, K. (2010) 'Quality in childhood settings', in K. Sylva, E. Melhuish, Siraj-Blatchford, I. and Taggart, B. (eds) *Early Childhood Matters: Evidence from the E!ective Preschool and Primary Project*, London: Routledge, pp 70-91.

Sylva, K., Melhuish, E., Sammons, P., Siraj-Blatchford, I. and Taggart, B. (2004) *The Effective Provision of Pre-school Education (EPPE) Project: Effective Pre-school Education. A Longitudinal Study Funded by the DfES 1997–2004,* Annesley: DfES Publications.

Sylva, K., Siraj-Blatchford, I. and Melhuish, E. (1999) *The Effective Provision of Pre-school Education (EPPE) project,* Technical paper 6: *Characteristics of the Centres in the EPPE Sample,* London: Institute of Education.

Tickell, C. (2012) *The Tickell Review – The Early Years: Foundations for Life, Health and Learning,* London: Department for Education.

Waldfogel, J. and Garnham, A. (2008) *Childcare and Child Poverty,* York: Joseph Rowntree Foundation.

THREE

Towards universal quality early childhood education and care: The Norwegian model

Anne Lise Ellingsæter

Introduction

Historically, Norwegian early childhood education and care institutions have developed from targeted services for the needy towards a universal arrangement (Ellingsæter and Gulbrandsen, 2007). Today, universal access is reflected both in that a place is institutionalised as a social right for children aged one to five, and that the great majority of children in this age group – 90% – are enrolled in services. The present model has developed gradually in a dynamic interplay of supply and demand over the past 30 to 40 years (Ellingsæter and Gulbrandsen, 2007).

Although sharing similarities with the other Scandinavian welfare states, the Norwegian model exhibits some distinctive features. Central government is responsible for funding and legal/regulatory aspects, and thus vital in ensuring the establishment and expansion of services and a relatively uniform standard. But ownership is a public–private mix, and since the mid-1970s about half of all institutions have been privately owned. Meeting parents' demand, especially for places for children under the age of three, and the institutionalisation of childcare as a legal right, has been much slower than in the other Scandinavian countries. However, the 2000s saw concerted political commitment to expand access to services at reasonable costs for parents. Under the new condition of full coverage, policy efforts are directed at strengthening the quality of services, aimed at including all children. A particular concern is the inclusion of immigrant children and children from low-income and low educational backgrounds. This chapter outlines the main features of the Norwegian early childhood education and care (ECEC) model and addresses key policy challenges.

Major policy reforms and rationales

The Day Care Institution Act of 1975 represented the start of modern childcare services in Norway. The act stated that childcare should be a service for all parents who wanted it. Childcare thus became part of universally oriented welfare services, supported by nearly all political parties. Today's Kindergarten Act (Act No 64 of June 2005 relating to kindergartens) entered into force in January 2006. Kindergarten (*barnehage*) is the official and common term for early childhood education and care institutions. Here the terms 'kindergarten', 'childcare services' and 'childcare centres' are used interchangeably.

It has taken more than three decades to achieve 'full coverage', meaning the provision of places to all parents who want one for their child. In the 1980s political debate about the development of childcare services, the political left prioritised more childcare places with longer hours, while the political right considered too much childcare as harmful to children (Vollset, 2011). In the 1990s, parents' demand for childcare was overshadowed by the paramount policy debate of 'more time for children' and 'parental choice' (Ellingsæter, 2003). Two major family policy reforms were introduced during this decade: the extension of parental leave to one year in 1993 and, in 1998, a cash-for-care benefit for one- and two-year-olds who do not use publicly subsidised childcare services. The latter was promoted by centre-right parties, with parties on the left in fierce opposition. The main aim of the cash-for-care reform was to improve parents' opportunities to provide good childcare, based on the assumption that parental care is the best for the youngest children. Other main rationales were giving families a real choice of form of care and equal distribution of government care subsidies among families; private childminders should be subsidised like publicly funded childcare.

After the introduction of the cash-for-care benefit a new political situation emerged, giving space for a stronger focus on childcare services (Ellingsæter and Gulbrandsen, 2007). The 2000s saw important reforms influencing the supply and demand for childcare. In 2003, an all-party childcare compromise was reached on changes in economic and legal measures (Ministry of Children and Family Affairs, 2003b). The main aims were lower parents' fees, equal treatment of public and privately owned institutions and sector expansion. Main measures were an increase in state financial input and a strengthening of the municipalities' responsibility for the kindergarten sector. Public subsidies to services were to be increased substantially, to 80% of running costs. A maximum parental fee was to be introduced. A legal obligation was imposed on municipalities to offer childcare services. The principle of equal public subsidies to publicly and privately owned childcare institutions was stated.[1] Moreover, when 'full coverage' had been achieved, earmarked state grants to services should be replaced by block grants to municipalities, and a legal right to childcare services should be introduced.

Modern Norwegian kindergartens have been guided by a social pedagogical tradition common to the Nordic countries, typified by a holistic approach to child development and learning. Childhood is perceived as a life stage with its own value, and care, play and learning are seen in relation to each other (NOU, 2010). The holistic approach is also reflected in the organisation of kindergarten as a social institution: it covers all children under five; thus there is no division between care for the under threes and preschool for children aged three and over, as in many other European countries.

The pedagogical aim of kindergartens in the best interest of the child has been the main legitimation of childcare services. Attitudes towards working mothers and full-time childcare services were long ambivalent (Ellingsæter and Gulbrandsen, 2007). Today, parents' need for childcare is acknowledged: 'pedagogy and care go hand in hand in the Norwegian kindergarten tradition' (Ministry of Children and Family Affairs, 2003a, p 7). Like in many other countries, a shift towards social investment has taken place in recent years (for example, Jenson, 2004). The kindergarten is seen as part of lifelong learning and investment in future productive citizens (Ministry of Children and Family Affairs, 2003a). Responsibility for kindergartens was transferred from the Ministry of Children and Equality to the Ministry of Education and Research in 2006, signalling that kindergartens increasingly are seen as part of the educational system (NOU, 2010). Emphasis on play and development of social competence is somewhat weakened, while cognitive development is more accentuated (NOU, 2010). In tandem with the efforts to achieve full coverage, quality of services has become a key policy issue, reflected in a number of policy documents and government-commissioned expert reports in the 2000s (NOU, 2007, 2010, 2012; Ministry of Children and Family Affairs, 1999; Ministry of Education and Research, 2009). Kindergartens of high quality are considered an important arena for securing equal opportunities and reducing social inequality (NOU, 2009, 2010, 2012).

Children enrolled in childcare services

The Kindergarten Act regulates the authorisation, operation and supervision of childcare services.[2] Municipalities are the local authorities for kindergartens, and must approve kindergartens, provide guidance to them, and ensure that kindergartens are operated in accordance with existing rules. Privately owned kindergartens have a legal right to approval if they are suitable in terms of purpose and content and fulfil the requirements stated by the Act. Childcare services are in the main provided at the municipal level (429 municipalities). In 2011, there were 6,579 kindergartens, enrolling 277,000 children (Statistics Norway, 2012). Kindergarten opening hours vary, but 89% are open 9.5–10 hours per day (NOU, 2012). Children's actual hours spent there are, on average, 30–35 per week (NOU, 2012: 91–2). Services are for the most part organised in ordinary kindergartens, but there are also some 'family kindergartens' – small units in private homes – providing a regulated alternative to private nannies. The usual arrangement is one employee taking care of four to five children in one of the parents' home, including 7,568 children, mostly under three years-old, in 2010 (NOU, 2012). In addition, there are 'open kindergartens', where children are not enrolled and parents or other care persons are present, including 5,720 children in 2011 (Statistics Norway, 2012).

For several decades, there was a huge gap between the supply of childcare services and the demand of parents (Ellingsæter and Gulbrandsen, 2007). Expansion was slow. In the 1990s, coverage rates improved when parental leave was extended to one year in 1993 and school age was lowered from seven to six years in 1997, but the places added were actually lower than in the two preceding decades. Also, a significant number of the new places for the youngest children were in family kindergartens, which are less expensive to run as less staff are required per child compared to ordinary kindergartens. These units resemble private childminder arrangements, except for the public subsidy and some public control of the operation.[3] Family kindergartens were thought to be more 'family like', and thus better suited for the youngest children, but the great majority of parents prefer ordinary kindergartens (Ellingsæter and Gulbrandsen, 2007).

The 2000s may deserve the characterisation of a childcare revolution: in 2000, two out of three children aged nought to five were enrolled in kindergartens; in 2011, nine out of ten were enrolled. Differences in coverage rates among municipalities were significantly reduced (Borge et al, 2010). There is still some geographical variation in coverage rates, ranging between 85% and 95% among the counties. The capital, Oslo, had the lowest rate (Statistics Norway, 2012), which might reflect its higher immigrant population. Nearly all three to five-year-olds (97%) had a place in childcare in 2011, for this group growth in rates levelled off in the most recent years (Table 3.1). A remarkable increase took place among the one- and two-year-olds, labelled a 'toddler invasion' by some scholars (Løvgren and Gulbrandsen, 2012). In 2000, 37% of one- to two-year-olds were enrolled in childcare, compared to 80% in 2011; 88% among two-year-olds and 71% among one-year-olds. Children under three constituted 36% of all children in childcare (Statistics Norway, 2012). Parents' demand for full-time places was also met in this decade; 90% of one to five-year-olds were enrolled full time in 2011. Norwegian coverage rates for children aged two to five are on a par with Denmark and Sweden, while coverage rates for one-year-olds are somewhat lower than in Denmark, but higher than in Sweden (Table 3.2). The differences are related to variation in the length of the parental leave.

A main demand factor is the high employment rates among mothers: 83% with the youngest child aged one to two, and 86% with the

Table 3.1: Norway: Coverage rates in childcare services by children's age, 1980–2012 (%)

Age	1980	1985	1990	1995	2000	2005	2010	2012
1–2	7	9	15	31	37	54	79	80
3–5	27	38	52	66	78	91	97	97
1–5	19	27	36	52	62	76	89	90

Source: Kindergartens statistics, Statistics Norway

Table 3.2: Percentage of children in childcare by age in the Scandinavian countries, 2010[a]

Age of child	Denmark	Norway[b]	Sweden
Total 0–5	82	76	72
0	18	4	–
1	86	71	49
2	94	88	91
3	97	95	96
4	99	97	98
5	97	97	98

Notes: [a] Total or partly publicly funded childcare. [b] 2011, Statistics Norway (2012)
Source: Nordic Council of Ministers (2011)

youngest child aged three to five, are employed (Moafi and Bjørkli, 2011). Moreover, demand for childcare services are influenced by other national childcare policies. The parental leave system and the cash-for-care benefit are important. The paid parental leave is 47 weeks at 100% wage replacement, or 57 weeks at 80% (2012). Nearly three out of four parents choose the longest leave alternative (Grambo and Myklebø, 2009). The cash-for-care benefit for one- to two-year-olds was offered until 2012. Until then, the tax-free benefit had been NOK3,303 per month – approximately €400. Children enrolled part time in kindergartens received a reduced benefit. When the benefit was introduced, a high proportion of Norwegian parents received it, but take-up has fallen ever since. At the end of 1999, 75% of parents of one- to two-year-olds received the benefit, compared to only 25% at the end of 2011: 30% among one-year-olds, and 20% among two-year-olds. The share of parents taking up full benefit also declined. The massive decline is associated with the expansion of services and reduced parental fees. As of 1 August 2012, the majority red-green government discontinued the benefit for the two-year-olds, and the benefit for the one-year-olds was restructured (Ministry of Children, Equality and Social Inclusion, 2011).[4] The motivation for the reform was the benefit's negative impact on mothers' employment and use of childcare, considered particularly negative to the integration of women and children with immigrant backgrounds, and thus to the development of children's language skills (Ministry of Children, Equality and Social Inclusion, 2011).

Socioeconomic variation in enrolment rates

In the late 1980s, the socioeconomic profile of parents using childcare services was documented for the first time, showing a skewed distribution among socioeconomic groups; middle-class children were enrolled more often than children from families with fewer resources (Gulbrandsen and Tønnesen, 1988). Differences still exist, but have been reduced in tandem with increasing supply of places and lower parental fees in the past decade. For example, a study of the period 2004–08 indicates that kindergarten attendance was higher among families with higher incomes, but the *increase* was higher among families with lower incomes (Sæther, 2010, p 6). The gap between children from families with a high level of education and those with upper secondary education was also reduced.

A survey of families' use of different forms of childcare in 2010 shows that kindergarten attendance is correlated with parents' employment status, educational level and income, but to a lesser degree among children aged three to five than among those aged one to two (Moafi and Bjørkli, 2011). Actually, enrolment among children aged three to five is quite high in all family types; the lowest rate, 87%, is found in families with no, or just one, wage earner. In single-parent or dual-earner families, more or less all children are enrolled in kindergartens (Table 3.3). Variation among children aged one to two is larger: the highest enrolment rate is found among employed single parents (100%) and dual-earner families (85%). Also, the majority of children from single-income families, 58%, were enrolled, while families with no wage income had the lowest rate.

Enrolment of three- to five-year-olds by parents' education varies between 97% among the highly educated, and 88% among those with only primary education (Table 3.3). Figures for low-income groups show a similar pattern. Variation in enrolment by educational levels is considerably higher among the one- to two-year-olds: 82% among

Table 3.3: Norway: Percentage of children enrolled in kindergartens, by socio-economic characteristics, 2010

	Children 1–2 years old	Children 3–5 years old
Family type		
Single provider, no wage income	60	94
Single provider, wage income	91	100
Married/cohabiting, no wage income	31	87
Married/cohabiting, one wage income	58	87
Married/cohabiting, two wage incomes	85	99
Parents' educational level		
Primary education	53	88
Secondary education	76	96
Higher education	82	97
Low income families		
Low income (OECD 50%)	58	84
Not low income (OECD 50%)	80	97
Low income (EU 60%)	55	89
Not low income (EU 60%)	81	97
Mother's country of birth		
Norway	81	97
EU, USA, Canada, Australia, New Zealand	82	98
Asia, Africa, Latin America, other non-Western countries	58	90

Source: Moafi and Bjørkli (2011, Tables 2.2, 2.3)

the highly educated compared to 53% among those with the lowest educational levels. Children with a non-Western background have lower enrolment rates, and many in the low-income/education groups are immigrants. But among the three- to five-year-old immigrant children, the enrolment rate is high at 90%, although seven percentage points lower than among children with western backgrounds (Table 3.3). A slight majority of children aged one to two with non-Western backgrounds (58%) attend kindergartens, which is 22 percentage points lower than children with Western backgrounds. The number of immigrant children in childcare services has been increasing; in 2011 they constituted 11% of all children in childcare (Statistics Norway, 2012). Children with disabilities have priority access to childcare (Ministry of Education and Research, 2009, p 91). In 2008, this group amounted to 5.5% of all children in childcare services.

Children not attending kindergartens are becoming a minority, especially children aged three or more. Parents of these children have lower education and income than parents with children in childcare services (Sæther, 2010). Qualitative studies report some cultural differences in how parents talk about childcare. One study finds that working-class parents believe that one- and two-year-olds need peaceful surroundings, while middle-class parents place more emphasis on the child's individual development (Stefansen and Farstad, 2008). That children need peaceful surroundings is also mentioned in a study of parents who do not use childcare services for their three- to five-year-olds (Seeberg, 2010). These parents see kindergartens as part of an organised and stressful life based on the premises of working life. Parents are considered the best care persons for their children, and mothers' opportunity to stay at home is seen as a privilege and a choice they have the right to make. The latter study found differences related to class and ethnicity, but there were also many similarities. Some class differences in opinions on kindergarten pedagogics are also reported from a qualitative study (Stefansen and Skogen, 2010).

Several explanations have been suggested for the lower use of childcare among immigrant children (NOU, 2012). The introduction of the cash-for-care benefit for one- and two-year-olds was associated with a decline in immigrant parents' use of childcare. However, the take-up of the benefit has fallen also among parents with backgrounds from Asia and Africa, but much less than the general trend. Parents' fees seem important to the use of services. For example, pilot projects in parts of the capital Oslo offer free childcare for 20 hours per week for all four- and five-year-olds. Evaluation reports show that almost all children participate, and there has been a shift towards more full-time childcare as the total costs have become lower (NOU, 2010). However, when a parent fee of NOK650 (about €80) per month was introduced, about one-third of those in the target group failed to appear (NOU, 2012). Free part-time services provide language training, but the effect may be limited when almost all children participating have a minority background (majority share 2–10%).

Childcare as a social right – principle and practice

In 1975, the Day Care Institution Act established that municipalities had the responsibility for developing and managing childcare facilities, but this did not entail an obligation to establish such services (NOU, 2012). Only in 2004 were municipalities assigned the obligation to provide a sufficient number of places. In 2009, the majority red–green government established a legal right to childcare services for children aged one to five. The right is independent of parents' labour market status, in contrast to, for instance, Sweden, where the right to childcare is reserved for economically active parents.

The right to childcare comes into force when the child is aged one – that is, the municipality has to offer services from August to children who have turned one before 1 September.[5] This date is related to the main annual uptake of children to kindergartens; nearly 60,000 places are made available each year when the six-year-olds start school. Children who turn one after this date do not have the right to a place before August the next year, and thus may have to wait up to a year if places are not available. For parents, it may entail a period on unpaid leave and thus economic loss, or complex temporary care arrangements. It is claimed that parents have adapted to the new regulation by planning their births; midwives at maternity wards report the top months of child births to be the summer months, compared to previous reports that spring month births were most common.[6] However, this growing trend in summer births started before the legal right was established probably related to the date for the annual intake.[7] Municipalities practice the regulation differently, and two annual intakes are suggested by a government-appointed expert commission (NOU, 2012). Continuous uptakes have also been suggested, but this requires excess capacity and is very costly.

The discontinuation of the cash-for-care benefit for two-year-olds is expected to increase the demand for childcare services further. However, 19 municipalities have decided to offer the benefit for two-year-olds; most of them are centre-right local governments in the more conservative regions of Norway.[8] For example, the fourth largest city in Norway introduced a cash-for-care benefit of NOK4,000 (about €500) for two-year-olds in the autumn of 2012, provided that the child does not use childcare services at all.[9] The argument was that it would support the 'choice' of families, but it is also emphasised that it would strengthen the economy of the local municipality. A place in the childcare services is more expensive than the cash benefit. The number of kindergarten places for two-year-olds would then be reduced. However, few parents in the municipalities offering the benefit have applied for it. If interest increases, the government is considering taxing this benefit.[10]

Financing of services

Kindergartens are financed by the state, the municipalities and the parents. Contributions from companies are not common. Government grants have been the key incentive for expansion and operation of services. Government-earmarked grants to childcare services amounted to NOK26.3 billion in 2010 (about €3.3 billion). In 2011, municipalities took over the responsibility of financing childcare services – both municipal and non-municipal institutions. Government funding of childcare services was then shifted from earmarked grants targeted for this specific service, to general-purpose grants to municipalities – block grants that are not earmarked for particular services. Block grants are used for well-established services. General-purpose grants have been the key principle in government transfers to municipalities since 1986 (NOU, 2010). They are considered important for local decision making, encouraging local initiatives and giving the municipality the opportunity to prioritise resources according to local costs and the population's service needs. The earmarked grants were based on the number of children in kindergartens, their age and the number of weekly hours spent. Block grants are distributed to municipalities according to potential *demand*: the number of children aged three to five, the number of children aged one to two who do not receive the cash-for-care benefit, and the educational level of the population. The latter implies that a population with higher educational levels generates higher demand. Thus, this model does not take into account variation in the presence of children from low-income or immigrant families, and in reality appears to do the opposite.[11] Some state grants to municipalities are still earmarked, for example, investment grants and support for improving language skills among minority children.[12] Kindergartens with children that need extra resources receive extra grants from the state and the municipality. In 2008, 3.3% of all children in kindergartens received extra economic resources, in most cases used for increasing personnel resources. Children with needs that cannot be handled within ordinary arrangements and resources have an individual right to special pedagogical support (Education Act 1998).

In 2011, the financing of childcare services included 1% state grants, 83% municipal grants and 15% user fees (Statistics Norway, 2012). Childcare services constituted 14.9% of the total net operational costs of municipalities, and were the third largest municipal service sector, next after care services and primary education. A national standard is established for grants per place paid to private kindergartens, but still the amount varies significantly among municipalities.[13]

Block grants are a significantly different way of distributing finances to childcare institutions; childcare services will have to compete with other municipal welfare services (NOU, 2010). How the shift from earmarked funding to block grants to municipalities may affect the provision of places and quality in the long term is uncertain. The childcare sector is not yet stable, new day centres are still built and the lack of kindergarten teachers is considerable (NOU, 2010). In the short term, the shift from earmarked to block grants does not seem to have caused changes in the municipalities' provision of places. But a government-appointed expert commission maintains that block grants might lower quality and thus necessitate additional regulation of content and quality in the Kindergarten Act (NOU, 2012).

Equity in funding of publicly and privately owned institutions

Most of the early institutions were private; in 1963, only 21% were publicly owned (Gulbrandsen, 2007). Since the mid-1970s the public–private ownership distribution has been about fifty-fifty, with a somewhat higher public share until the mid-1990s, and a somewhat higher private share during the 2000s, as the recent sizable expansion also relied on the initiative of private owners. In 2010, 54% of kindergartens were privately owned, while 53% of all children were enrolled in publicly owned kindergartens – often larger than private ones (NOU, 2012). Almost all publicly owned kindergartens are owned by municipalities. When municipalities in previous decades failed to accommodate the increasing demand, the public grant system made it possible for parents and other actors to move in. A substantial proportion of private centres have been owned by parents (24% in 2006), while 37% were owned by individuals (mostly small family kindergartens) (Borge et al, 2010). Company-owned kindergartens, including student welfare organisations, constituted 10% of the privately owned institutions. Religious organisations owned 8%, while special pedagogical or voluntary organisations owned 5%. About 15% of private kindergartens had other types of ownership, including limited liability companies.

Equal treatment of municipal and non-municipal kindergartens implies a gradual increase in municipal grants to non-municipal services (to reach 100% in 2014). This will enable non-municipal kindergartens to offer equal working conditions and pay in relation to municipal institutions (NOU, 2010: 52). Cost estimates suggest that non-municipal kindergartens have had lower costs than municipal ones (92% in 2010), mainly generated by lower employee-to-child ratio and personnel costs (NOU, 2012).

The ownership structure is changing. In particular, increasing for-profit ownership poses new policy challenges (Ministry of Education and Research, 2012). Since 2003, several new organisational forms have been established in the private sector, some with commercial motives. There is a shift towards limited liability companies among private owners.[14] The role of private for-profit commercial owners is a disputed issue in relation to welfare services in Norway; profit extraction is not allowed for private schools, for example. The main opportunity to generate profit in the private childcare sector would be through cost adjustments – that is, by operating with lower costs than municipal services. Profit extraction is not widespread today, but remains a problem in some cases.

In order to 'secure that equal financing leads to equal quality in the kindergartens [...] and that municipal grants and parental fees in non-municipal kindergartens are put to the benefit of children' (Ministry of Education and Research, 2012, p 5), the majority red–green government has introduced new regulations in the Kindergarten Act, effective from 2013. Private institutions are allowed a limited profit, defined as 'a reasonable annual result'. The Act states that the annual result is not considered 'reasonable' if the personnel costs are substantially lower than in municipal kindergartens. If the requirement of 'reasonable annual result' is not fulfilled, the municipality can reduce or withhold grants. The centre-right parliamentary opposition voted against the law, contending that the regulation was based on a general mistrust of private ownership, and a view that grants in the private sector are not put to the benefit of children (Innst 352 L, 2011–2012, p 8). Thus this is a disputed issue, and policies may change in the future.

Parents' fees

The maximum fee is decided in the government's annual budgets. In 2012 it was NOK2,330 per month, about €300.[15] The Kindergarten Act states that for the second child, fees should be reduced by at least 30%, and for the third child and subsequent children the reduction should be at least 50%.[16] Municipalities also have an obligation to establish arrangements that offer families with the lowest ability to pay a reduction or exemption of parental fees, including non-municipal kindergartens. The arrangement is up to the municipality. In 2011, 21% of the municipalities reporting had income-graded fees (income caps vary considerably), covering 53% of all children enrolled in kindergartens (income-graded fees are most common among densely populated municipalities). About 5% of the enrolled children in these municipalities paid reduced fees (NOU, 2012). Of the municipalities that did not have income-graded fees, 60% offered social assistance schemes, covering 28% of the enrolled children. Providers who cater for children for whom reduced or no fees are paid, are compensated for the income loss.

Parental fees have been substantially reduced since 2005 due to the maximum fee. But families with the lowest incomes have had a lower real reduction in fees than parents with a high income (NOU, 2010). Low-income families spend two or three times more of their income on childcare compared to high-income families (Ministry of Education and Research, 2009). Pay reductions given by municipalities seem to be rather modest (NOU, 2012).

A stronger state regulation of schemes for families with low ability to pay has been proposed by a government-appointed expert commission (NOU, 2010).

Regulations and quality of services

The Kindergarten Act is the most important tool to secure quality in the services. The Act states aims and content, which to a large extent define what are considered good kindergartens, with high-quality childcare (NOU, 2010, 2012). The Framework Plan, a regulation to the Kindergarten Act, specifies the content and tasks of kindergartens further.[17] The Act states that kindergartens shall lay a sound foundation for the child's development, lifelong learning, and active participation in a democratic society. There are few standard requirements, however, which give space for local accommodations (NOU, 2010). The owner and employees decide work methods, equipment and organisation, based on children's needs. A coordinating committee must establish an annual plan for the pedagogical activities. The Framework Plan establishes a national curriculum, and there is a clear connection between the Framework Plan and the curricula of Norwegian primary schools. Children and parents have a right to participation. The Kindergarten Act states that each kindergarten shall have a parents' council and a coordinating committee to ensure collaboration with the children's homes. The Act also states that children in the kindergarten shall have the right to express their views on the day-to-day activities of the kindergarten, and should be given the opportunity to take part in planning and assessing activities. Children's views are given weight according to their age and maturity.

According to the Kindergarten Act, the municipality is required to supervise the operation of municipal and non-municipal kindergartens. The method and frequency is left to the discretion of the municipality. The Ministry of Education and Research's guidelines include the obligation that municipalities must develop a plan for supervision and indicate the central points to consider (NOU, 2012). The county governor guides and supervises municipalities.

Staff

There are three main staff categories in kindergartens: the headteacher (daily manager), pedagogical leaders (of the children groups) and assistants. Among the few specific requirements in the Kindergarten Act are staff qualifications and pedagogue-to-child ratios. According to the Act, kindergarten teachers are required in all kindergartens. The education requirement for kindergarten teachers is a three-year university bachelor degree. Headteachers and pedagogical leaders must be trained kindergarten teachers or have other college education that is relevant to working with children, as well as pedagogical expertise. Educational requirements can be exempted if there are no qualified applicants. The norm for pedagogue-to-children ratio stated is a minimum of one pedagogical leader per 14–18 children when children are three years or older, and a minimum of one pedagogical leader per seven to nine children when children are younger than three years old. The norm for time spent in the kindergarten is six hours or more per day.[18] There is no specification of a general staff-to-children ratio; the act just states that staffing should be adequate. A recent survey found that the average number of children per employee was 3.4 children in groups with children under three, and 5.5 children per employee in groups with children aged three to five (Vassenden et al, 2011). In age-mixed groups, the average was 4.6 children per employee. Some municipalities have local agreements about staff-to-children ratios. For example, since 1987, the agreement in the municipality of Oslo has been three employees per nine children among children under three, and three employees per 18 children among children three or older. In 2012 the municipality wanted to terminate this agreement, to allow for more flexibility, causing a strike among employees and parents.

A government-appointed expert commission has proposed a new regulation specifying the required staff-to-child ratio (NOU, 2012): for children under three, one member of staff per three children and one pedagogue per six children; for three- to five-year-olds, one member of staff per six children and one pedagogue per 12 children. This proposal would formalise a general staff-to-children ratio close to actual practices, and increase the pedagogue density. It would give a 50% share of pedagogues, and is estimated to cost NOK1.4 billion (NOU, 2012).

A total of 88,800 people were employed in kindergartens in 2011 (Statistics Norway, 2012). During the recent decade of services expansion there has been a significant increase in the number of places available to study to become kindergarten teachers (NOU, 2010). Despite this, there remains a lack of qualified staff in Norwegian kindergartens. A government-appointed expert commission has expressed worries about what is describes as the 'competence situation' (NOU, 2010). In 2010, 96% of headteachers and 83% of the pedagogical leaders had the required pedagogical education (NOU, 2012). Kindergarten teachers are stable employees: 84% of those employed in kindergartens in 2003 were still employed in the sector four years later, compared to 63% of staff without such education (NOU, 2012). Among the assistants, 26% had some pedagogical education. A rather high proportion of all staff, 23% in 2007, had only primary education, while 39% had only secondary education (Gulbrandsen, 2009). The lack of kindergarten teachers is most acute in the capital and the surrounding region (Oslo-Akershus). This may result in less qualified staff being employed in the less attractive neighbourhoods, where most immigrant children live. In 2007, 7.5% of kindergarten employees were immigrants, and only 19% of them had any pedagogical education (NOU, 2012). A positive scenario is that the general lack of qualified kindergarten teachers will vanish in the near future due to a young and increasingly stable workforce (Gulbrandsen, 2009).

Full coverage means that the kindergartens are changing: the composition of children has changed. There are more toddlers, more immigrant children and more children with special needs. Parents may also have greater demands. This situation is demanding for the staff, requiring competencies that many are lacking (NOU, 2010: 51). Kindergarten employees have met 'the toddler invasion' with some reservation: about half of them think that children should start later and spend fewer hours in kindergarten than they do in reality (Løvgren and Gulbrandsen, 2012). Older employees are somewhat more conservative than younger ones. The best educated employees are the most positive.

Kindergarten teachers enjoy their work, but the work environment may be challenging. Problems reported have included noise, poor indoor climate, increasing workloads and lack of time to do work properly (Utdanningsforbundet, 2007). The level of sickness absence is rather high in kindergartens, and a main problem is to find cover for staff who are sick (NOU, 2012). Wages of kindergarten teachers are low compared to other groups with higher education. While doctors, lawyers and engineers earn 40%–60% more over the life course compared to a reference group with only upper secondary education, kindergarten teachers earn almost 20% *less* (nurses and teachers earn 13% and 10% less, respectively) (Kirkebøen, 2010). The same patterns appear for both genders. Assistants are also relatively low paid.

Policies on quality development

Quality of childcare services is the major policy concern of the further development of childcare services. Efforts to increase quality have intensified. In 1999, a government White Paper announced a three-year programme to improve quality, starting in 2001 (Ministry of Children and Family Affairs, 1999). Three issues were considered crucial for quality development: a kindergarten for all children, varied and user-oriented services in line with the needs of parents and children and competent staff. Quality has been the major topic of all succeeding policy documents dealing with kindergartens. In 2009, the government presented a White Paper to Parliament focusing exclusively on the quality of kindergartens (Ministry of Education and Research, 2009).[19] Three main aims were stated: ensure equity and high quality in all kindergartens; strengthen the kindergarten as a learning area; and offer all children the possibility to participate in an inclusive kindergarten community. Emphasis was on the further development of three quality indicators:

- staff competence
- quality of the kindergarten's learning milieu
- children with specific needs.

A survey among kindergarten managers conducted in 2002 suggested that the work on quality improvement had started well (Gulbrandsen and Sundnes, 2004). By the end of 2003, all kindergartens should have established routines – tools and systems designed to maintain and further develop and secure the quality. However, a new survey in 2004 suggested that only one in five managers felt that their kindergarten had attained the stated goals (Gulbrandsen and Sundnes, 2004). A vital question is how the strong expansion of childcare places has affected quality. The main finding from a survey among kindergartens in 2008 actually shows that structural quality improved in parallel with sector expansion (Winsvold and Gulbrandsen, 2009). The indicators included, for instance: material standards, personnel qualifications, stability and training, the existence of user surveys and mapping of children's wellbeing and development. The study indicated that the larger the kindergarten, the more goals from the previous quality improvement programme had been achieved.

The percentage of educated kindergarten teachers in kindergartens varies considerably. In one in four kindergartens, 27% or fewer of the staff had kindergarten teacher education (Winsvold and Gulbrandsen, 2009). In another fourth of the kindergartens, 43% or more were educated kindergarten teachers. Still, compared to 2004 there had been no decrease in the proportion of kindergarten teachers. The proportion had increased more in the private kindergartens than in municipal kindergartens. Municipal kindergartens were best at planning and providing training and post-qualifying education facilities for their staff. The contact between kindergartens and the municipality did not improve, however, and the least contact was with private kindergartens. This is problematic when seen in the light of the municipality's authority to supervise and control kindergartens (Winsvold and Gulbrandsen, 2009).

Organisation, size and quality

There are trends towards larger kindergartens, larger children groups and more flexible forms of organisation. New centres are usually larger than those previously established. The average number of children per kindergarten is 47 (NOU, 2012). In total, 62% of kindergartens have less than 52 children, covering a third of all children, while 14% have more than 75 children, accounting for another third of all children. Municipal kindergartens are, on average, larger than the private ones. Very large centres are still quite rare; centres with more than 100 children represent only 4% of all kindergartens and 10% of all children.

Worries have been voiced about very large kindergartens. Parents often do not have a choice; they go to the nearest one.

A study from 2010 draws a complex picture of how structural quality is ensured in kindergartens with different sizes and organisational forms (Vassenden et al, 2011). A wide range of indicators of structural quality were measured – for example, staff composition, competence, experience and areas of responsibility, stability, the number of children per group and per adult in the groups, physical space and routines for user participation.

A narrow majority in the sample were organised as traditional group-based kindergartens. There was no clear correlation between size and organisational form, but the majority of the largest centres (100 children or more) had either flexible grouping or a combination model. In small kindergartens (less than 45 children), groups of one-to two-year-olds varied between nine and 11 children, compared to 13 to 14 in large kindergartens (80 children or more) (Vassenden et al, 2011). Kindergartens with flexible grouping operated with larger groups of children than the group-based kindergartens. The qualitative in-depth study of educational quality suggested that the most significant difference was between the small, group-based kindergartens and the large kindergartens with flexible grouping. The former were characterised by a small and stable staff, with high levels of trust and social integration between staff, children and parents. But their potential for staff development was limited. The larger kindergartens with flexible grouping were found to be less stable and not as integrated or transparent. Within more complex organisations, staff's opinions related to structure and communication were mixed. However, they had a larger, varied and more qualified staff and better possibilities for professional development. The medium-sized, group-based kindergartens seemed to be able to combine the respective strengths of the other two: trust and stability combined with professional development.

The Norwegian model: characteristics and challenges

The kindergarten has become an important social institution in Norway, as part of normal childhood and parenthood, and in terms of public finances and employment. This has generated a new understanding of its importance to society and increased attention to quality. Full childcare coverage has been achieved by sector expansion, the institutionalisation of children's right to childcare and the introduction of maximum parental fees. Municipalities have succeeded in providing services to most parents who want a place for their child.

There are variations in the childcare services with regard to size, organisation, personnel and quality (Ministry of Education and Research, 2009). However, the great service expansion in the past decade did not lower quality. Nevertheless, educating enough skilled pedagogical staff continues to be a key challenge. The traditional social pedagogical model has been somewhat weakened, with a growing emphasis on investment in human capital and on cognitive development and learning. Larger and more flexibly organised kindergartens and the changing age composition (with more toddlers) create new challenges to kindergarten quality.

High coverage rates indicate that most parents prefer kindergartens. For children aged three or older, attending kindergarten is considered an undisputed good, and kindergarten is to a considerable degree accepted as positive also for the development of one- and two-year-olds. Surveys over the past 20 years indicate that parents are very satisfied with childcare services and experience the cooperation with the kindergarten as good (Ministry of Education and Research, 2009). In a situation of full coverage, however, parents may become more demanding in relation to the quality of services. In order to secure and increase quality of services, government expert committees have proposed stronger regulative measures – for example, with regards to staffing (NOU, 2012). Others believe in increasing competition – for example, the Conservative Party wants kindergartens to compete in attracting children, and proposes a web-based national 'kindergarten barometer' with standardised information about each kindergarten, to that end.[20]

Because of the positive effects associated with kindergarten attendance, it is a stated government policy aim that all children should be able to participate (NOU, 2012). If a future high attendance rate is to be achieved, sufficient provision of places and maximum parental fees should be continued, supplemented by schemes for the reduction or exemption of fees (NOU, 2012). Children not attending kindergarten are becoming a small minority, especially among three- to five-year-olds. Children from low-income/education and immigrant families are over-represented, and this undermines the aim of the kindergarten as an arena for reducing socioeconomic inequalities in society. Research indicates that children from such backgrounds benefit the most from attending day care (NOU, 2009).

Although kindergarten fees have been substantially reduced over the past decade, there are still families who do not use kindergartens due to economic constraints. This raises the need for additional policies to reduce fees. An expert commission observed that there are considerable differences among municipalities in what is considered low ability to pay, the size of fee reduction and whether fee reductions are given at all (NOU, 2012). The commission proposed that the municipalities' obligation to offer fee reduction schemes should become statutory (including fee reduction for siblings). A minimum amount should be defined as a basis for fee exemption, and national guidelines for income grading should be established. In order to widen access to low-income families, several expert commissions have proposed a certain number of weekly hours free of charge to all children (NOU, 2009, 2012). One commission proposed 20 hours to give parents genuine choice (NOU, 2009). It was argued that kindergarten attendance is important in creating a good foundation before the start of school. One important aim in this respect is to improve the language skills of certain minority groups. The offer needs to be universal, covering all groups of children, because targeted arrangements present their own challenges in terms of establishing criteria that successfully identify those children who ought to participate.

Notes

[1] Also, rules for tax exemption for employer owned/run services were established.

[2] www.lovdata.no/all/hl-20050617-064.html

English version: www.regjeringen.no/upload/KD/Vedlegg/Barnehager/engelsk/Act_no_64_of_June_2005_web.pdf

[3] Family kindergartens are regulated by the Kindergarten Act.

[4] Either a full or a 50% benefit will be paid (for children in kindergarten less than 20 hours a week). Children aged 13–18 months and 19–23 months receive NOK5,000 and NOK3,303/month respectively, in full benefit.

[5] Parents must be registered residents in the municipality.

[6] 'Flere sommerbarn utfordrer fødeavdelingen', *Aftenposten*, 7.8.2012.

[7] Own calculations, Statistikkbanken, Statistics Norway.

[8] 'Liten interesse for lokal kontantstøtte', *Kommunal rapport*, nr 22/12.

[9] www.kristiansand.kommune.no

[10] 'Vil vurdere skatt på kontantstøtte', *Kommunal rapport*, nr 22/12.

[11] The provider receives grants according to the number of children enrolled, differentiating between those under and over three years old (places for children under three receive 80% higher grants) and hours of attendance.

[12] Of all municipalities, 92% have schemes to map children's language skills in municipal kindergartens; 75% of the municipalities with non-municipal facilities also have such schemes in these institutions (Ministry of Education and Research, 2009).

[13] 'Enorme forskjeller i tilskudd', *Kommunal Rapport*, 6.4.2011.

[14] Some are owned by corporations registered in tax havens, *Klassekampen*, 3.8.2012.

[15] Kindergartens are allowed to charge parents extra for meals.

[16] Parental allowance for documented costs associated with childcare can be deducted from taxes: NOK25,000 for one child and an additional NOK5,000 for each subsequent child.

[17] www.lovdata.no/for/sf/kd/kd-20060301-0266.html

[18] In kindergartens where the majority of children have shorter hours of attendance the number of children per pedagogical leader can be increased somewhat (NOU, 2012).

[19] Fact sheet in English: www.regjeringen.no/upload/KD/Vedlegg/Barnehager/Kvalitesmeldingen/FactsheetSTMeld41.pdf

[20] For example: opening hours, diet, indoor climate, outdoor milieu, sickness absence among employees, reports from inspections, and so on. 'Høyre vil la barnehagene kjempe om barna', *Aftenposten*, 3 August 2012.

References

Borge, L.E., Johannesen, A.B. and Tovmo, P. (2010) *Barnehager i inntektssystemet for kommunene* [*Kindergartens in the Municipal Revenue System*], Trondheim: Senter for økonomisk forskning.

Ellingsæter, A.L. (2003) 'The complexity of family policy reform. The case of Norway', *European Societies*, vol 5, no 4, pp 419–43.

Ellingsæter, A.L. and Gulbrandsen, L. (2007) 'Closing the childcare gap: The interaction of childcare supply and mothers' agency in Norway', *Journal of Social Policies*, vol 36, no 4, pp 649–69.

Grambo, A.C. and Myklebø, S. (2009) *Moderne familier – tradisjonelle valg: En studie av mors og fars uttak av foreldrepermisjon* [*Modern Families – Traditional Choices: A Study of Mothers' and Fathers' Uptake of Parental Leave*], Oslo: Nav.

Gulbrandsen, L. (2007) *Full dekning, også av førskolelærere?* [*Full Coverage – Also of Kindergarten Teachers?*], Oslo: Nova.

Gulbrandsen, L. (2009) *Førskolelærere og barnehageansatte* [*Kindergarten Teachers and Kindergarten Employees*], Oslo: Nova.

Gulbrandsen, L. and Sundnes, A. (2004) *Fra best til bedre? Kvalitetssatsing i norske barnehager* [*From Best to Better? Commitment to Quality in Norwegian Kindergartens*], Oslo: Nova.

Gulbrandsen, L. and Tønnesen, C. (1988) 'Barnehageutbyggingens fordelingsmessige virkninger' ['The distributional effects of kindergarten expansion'], *Tidsskrift for samfunnsforskning*, vol 29, no 6, pp 539–54.

Innst 352 L (2011–12) 'Innstilling til Stortinget fra familie- og kulturkomiteen' [Recommendation from the Family and Cultural Affairs Committee to the Storting (Parliament)].

Jenson, J. (2004) 'Changing the paradigm: Family responsibility or investing in children', *Canadian Journal of Sociology*, vol 29, no 2, pp 169–92.

Kirkebøen, L.J. (2010) *Forskjeller i livsløpsinntekt mellom utdanningsgrupper* [*Differences in Life Cycle Income among Educational Groups*], Oslo: Statistics Norway.

Løvgren, M. and Gulbrandsen, L. (2012) 'How early and how long?', *Nordic Early Childhood Education and Research*, vol 5, no 7, pp 1–9.

Ministry of Children and Family Affairs (1999) *St meld nr 27 (1999–2000) Barnehage til beste for alle barn* [*Kindergarten in the Best Interest of All Children*], Oslo: Ministry of Children and Family Affairs.

Ministry of Children and Family Affairs (2003a) *St meld. nr 24 (2002–2003) Barnehagetilbud til alle – økonomi, mangfold og valgfrihet* [*Kindergarten Provision for All – Economy, Diversity and Freedom of Choice*], Oslo: Ministry of Children and Family Affairs.

Ministry of Children and Family Affairs (2003b) *Ot prp nr 76 (2002–2003) om endringer i barnehageloven* [*About Changes in the Kindergarten Act*], Oslo: Ministry of Children and Family Affairs.

Ministry of Children, Equality and Social Inclusion (2011) *Prop 1S (2011–2012)*, Oslo: Ministry of Children, Equality and Social Inclusion.

Ministry of Education and Research (2009) *St meld nr 41 (2008–09) Kvalitet i barnehagen* [*Quality in the Kindergarten*], Oslo: Ministry of Education and Research.

Ministry of Education and Research (2012) *Prop 98 L (2011–12) Endringer i barnehageloven (tilskudd og foreldrebetaling i ikke-kommunale barnehager)* [*Changes in the Kindergarten Act (Grants and Parental Fees in Non-municipal Kindergartens)*], Oslo: Ministry of Education and Research.

Moafi, H. and Bjørkli, E.S. (2011) *Barnefamiliers tilsynsordninger, høsten 2010* [*Care Arrangements among Families with Children, Autumn 2010*], Oslo: Statistics Norway.

Nordic Council of Ministers (2011) *Nordic Statistical Yearbook 2011*, Copenhagen: Nordic Council of Ministers.

NOU (2007) *Formål for framtida. Formål for barnehagen og opplæringen* [*Aims for the Future. Aims for Kindergarten and Training*], Oslo: Ministry of Education and Research.

NOU (2009) *Fordelingsutvalget* [*The Allocation Commission*], NOU 2009: 10, Oslo: Ministry of Finance.

NOU (2010) *Med forskertrang og lekelyst: Systematisk pedagogisk tilbud til alle førskolebarn* [*Systematic Pedagogical Offer to All Preschool Age Children*], NOU 2010: 8, Oslo: Ministry of Education and Research.

NOU (2012) *Til barnas beste: Ny lovgivning for barnehagene* [*In the Best Interest of Children: New Legislation for Kindergartens*], NOU 2012: 1, Oslo: Ministry of Education and Research.

Seeberg, M.L. (2010) *Siste skanse: En undersøkelse av 3–5-åringer som ikke går i barnehage* [*The Last Bastion:A Study of Three to Five Year-Olds Who Are Not Enrolled in Kindergartens*], Oslo: Nova.

Statistics Norway (2012) *Andelen barn i barnehage flater ut* [*The Proportion of Children in Kindergartens Is Levelling Off*], Oslo: Statistics Norway (www.ssb.no/emner/04/02/10/barnehager).

Stefansen, K. and Farstad, G. (2008) 'Småbarnsforeldres omsorgsprosjekter' ['Parents' childcare strategies'], *Tidsskrift for samfunnsforskning*, vol 49, no 3, pp 343–72.

Stefansen, K. and Skogen, K. (2010) 'Selective identification, quiet distancing: Understanding the working-class response to the Nordic childcare model', *Sociological Review*, vol 58, no 4, pp 587–603.

Sæther, J.P. (2010) *Barn i barnehage – foreldrebakgrunn og utvikling de seneste årene* [*Children in Kindergartens – Parents' Background and Development in Recent Years*], Oslo: Statistics Norway.

Utdanningsforbundet (2007) *Arbeidsmiljøet i barnehagen – en undersøkelse om førskolelærenes arbeidsmiljø* [*Work Environment in the Kindergarten – A Study of Kindergarten Teachers' Work Environment*]. Oslo: Utdanningsforbundet.

Vassenden, A., Thygesen, J., Brosvik Bayer, S., Alvestad, M. and Abrahamsen, G. (2011) *Barnehagenes organisering og strukturelle faktorers betydning for kvalitet* [*The Organisation of Kindergartens and the Significance of Structural Factors for Quality*], Stavanger: International Research Institute of Stavanger.

Vollset, G. (2011) *Familiepolitikkens historie – 1970 til 2000* [*The History of Family Policies – 1970 to 2000*], Oslo: Nova.

Winsvold, A. and Gulbrandsen, L. (2009) *Kvalitet og kvantitet. Kvalitet i en barnehagesektor i sterk vekst* [Quality and Quantity. Quality in an Expanding Kindergarten sector], Oslo: Nova.

FOUR

Equal access to quality care: Lessons from France on providing high-quality and affordable early childhood education and care

Jeanne Fagnani

Introduction

Along with the Nordic countries, France leads the European Union (EU) in public childcare provision and benefits aimed at reducing childcare costs for families. It has also widely been recognised that the French childcare system has many strengths (OECD, 2012). In recent years, however, in the context of economic uncertainties, policy makers have been confronted with new tensions and dilemmas. While over the last decade France has continued to progressively consolidate and enhance its promotion of policies to support the work–family life balance, the introduction of new laws in the domain of early childhood education and care (ECEC) has mirrored the growing hold of employment policies over childcare policies.

What has been at stake when it comes to accessible, affordable and good quality ECEC? To what extent is the system meeting the challenge of providing equal access for all children under six? What were the rationales underpinning changes and what were the key drivers of change? Against the background of budgetary constraints, what are currently the main priorities? What is the impact of the rising demand of formal childcare provisions on quality framework and tools? These are the questions addressed in this chapter.

The first part of this chapter is devoted to the ECEC system. In particular, I investigate whether socio-economically disadvantaged children are accessing high-quality ECEC to the same extent as their more advantaged peers. Funding and cost of care to families follows. Then I focus on the quality issue and the recent decisions made in this domain. To conclude, I highlight some of the challenges policy makers currently face and the tensions they have to deal with.

For the rest of the chapter I use the term 'early childhood education and care' (ECEC), as well as other terms such as *crèches*,[1] childminders, écoles maternelles (nursery schools) and *multi-accueil* (multi-functional childcare centres), which more aptly describe the services available in France, as the chapter will make clear.

An extensive and segmented system of public provision: day-care and *écoles maternelles*

France has a well-established and longstanding early childhood system dating back to the end of the nineteenth century. The system has two tiers, falling under separate ministerial auspices: on the one hand, formal childcare provision (publicly subsidised centre-based as well as home-based arrangements); and on the other, écoles maternelles. This dual system is a legacy of the past.

As Table 4.1 illustrates, the services available depend on the age of the child. While almost all children aged three to six are enrolled in écoles maternelles, which are free and fully integrated into the school system, the system of services for children under three is more varied and the coverage rate lower. For this reason, in this section the emphasis is on children under three.

Setting the scene for the institutions in charge of formal childcare provisions

In relation to children under three, responsibility for services is shared by several institutional actors: the national Family Allowance Fund (*Caisse nationale des allocations familiales*, CNAF), the national ministries in charge of social policies and health, local authorities and social partners, such as the National Union of Family Associations (*Union nationale des associations familiales*, UNAF). Enterprises, non-profit/ voluntary organisations and the market still play a minor role in comparison to the state. Currently, however, for-profit providers are increasingly being considered as real partners in policy development and service delivery in France.

These services are, nevertheless, poorly coordinated. The most recent report of the National Audit Office (*Cour des comptes*), released in July 2008, therefore recommended reinforcing the coherence of their respective intervention.

Table 4.1: France: Main services and provisions (ECEC) available by child age

Age of the child	Maternity and paternity leave[a]	Parental leave (with or without a benefit)[a]	EAJE (crèches and multi-accueil)	Licensed childminders	Nanny/day-care employee	Nursery schools (écoles maternelles)
Under age 1	*Length of maternity leave:* 16 weeks Mothers having a third or higher order child: 24 weeks of leave. *Paternity leave:* 2 weeks	Until the child reaches three years. Under certain conditions parents can be provided with a flat-rate benefit (€566 per month in 2012) paid by CAF	The child can attend up to a maximum of 10 hours per day. Licensing and supervision by the local PMI services (at the department level). Funded by local authorities and CAFs; fees for parents are income-related	Main formal childcare arrangement outside the parents. Childcare allowance paid by CAF. Licensing and supervision by the local PMI services (at the department level)	Very few parents can afford to hire someone at home. Parents are provided with a childcare allowance and tax breaks. The employee is not supervised by PMI services	–
Aged 1	–	Similar to children under age 1	Similar to children under age 1	Similar to children under age 1	Similar to children under age 1	–
Aged 2	–	Similar to children under age 1	Similar to children under age 1	Similar to children under age 1. Children who attend nursery school only half time can be looked after by a childminder the rest of the day	Similar to children under age 1. Children who attend nursery school only half time can be looked after by a nanny the rest of the day	*Toute petite section* (very little section) or children may be integrated with the three- to five-year-olds
Aged 3–6	–	–	–	Children who attend nursery school only half time can be looked after by a childminder the rest of the day	Children who attend nursery school only half time can be looked after by a nanny the rest of the day	Almost all children aged three to six attend it full time or part time

Notes: [a] For more details, see Fagnani and Math (2011), and Boyer (2012).

The CNAF and its large network of decentralised CAFs (*Caisses des allocations familiales*) (123 local family allowance funds) play a key and pivotal role in the funding and provision of childcare services. In theory, social partners such as family organisations, employers' representatives and workers' trade unions, which are represented on the executive board of the CNAF, periodically determine the orientations for intervention in family and childcare policies. In practice, decisions are made by the government, whether approved or not by the executive board. It is solely at the local level that the executive boards of the CAFs have any real decision-making power, and in particular, a margin for manoeuvre in the funding and development of childcare services.

Since 2002, early childhood commissions have been working at the *département* level: they are in charge of bringing together all the relevant actors (local authorities, representatives of the Ministry of Education, CAF, the trade unions and family associations) to enhance coherence, coordinate services, provide information to families (through, for instance, the internet site Monenfant.fr), increase equality of access to services, and to support innovation in the field.

A complex combination of subsidised centre- and home-based arrangements and a system based on the principle of universality

The majority of children under three are, however, mainly cared for by one of the parents (mostly the mother, working or not) during the week (see Table 4.2).

The French childcare system is based on the principle of universality, and the rationale underlying this system is to provide equal access to all public facilities whatever the income or the social background of the family; this means that *crèches* are not targeted at low-income families. However, lone mothers in employment or registered as unemployed are frequently given priority, in particular in disadvantaged areas. Indeed, there is a consensus among policy makers and public opinion that the best way to lift families and their children out of poverty is to help the mother to sustain employment.

Although formal childcare provision (*crèches* and childminders) is highly subsidised and fees are income-related, for low-income families these services remain expensive. Indeed, almost all children from the lowest-income families are cared for mainly by their parents (see Table 4.3). For working parents this means coordinating so that working schedules do not overlap. Among low-income families, the take-up rate of the parental leave benefit is much higher than among better-off families (Boyer, 2012). This flat rate benefit (€566 per month

Table 4.2: France: Childcare arrangements for under threes during the week (%)

	All children		Both parents work full-time
	Main childcare arrangement	**Second childcare arrangement**	**Main childcare arrangement**
Crèches	10	8	18
Registered childminders	18	8	37
Nanny/day-care employee (publicly subsidised)	2	–	4
Total formal arrangements	30	16	59
Looked after by relatives	4	11	9
Looked after by parents	63	33	27
Other arrangement	3	7	5
No second arrangement		33	
TOTAL	100		100

Notes: Main childcare arrangement refers to the arrangement in which the child spends most of the hours between 9am and 7pm from Monday to Friday. Second childcare arrangement is ranked second in terms of hours spent, as above. 'Other arrangement' includes friends, neighbours, babysitters or other person not related to the family, *jardin d'enfants*, nursery school or setting for children with additional needs or learning disabilities.

Source: Boyer et al (2012, pp 22–3). Data refers to 2007

Table 4.3: France: Children under three: breakdown according to the main childcare arrangement during the week and the family income level (%)

Income per consumption unit	Parents	Relatives	Licensed childminder	Childcare centres (EAJE)	Ecole maternelle	Nanny/ day-care employee	Other	Total
First quintile	91	1	2	4	1	0	1	100
Second quintile	84	2	5	5	2	0	2	100
Third quintile	64	6	18	9	2	0	1	100
Fourth quintile	44	7	29	16	2	1	1	100
Fifth quintile	31	5	37	16	3	7	1	100

Source: Borderies (2012)

if the parent stops working) can be provided until the child reaches the age of three. In 2009, 61% of low qualified mothers compared to 22% of highly qualified mothers claimed this benefit (Boyer, 2012).

Besides differences in ECEC usage across income levels, it is worth noting that there are large geographical disparities in the supply of places in centre-based provision (Borderies, 2012). In deprived areas, often located in the outer suburbs, if parents cannot get a place in those centres mothers are therefore prone to stop seeking work or to be in employment.

Centre-based provision: crèches and multi-accueil

Nearly 15% of all children under three attend centre-based services, which mainly take the form of *crèches collectives*, open up to 11 hours a day all year round. Over the last decade, there has been an increase in the number of multi-centres (*multi-accueil*), now termed *etablissements d'accueil du jeune enfant* (EAJE) (early childhood care centres). Nearly three-quarters of *crèches* are based in such centres (CNAF, 2012a). The rationale is to group together in one place different childcare services, offering multiple and flexible arrangements: *crèches*, *halte-garderies* (half time and occasional day-care), *jardins d'enfants*, *crèches parentales* (where parents can also be involved in the management and daily work), emergency care for children at risk and rooms for childminders. The objective was to meet parents' needs by providing them with opportunities to modify their childcare arrangements in relation to job demands: from part time to full time, for instance, on a regular basis or from time to time, and so on. The use of some slots in *multi-accueil* are therefore not defined in advance.

Since 2003, the provision of childcare services is also open to for-profit providers with the explicit objective of increasing the availability of childcare places. They have access to public subsidies (from the local CAF) if they meet the specific quality requirements (discussed below) and if they operate income-related fees.

Moreover, while the vast majority of collective childcare centres are located in the neighbourhoods where families live, a few employers have created childcare centres called *crèches d'entreprise* (workplace *crèches*, mostly run by for-profit providers) for their staff. They also have access to public subsidies if they meet specific quality requirements (see later). There are currently about 500 *crèches d'entreprise* (representing around 2.7% of the total of places in collective childcare centres). Cooperating with local authorities and CAFs, companies can also contribute to the setting up and running costs of public centre-based services (including around-the-clock home-based childcare) and in exchange, some places are reserved for their employees' children.

In disadvantaged areas,[2] over the last decade, the government and CNAF have made important efforts to increase access to collective childcare settings. One of the main objectives of the national programme *Plan crèches espoir banlieues* (literally, 'Project Childcare Hope in Disadvantaged Areas') is to encourage the creation of 'innovative' and 'flexible' childcare places suitable for parents with non-standard working schedules. The programme, however, does not mean that children from the most deprived families have systematically priority access to day-care centres for under threes because the system remains based on the principle of universality, and one of the criteria of the choices (among candidates on the waiting list) made by the local council is to mix children from diverse social backgrounds.

Importantly, *crèches* are highly valued by families, as a result of the staff's qualification requirements in place (see below) and of the prevalent idea that *crèches* provide an ideal preparation for the transition to nursery school and consequently to primary education. Therefore the demand emanating from middle-class families is high. The early socialisation (a longstanding tradition in France dating back to the end of the nineteenth century) this provides is held in high esteem, and the probability that a child will attend a *crèche* increases significantly when the child's mother has reached a high level of educational attainment. Twenty-one per cent of those children whose parents are in senior or middle management or occupying supervisory roles are enrolled in a *crèche* as their main childcare during the week, compared with only 5% of children from working-class families (Ananian and Robert-Bobée, 2009). Table 4.3 also shows that children living in the wealthiest families are over-represented in childcare centres.

Registered childminders: a major contribution to the supply of childcare services

Since the 1990s, the primary method for bridging the gap between supply and demand for childcare has been to increase government support for licensed childminders who look after children in their private home.[3] By 2010, the number of childminders looking after children reached 306,256 (including 1,434 men). They are required to register with local authorities, a procedure that is mandatory if parents who rely on them wish to be eligible for the related childcare allowance paid by the local CAF and the tax deduction.

When both parents work full time, childminders are the main and primary form of care arrangement for under threes: 37% are looked after by a childminder. The same is true for the whole population of children looked after in any formal care arrangement (see Table 4.2 above).

Some registered childminders are directly employed by municipalities or by non-governmental organisations (NGOs) (termed *crèches familiales*). In rural areas, some local authorities have developed *micro crèches*, where childminders look after children in a collective place, mixing individual childcare by childminders and collective care.

In socio-economically deprived areas, low qualified women are being encouraged to become childminders, both to increase the supply of places in formal childcare and to support women's employment. A counsellor of the local employment agency advises them and they may be provided with financial support from CAF to help them adapt their home to regulatory requirements.

Working parents can also hire a babysitter or a nanny to look after their children, either on a full-time basis or to provide after-school care and to cover Wednesdays. Provided that he/she is declared, a childcare allowance covers part of the social security contributions that must be paid by these families. In addition, they may deduct 50%, up to €6,000 per year, of the real costs from their income tax. However, only a few parents can afford this care arrangement (see Table 4.3 above).

Nursery schools: écoles maternelles

Écoles maternelles are free for parents and are fully integrated into the school system under the national Ministry of Education, with the same guiding principles, opening hours and administration as elementary schools. According to the French education code every child, on reaching the age of three, has the right (but it is not compulsory) to attend a nursery school, and almost all children aged three to six attend it full or part time. Children are usually grouped into three classes, according to age. Mixed age grouping is relatively uncommon.

Nursery schools are generally open from 8.30am to 4.30pm and have canteen facilities (under the supervision of a dietician) where fees are income related. They are routinely closed on Wednesdays, but are supplemented by half-day Saturday sessions.

Over the last decade, policies targeted to children from disadvantaged backgrounds have channelled additional resources towards schools located in more deprived areas. An area is designated as a *zone d'éducation prioritaire* (ZEP) (priority education area) when it includes a high proportion of those children, defined according to a variety of criteria outlined by the national Ministry of Education. The government passed a law in 2005 to encourage and extend in these areas access of under threes to *écoles maternelles* by providing them with priority access. In schools with many two-year-olds, there may be a *toute petite section* (very little section), or children may be integrated with the three- to five-year-olds. The child-to-staff ratio most often falls to 20 children plus an assistant, and is capped at 25.

The shortfall of places in *crèches*, and the fact that this service is free, has given parents living in ZEPs a strong incentive to ask for a place in a nursery school. However, the share of children aged between two and three in *écoles maternelles* has fallen off sharply, from 37% in 2000 to 11.6% in 2011. This is mainly due to the dramatic increase in the number of children aged between three and six (following a growth in the fertility rate since 1999) who are given priority over the two-year-olds and to funding restrictions at the national Ministry of Education (resulting in a reduction in the number of teachers and assistants). On the other hand, the enrolment of two-year-olds remains a controversial issue: some children's experts underline that an école maternelle is not appropriate to the needs of under threes while some research shows the benefits of early schooling for children from economically disadvantaged backgrounds (Ministere de l'éducation nationale, de la jeunesse et de la vie associative, 2011). It is important to note, however, that most of the under threes attend school only in the morning (Vanovermeir, 2012).

Funding structures: the state, the CAFs and local authorities

Funding structures are very complex and vary according to the type of care arrangement. Many stakeholders are involved in funding: the state (through the Ministry of Education and tax breaks related to childcare allowances), CAFs, the local authorities and the families. It is worth noticing that despite a general tightening of purse strings in public expenditure, childcare policies have continued to see increases in funding, and remain a growth area in the French welfare state.[4] Therefore the system of public *crèches*, and more generally EAJE, has suffered no funding cutbacks.

CNAF is the leading contributor (73%) to childcare for under threes. It allocates funds to each decentralised CAF to help local authorities create and run childcare centres. Both public *crèches* and the few for-profit ones receive funding from CAF on a per child basis if they use the national sliding fee scale based on family income. Because individual settings cannot charge top-up fees, there is little incentive for them to select well-off families as they receive the same amount of money per child by the local CAF. The aim of this flat funding is precisely to ensure social mix in collective centres. By contrast, on the whole, costs to the CNAF vary greatly according to the level of income of families accessing *crèches*, with low-income families receiving higher subsidies (Boyer, 2012).

Employers are involved in an indirect way in funding childcare because CNAF is mainly funded out of social security contributions paid by employers (around 65%). The state, through income tax and other taxes, is the other contributor.

Local authorities – *départements* (departments) and *communes* (municipalities) – also make a significant financial commitment (Boyer, 2012). They have, however, substantial autonomy in offering *crèches* and EAJE in general: they are not required to create childcare facilities and sometimes prefer to encourage and help women to become childminders (through the funding of training programmes) because it is much less expensive for them than to develop day-care centres. This partly explains why there is a substantial variation in enrolment rates in *crèches* across the country. Local authorities also fund part of the running costs of nursery schools but the national Ministry of Education pays teachers' wages.

In regard to collective childcare settings, the rules that govern the levels of public funding (by the state and CNAF), and the levels of (income-related) fees to be paid by the parents are set up nationally following guidelines fixed through agreements signed every four years between the government and CNAF. The cost of childcare to parents depends on the type of care arrangement chosen, the number and ages of the children and the income level. Indeed for all forms of subsidised childcare provision (outside écoles maternelles which are free) parents pay on a sliding scale according to their income.

Childminding is subsidised both by the state and by the CAFs. The state allows tax deductions from income tax, up to a limit of €1,150 per year, and offers tax credits for families who are not liable to income tax. The CAFs, on the other hand, subsidise childminding through an allowance (*complément de libre choix du mode de garde*, CLMG; literally, supplement for the freedom of choice of the childcare arrangement).[5] CLMG covers the social security contributions to be paid by the employer of the registered childminder, and also provides the family with an additional and income-related financial contribution. The amount of this allowance also varies according to the age of the child (less than three, and three to six) and the number of children living in the family.

In order to be eligible to receive the allowance, parents must pay the childminder at least the statutory minimum income[6] defined by

CNAF to be eligible for the CLMG: €46.10 per child and per day corresponding to 10 hours of care for the child.[7] The net median wage per hour and per child was €2.96 by 2010 and the net average wage per hour and per child €3.03 (Fagnani and Math, 2012).

In 2004 a significant increase in the allowance that low-income families receive made childminding more accessible than it was. However, for most of them, it remains too expensive, and in 2007 only 4% of the families with incomes below €1,100 per month could afford a childminder to care for their child aged below three compared to 22% of the families whose income was between €1,100 and €1,700 and 37% of the families earning more than €2,300 (Borderies, 2012) (see also Table 4.3).

As far as *crèches* are concerned, parents pay on a sliding scale according to their income. The cost of a place in a *crèche* also depends on the number of hours of attendance. For instance, in a family with a single child cared for 9 hours a day and 18 days per month, net out-of-pocket expenses amounts to an average of €400 per month to parents with an income level of €5,471 and more, while for an income level of €2,163 this amount represents €100 per month (Boyer, 2012).

For low-income families, despite the related childcare allowance (CLMG), the cost of a childminder is twice the cost of a place in a *crèche*. The shortage of places in *crèches* is therefore detrimental to them, in particular to lone-parent households, and presents a barrier to full-time work. Consequently when they are in employment they most often rely on relatives or to undeclared childminders.

Quality of provision and the current regulatory framework

PMI services: a crucial role in ensuring quality

The national public system of preventive healthcare and health promotion for all mothers and children from birth through age six, *protection maternelle et infantile* (PMI), plays a crucial role and is responsible for upholding the quality of public childcare provision (childcare centres as well as licensed childminders). Created in 1945 and subsequently developed (Fagnani, 2006) local PMI services fall under the remit of the *départements* (local authorities) and are supervised by the national Ministry of Social Affairs (Department of Social Security).

Local PMI services are in charge of licensing and monitoring all care services that fall outside the remit of the public school system and intervene regularly across many areas. Primarily, they ensure that providers (including childcare centres run by private providers but publicly subsidised) abide with regulation concerning health and safety (including preventive health exams and vaccinations), nutrition and staffing standards. Doctors or *puéricultrices* employed by PMI services regularly inspect services.

Health services are also integrated into *écoles maternelles*: they have a doctor and psychologist on their staff several hours per week or available for consultation as needed to provide evaluations and referrals. Preventive health exams are mandated for all four-year-olds. Trained medical staff from the local PMI services also play a role in helping integrate children with additional needs or learning disabilities, whether in schools or childcare settings.

Policy priorities, goals and requirements affecting childcare provision

There is a different understanding of quality in nursery schools and in services for under threes. This reflects the dual nature of the system of services. In relation to all publicly subsidised childcare services (except nannies or home helpers) the policy priorities and goals can be summarised as follows:

- ensuring children with safety, health and a sense of wellbeing by focusing on education, socialisation and cognitive development;
- giving parents 'freedom of choice' over childcare arrangements;
- enabling parents (in particular mothers) to participate in the workforce;
- enhancing equal opportunities for children;
- complying with the principle of social justice (income-related fees in childcare settings);
- encouraging a social mix that underpins social cohesion.

It is assumed that childcare centres can partly offset the negative outcomes for children living in families coping with hard living conditions (in particular overcrowded housing), but against the background of a high unemployment rate, there is also an underlying rationale: creating a tool to fight unemployment by encouraging parents to hire someone to look after their children (licensed childminders and nannies).

Within this overall approach, different services have their specific quality regulatory framework, which is legally enforceable. In *crèches*, staffing standards are laid down nationally: one adult to five children who are not yet walking, and one adult to eight children for other children. To ensure psychological wellbeing, each child is under the specific supervision of a *personne de référence* (contact person).

Although there is no national curriculum for collective childcare settings, since 2000 *crèches* and *multi-accueil* have been required to elaborate an education and social project (*projet d'établissement*) that includes a *projet éducatif* (education programme) and a *projet social* (social project). The main goals embedded in the quality tools are: enhancement of cognitive and physical abilities, development of pedagogical activities, respect for biological rhythms, ensuring children with safety, health and wellbeing, and promoting and favouring social integration (mentioned earlier). Parents are also encouraged to participate in the everyday life of the setting. Emphasis is also put on the exchanges with stakeholders involved in childcare policies, as well as on coordination with different agencies.

Other objectives include enhancing equal opportunities for children, thereby contributing to prevent social exclusion and to foster gender equality by supporting mothers' participation in the labour market.

Childminders are closely supervised by PMI services, although with a frequency depending on the local authorities. Before being licensed, they are interviewed by a social worker, a paediatric nurse and a psychologist. The housing conditions and environment for receiving children should be approved, especially in terms of space, hygiene and safety. As of March 2012 PMI services have been required to use common standards for criteria related to the registration of childminders. And since 2005 registration procedures have to take into account the childminder's educational skills. The license is valid for five years and can be renewed for consecutive periods. It specifies the number (no more than four simultaneously) and the age of children that can be cared for by the childminder, either full or part time.

Given that childminding is the most common childcare arrangement for children under three, in recent years policy makers have been addressing the issue of their qualifications. Indeed, although their average educational achievement had improved since the 1970s, in 2005, 49% had no qualification whatsoever and 35% had very low qualifications. Therefore, efforts to reduce the cost for parents of this type of care have been coupled with measures attempting to professionalise childminding. Since 2004 childminders have been required to receive 60 hours of additional training (in total 60 before and 60 in the two years following their registration). The training programme is paid for and supervised by the local authorities.

Despite these significant improvements, however, childhood experts and childminders' trade unions still point out the persistent shortcomings and the heterogeneity of the training programmes across the country, and are calling for further development of qualifications available to childminders (Fagnani and Math, 2012). However, parents cannot always afford to rely on a qualified childminder despite generous childcare allowances: such a person can be more demanding in this regard than a less trained counterpart.

In order to enhance early socialisation of children, childminders are encouraged to participate in childminders' centres (*relais assistants maternels*, RAM), where they can exchange on their own experience with other childminders and also receive advice from a qualified child nurse, while children can participate in collective activities. RAMs are highly valued by childminders (Fagnani and Math, 2012) but, despite their rapid increase over the last few years (the numbers currently reach 500), there is still a lack of these facilities.

In 2005 the employment regulation of childminders was revised. The aim was both to enhance the quality of care by improving working conditions and to make this profession more attractive through stricter regulation. Such regulation has made the childminders' employment contract more in line with that of other employees. The objective of the reform was to make work regulations closer to the common work rules, especially with regard to the labour contract, to earnings and working-time regulations. The *professionalisation* programme renewed childminders' collective agreement, thus settling labour relations between employers (parents, municipalities, NGOs) and the childminders. The national employment contract is binding, defines minimum payments (mentioned earlier) and limits the legal working hours to 45 hours per week. Childminders' salary should be paid monthly in order to provide childminders with regular earnings throughout the year as well as entitlement for annual paid leave. Finally, childminders became entitled to tax breaks on part of their earnings.

Staff qualifications and training programmes

Compared with childminders, staff in *crèches* (including in private *crèches* and in *crèches d'entreprise* subsidised by CAFs) and *multi-accueil* are well trained, closely supervised and relatively well remunerated (compared to the childminders). There are three categories of staff. First is the *puéricultrice* (pediatric nurse) with four-year post-secondary education. The *puéricultrice* usually works as the director of a *crèche* and *multi-accueil*. But the director may also be the doctor or midwife. All of them have to complete a year of specialisation in children's development, health and wellbeing. At the end of the training programme, practical work experience takes place: the student is required to work in a maternity ward, neonatal unit, paediatrics as well in a sector of PMI services and in a *crèche*. The training programme is updated each year to take into account new health concerns.

The second category of staff is the *éducatrice de jeunes enfants* (early childhood educator), who is required to have a high school diploma and to undergo a period of 27 months of vocational training programme comprising both theoretical training and practical field experience. *Auxiliaires de puéricultrice* – the third category of staff – can also attend this programme if they have three years of professional experience. If the centre has more than 40 places, there must be at least one *éducatrice de jeunes enfants*. They can develop educational projects and foster partnerships with families, schools and other social and cultural settings.

At least half of the staff in centres must be *auxiliaires de puéricultrice* (assistant pediatric nurses). The *auxiliaire* is required to attend an *école d'auxiliaires de puéricultrice* where they are provided with a vocational qualification programme over a period of 12 months (1,575 hours comprising theoretical and practical fieldwork). Training is open to candidates who have passed the entry exams and have either a professional certificate or have completed four years of secondary education. The training includes pedagogy and human development; education and care; child development and educational practice; group management; law; economics and social studies; and professional studies and methods. Training centres are mainly run privately, but accredited by the national Ministry of Health.

In *écoles maternelles*, on the other hand, all teachers (*professeurs des écoles*) are public servants and must have passed a national exam that is open to those who have a three-year college degree before teaching. The exam includes written papers in French, maths, science and art, a practical exam in sport and an oral exam on workplace experiences. Those who pass the exam enrol in one of the public academic institutes for a year of professional training (about 450 hours), which generally includes studies in education; philosophy; history of education; sociology; psychology; subject study; and preparation for administrative tasks.

To help teachers with daily activities such as cleaning up and toileting as well as in carrying out pedagogical activities, assistants named as *agents territorial spécialisé des écoles maternelles* (ATSEM) are employed by local authorities. Since 1992, ATSEM are required to hold a certificate in early childhood education (*CAP petite enfance*), a professional qualification level accessible from the age of 16 without being required to have any diploma. The mayor appoints these aides and they work under the supervision of the director of the school.

In *écoles maternelles* there are no national regulations for staff-to-child ratios. In 2010–11, there was on average one teacher to every 25.7 children. The assistants, ATSEM, are not included in this calculation because not all local authorities fund enough assistants, especially with older children, and, moreover, they are not present the whole day.

Tensions and inconsistencies

French childcare policy is currently facing new challenges linked to the numerous and dramatic changes that have occurred both in the labour market and in the family sphere. Policy makers therefore have to deal with tensions and difficult trade-offs. In a context where their room of manoeuvre is limited, ensuring high-quality provision seems at odds with affordability and availability of places for under threes. How can children's interests be reconciled with other interests, for example, gender equality, employment and employers? Alongside some progress it is clear that reforms recently introduced appear to be driven more by labour market pressure and mothers' rights to paid work than always being couched in terms of the 'best interests' of the child.

Indeed, over the last decade the ministry in charge of family policies, local authorities and CNAF has refocused its energies and currently places more emphasis than before on the following issues: how to increase the number of available slots in the formal childcare sector (in response to the rise in the number of births and the need for many women to be in paid employment) and enable parents confronted with non-standard or family-unfriendly flexible work hours to combine their job with family responsibilities (Fagnani, 2010), and at the same time, how to promote female employment in economically disadvantaged neighbourhoods.

Tensions between quality of care and a shortfall of crèche places

Although measures were being taken over the last decade to compensate for a persistent shortfall in supply, policy makers have yet to satisfy the ceaseless demand for places in childcare facilities and the services of registered childminders.[8] This problem has been aggravated by the difficulties local authorities and CAFs have to cope with in recruiting qualified staff (due to funding restrictions, there is a dearth of places in training centres for people looking to qualify for jobs in the childcare sector) and thereby to reach the required standards imposed by PMI services (50% at least of the staff in EAJE has to be made up of *puéricultrices, éducatrice de jeunes enfants, auxiliaires de puéricultrice*, nurses or psycho-motor therapists). This problem has also been reinforced by the fact that the number of children born in 2010 reached 833,000, representing a steady rise from the 757,000 reported in 1997. Moreover, the enhancement of women's employment has continued to be an explicit objective of French family policies (Fagnani and Math, 2011). The increase in the number of places has therefore been given higher priority on the policy agenda. The results of a recent survey of local elected officials are indicative of this trend: over the last four years, 46% declared that they put at the forefront of their care policies the development of childcare places (CNAF, 2012a).

Tensions between quality and affordability

The objective of the enhancement of women's employment – in particular in disadvantaged areas – does not always go hand in hand with easy access to affordable childcare. And as far as registered childminders are concerned, the move towards their professionalisation has pushed up the price of this care arrangement. The increase in the amount of the CLMG, decided in 2004, did not fully offset this phenomenon. It is therefore detrimental to low-income parents who are likely to be less demanding in terms of quality of care provided by childminders since demand far outstrips supply in childcare settings.

Concomitantly policy makers are once again confronted with another dilemma: taking into account the shortage of childminders in many urban areas, how do they make this profession more attractive without increasing their earnings (Himmelweit, 2007)? But against the background of budgetary constraints, will parents be willing to pay more to a better-trained childminder? Recent research based on a representative sample of parents relying on a childminder shows that only around a third would be willing to pay more (Fagnani and Math, 2012).

Tensions between quality and the objective of meeting the needs of parents confronted with atypical working schedules

Along with organisational changes in the workplace, staff in the childcare sector have been placed under pressure to adapt their own working hours to the needs of the increasing number of parents confronted with long and/or non-standard working hours. Moreover, a growing number of employees have a low degree of command over the scheduling of their work hours, in particular in low paying occupations.

Taking into account their family obligations, individuals employed in the childcare sector are all striving to protect their own interests and are reluctant to submit to ever more flexible working schedules. Registered childminders, if they can afford to,[9] will often refuse to look after a child outside of standard working hours. The result is that young children are often cared for by a rotating cast of characters and institutions within the same day. This is particularly true when both parents have non-standard work schedules, or when the parent is living alone (Bressé et al, 2007).

Recent decisions made at the expense of quality in childcare provision

Against this background, the following decisions have been made over the last decade on how to relieve some of the tensions inherent in current childcare policies.

New legislation was passed in June 2010 introducing significant reforms in the *Code de la santé publique* (Public Health Regulation). First, a decision was made to decrease from 50% to 40% the minimum share of staff required to qualify as skilled workers (*puéricultrices*, éducateurs *de jeunes enfants, auxiliaires de puéricultrice)* in childcare centres. This decision was motivated by the fact that a shortage of skilled workers had been acting as a brake on the swifter development of such centres.

Second, citing the fact that many young children registered in childcare centres do not attend every day or on a full-time basis, the government decided to raise the number of children these centres would be authorised to accept. From 2011, *crèches* with more than 40 slots are allowed to increase by 20% the number of children registered and attending the *crèche* (15% for *crèches* with less than 40 slots and 10% for those with less than 20 slots).

Third, in 2009 a law was passed, and registered childminders, instead of being limited to having only three children simultaneously under their care, are now allowed up to four. The aim was to increase the number of places in childcare provision and to provide childminders with the opportunity to earn more, thereby making the job more attractive. However, in a survey of local officials (Pillayre and Robert-Bobée, 2010) based in 94 departments and responsible for the supervision of childminders, 69% declared that this measure would result in less time devoted by childminders to each child, fewer opportunities to play with them and less availability to enhance their cognitive development. Almost one out of five underlined the risk involved as far as security was concerned and insufficient space in the home for each child to be able to rest.

None of these decisions have passed without controversy, and some trade unions and associations have denounced them as threats to the quality of childcare.[10] So far, the government has turned a deaf ear to these criticisms.

In 2004 the ministry in charge of family affairs introduced a measure to promote the creation of *crèches* in private companies (termed *crèches d'entreprise*) by providing them with tax deductions along with partial funding from CAFs. In the context of increasing commuting time, this type of solution can be detrimental to child wellbeing, as children would have to commute with their parents. Related to this, in an attempt to satisfy employers' demand for more atypical work hours, the last decade has witnessed an increase in the number of childcare services and *crèches* operating 24 hours a day and 7 days a week in order to allow working parents to meet the demands placed on them by employers. These company-run centres (partly funded by CAFs, as explained earlier) are a response to the new realities of the workplace. The need for extended childcare opening hours set to match is a shared one. The example of Renault (a leader in the French automotive industry) is emblematic of the new reality: since 2010 its employees have enjoyed access to childcare from 5.30am to 10.30pm, and this clearly illustrates that its employees' children are spending significant amounts of time in outside care, and thereby in commuting.[11]

Within the same approach, while the government supports the development of childcare centres in socio-economically disadvantaged areas (as discussed earlier), strong emphasis is put on the promotion of opening hours that are more in tune with 'the needs of working parents' and on the development of so-called 'flexible' and 'innovative' childcare arrangements. The operating hours of the childcare centres have been extended to over 10 hours per day, exceeding the current regulations granting children the right to attend a *crèche* as well as an école *maternelle* up to a maximum of 10 hours per working day.

In 2009, with the explicit objective of increasing the availability of childcare places, the government decided to create and support a new type of collective arrangement, called *jardins d'éveil*, where two- to three-year-old children could be cared for. They are supposed to serve as bridges between the home and the nursery school. Vocal criticisms, however, have been raised as the quality of this type of childcare which would be patchier than in *crèches* where the statutory child to staff ratio is 8:1 compared to 12:1 in *jardins d'éveil*, and the qualification requirements of the staff less strict.[12] These new centres are also widely viewed as an underhanded way to transfer more of the financial burden for care from the government to parents by reducing demand for places in nursery schools and siphoning it into these *jardins d'éveil*, although these centres have met with very little success.

Conclusions

Although the *EU Framework of Law for Children's Rights* (European Parliament, 2012) states that 'all EU policies must be designed and implemented in line with the child's best interests', new developments in France have given rise to increasing tensions and dilemmas despite attempts made to reconcile the quantitative with the qualitative in the formulation of consistent childcare policy. While the focus has continued to remain on supporting mothers' employment by subsidising formal individual care arrangements as well as collective ones, reforms introduced since the mid-1990s clearly illustrate the ways in which employment policies have encroached on the ground previously occupied by French family policy.

Moreover, reforms introduced by the government have created employment both on the supply side (the increased labour market participation of women) and on the demand side (the increased number of jobs in childcare services), but there are still important gaps in quality as far as childminders are concerned, and heterogeneity in this field is still the rule.

In all these domains, responsibilities (spread over different social partners) are all too often dissipated, which leads to a lack of accountability for actions taken, and no one is held responsible, for instance, for the mismatch between supply and demand of childcare at the local level. Spatial disparities in supply of places in centre-based settings also remain wide and continue to hinder access of all families to high-quality childcare.

Last but not least, the issue of the predominantly female workforce in the childcare sector has not yet been addressed although it would be a significant component of an holistic and comprehensive approach to promoting high-quality childcare.

Notes
[1] As the chapter will make clear, in France *crèches* offer regular, full-time childcare. French *crèches* thus are not to be confused with British crèches,

which provide occasional care, for example while parents are shopping or doing sports.

[2] Located in the 215 neighbourhoods designated as *zones urbaines sensibles* (sensitive urban areas) or in communes with a *contrats urbains de cohésion sociale* (urban social cohesion pacts).

[3] Referred to as *assistantes maternelles* (literally, maternal assistants).

[4] As far as collective childcare facilities are concerned, CNAF expenditure increased by 59.4% over the period 2006–11 (CNAF, 2012b).

[5] To be eligible both parents have to be employed or registered as unemployed or attending a training course.

[6] Beyond this statutory wage, parents are free to pay more, but the related social contributions will not be reimbursed by the CAF.

[7] There are also strong geographical disparities: childminders living in the metropolitan Paris area (in particular those located in Paris downtown) are those who are the best paid (€1,440 per month on average) as a result of the mismatch between supply and demand (Fagnani and Math, 2012).

[8] The gap between supply and demand for formal childcare has been estimated at a minimum of 350,000 places by the *Haut conseil de la famille* (High Council on Family Affairs) (HCF, 2009).

[9] For example, in cases where it is difficult for parents to make alternative arrangements or when the family hold the caregiver in high esteem.

[10] In April 2010 they drew up a petition against the new legislation under the banner of '*Pas de bébés à la consigne*' ('Left luggage: no babies allowed') and organised several demonstrations (www.pasdebebesalaconsigne.com).

[11] Strazdins et al (2006) have demonstrated that non-standard work schedules have detrimental effects on children's wellbeing and on the quality of interactions within the family.

[12] Regulation can be viewed at http://goo.gl/XbAFYc

References

Ananian, S. and Robert-Bobée, I. (2009) *Modes de garde et d'accueil des enfants en 2007* [*Early Childhood Care in 2007*], Paris: Direction de la recherche, des études, de l'évaluation et des statistiques (DREES), Etudes et résultats, no 678.

Borderies, F. (2012) *L'offre d'accueil des jeunes enfants de moins de 3 ans en 2010* [*The Supply of Early Childhood Care for Children under 3 in 2010*], Paris: Direction de la recherche, des études, de l'évaluation et des statistiques (DREES), Études et résultats, no 803.

Boyer, D. (ed) (2012) *L'accueil du jeune enfant en 2010, données statistiques* [*Early Childhood Care in 2010 – Statistics Report*], Paris: Observatoire national de la petite enfance, Caisse nationale des allocations familiales (CNAF).

Bressé, S., le Bihan, B. and Martin, C. (2007) *La garde des enfants en dehors des plages horaires standard* [*Early Childhood Care Outside Standard Hours*], Paris: Direction de la recherche, des études, de l'évaluation et des statistiques (DREES), Etudes et résultats, no 551.

CNAF (*Caisse nationale des allocations familiales*) (2012a) *La politique petite enfance vue par les communes* [*Early Childhood Policy from the Perspective of the Municipalities*], Paris: *L'e-ssentiel*, no 121 (www.caf.fr/sites/default/files/cnaf/Documents/Dser/essentiel/121-_cej.pdf)

CNAF (2012b) *Prestations familiales 201. Statistiques nationales* [*Family Allowances and Services 2011. National Statistics*], Paris: CNAF (www.caf.fr/sites/default/files/cnaf/Documents/Dser/donnees_tous_regimes/prestations_familiales_2011.pdf).

Cour des comptes (2008) *Rapport public annuel* [*Public annual report*], Paris: la Documentation française.

European Parliament (2012) *EU Framework of Law for Children's Rights*, Strasbourg: European Parliament Directorate General for Internal Policies (www.europarl.europa.eu/RegData/etudes/note/libe/2012/462445/IPOL-LIBE_NT(2012)462445_EN.pdf).

Fagnani, J. (2006) 'Family policy in France', in T. Fitzpatrick, N. Manning, J. Midgely, H. Kwon and G. Pascall (eds) *International Encyclopedia of Social Policy*, Oxford, New York: Routledge, vol 3, pp 501–6.

Fagnani, J. (2010) 'Childcare policies in France: the influence of organizational changes in the workplace', in S. Kamerman, S. Phipps and A. Ben-Arieh (eds) *From Child Welfare to Child Well-being: An International Perspective on Knowledge in the Service of Making Policy*, London, New York: Springer, pp 385–402.

Fagnani, J. and Math, A. (2011) 'France: Gender equality, a pipe dream?', in S. Kamerman and P. Moss (eds) *The Politics of Parental Leave Policies*, London and New York: Policy Press, pp 103–18.

Fagnani, J. and Math, A. (2012) 'Des assistantes maternelles mieux formées et plus qualifiées. Les parents consentiraient-ils à augmenter la rémunération?' ['Better trained and more qualified childminders. Would parents be willing to pay?'], *Politiques sociales et familiales*, vol 109, pp 59–73.

HCF (*Haut conseil de la famille*) (2009) *La lettre du Haut Conseil de la Famille, No 2* [*Letter from the High Council on Family Matters, No 2*] (www.hcf-famille.fr/IMG/pdf/Lettre_HCF_no2-3.pdf).

Himmelweit, S. (2007) 'The prospects for caring: economic theory and policy analysis', *Cambridge Journal of Economics*, vol 31, no 4, pp 581-99.

Ministere de l'éducation nationale, de la jeunesse et de la vie associative (2011) *L'école maternelle. Rapport à monsieur le ministre de l'éducation nationale, de la jeunesse et de la vie associative* [*Nursery School. Report to the Minister of National Education, Youth and Community Life*], Paris: Ministere de l'éducation nationale, de la jeunesse et de la vie associative (http://media.education.gouv.fr/file/2011/54/5/2011-108-IGEN-IGAENR_215545.pdf).

OECD (Organisation for Economic Co-operation and Development) (2012) *OECD Family Database*, Paris: OECD Publishing (www.oecd.org/els/social/family/database).

Pillayre, H. and Robert-Bobée, I. (2010) *Conditions d'attribution des agréments des assistants maternels* [*Conditions Regarding the Registration of Childminders*], Paris: Direction de la recherche, des études, de l'évaluation et des statistiques (DREES), Études et résultats, no 719.

Strazdins, L., Clements, M.S., Korda, R., Broom, D.H. and D'Souza, R. (2006) 'Unsociable work? Non-standard work schedules, family relationships and children's well-being', *Journal of Marriage and the Family*, vol 68, no 2, pp 394–410.

Vanovermeir, S. (2012) *L'accueil des jeunes enfants: axe majeur de la politique familiale française depuis les années 1970* [*Early Childhood Care: A Pillar of French Family Policy since the 1970s*], Paris: Dossier Solidarité Santé, DREES, no 31.

FIVE

Equal access to high-quality childcare in the Netherlands

Yusuf Emre Akgündüz and Janneke Plantenga

Introduction

The Dutch early childhood education and care (ECEC) system is essentially a two-tiered system, consisting of private day-care centres and publicly funded playgroups. Day-care centres provide care for young children whose parents are employed. Although almost all parents make use of these facilities on a part-time basis, the services may be offered up to 11 hours a day, five days a week and 50 weeks a year. Playgroups are more child-centred, focus only on children in the age category two to four and cover about 10 hours a week and 42 weeks per year. Because of the difference in focus, children attending playgroups tend to be more from lower-income families and from a minority background. In addition, specific programmes for disadvantaged children are often organised within the context of playgroups. This concerns the so-called VVE programmes, focusing on early childhood education and care. The programmes might cover approximately 15 hours a week, equivalent to about three or four mornings or afternoons.

Research seems to indicate that children benefit from the use of high-quality childcare, while low-quality care can have a negative effect on development (NICHD Early Child Care Research Network, 2006). Until now, however, there has been little information on the use of high-quality care in the Netherlands and the difference between households in that respect. High-quality childcare may not be available in low-income neighbourhoods, for example, or parents may lack the information to opt for the highest quality. There may also be systematic differences between the quality of childcare services and playgroups – and if playgroups score low on quality, this may have negative consequences for children of low socio-economic status.

In this chapter, we investigate the state of equality of access for high-quality care in the Netherlands for families of low socio-economic status and different cultural backgrounds. The results can have implications for whether the two-tiered Dutch childcare system with both private day-care centres and publicly funded playgroups is able to provide equal quality care across socio-economic and ethnic groups. For our analysis, the first wave of the Pre-COOL dataset was used, collected in 2010 and 2011. The dataset includes indicators on structural and process quality in both day-care centres and playgroups, data on children's development and socio-economic characteristics of the staff and parents. The Pre-COOL data focuses exclusively on two-year-olds; the ability to link parents' characteristics, children and formal childcare services' attributes makes it an ideal dataset to investigate equality of access to high-quality childcare.

The outline for the chapter is as follows: the next section gives a general overview of the childcare system in the Netherlands. We then introduce the Pre-COOL dataset and compare the quality of day-care and playgroups on the basis of this. The fourth section focuses on the use of formal childcare services, whereas in the fifth section we formally analyse the use of quality childcare by socio-economic status. The last section concludes.

Childcare in the Netherlands: availability, costs and quality

The female labour force participation rate in the Netherlands is relatively high. In 2010 almost 70% of all women were active in the labour market, according to Eurostat data (2011), which is 10 percentage points above the European Union (EU)-15 average. The large numbers of dual-earner households are likely to translate into a substantial need for non-parental childcare, all the more so as the parental leave entitlements are rather limited. Dutch legislation allows for 16 weeks of paid maternity leave and 26 weeks of parental leave, paid at a fairly low level by a fiscal benefit (Plantenga and Remery, 2009). In addition, the take-up rate of parental leave is less than 50% among mothers and about 20% among fathers. At the same time, the demand for formal childcare services is restrained by the specific Dutch working time regime. Over the last two decades part-time working hours have become increasingly popular, as a result of which in 2012 more than three-quarters of employed women worked on a part-time basis (Plantenga et al, 2012).

In fact, formal (institutionalised) childcare developed rather late in the Netherlands. At the end of the 1980s, the Netherlands had (together with Ireland and the UK) the lowest level of formal childcare facilities in the EU (Moss, 1990). It was only during the 1990s that the number of places started to increase. The growth accelerated after 2005 with the introduction of the Dutch Child Care Act. With the introduction of this new Act the financial organisation of the childcare sector changed from a system of supply-financing to one of demand-financing. Working parents in principle pay full childcare costs and are then compensated directly by the tax authorities. The explicit objective of the Child Care Act is to stimulate the operation of market forces so that childcare providers respond to parental wishes in an efficient way. As a result of the change towards a demand-driven financing system, publicly provided day-care in the Netherlands disappeared. Instead only private for-profit (60% of all Dutch childcare organisations) or not-for-profit providers (the remaining 40%) are now operating and competing in the childcare market (Noailly and Visser, 2009).

The change in the financing structure implied enormous growth in the childcare sector. It is difficult to find comparable statistics, but Table 5.1 indicates that the number of childcare places for young children by the end of 2009 could be estimated at approximately 165,000, whereas the number of out-of-school care places amounted to more than 187,000. Compared to figures for 2004 this implied a 33% growth in childcare services whereas out-of-school care more than doubled over a short period of time. Taking into account that most Dutch children use childcare services on a part-time basis, the number of children using childcare services is considerably higher. Following Gemmeke and Paulussen-Hoogeboom (2007), we assume that 1.9 children make use of one full-time place. As a result in 2009 the enrolment rate for the youngest age category can be estimated at approximately 40%, with increasing rates by age. Despite the strong growth, the enrolment rate for school-age children is still slightly more moderate, at approximately 15%.

Table 5.1: Netherlands: Development of childcare capacity, 2004–09

Type of care	2004	2006	2008	2009	Growth rate (%)
Day-care	124,000	130,000	147,500	165,000	33
Out-of-school care	74,000	95,000	158,000	187,500	253
Total	199,000	225,000	305,000	352,500	77

Note: Rounding as in the original source.

Source: Gemmeke and Paulussen-Hoogeboom (2007); Dekker and Paulussen-Hoogeboom (2010)

Whereas the Child Care Act regulates care services for dual-earner households, local authorities are responsible for the playgroups that are targeted towards children in the age category two to four, independent of the labour market status of their parents. In addition, local authorities may run specific programmes for children from a disadvantaged background that, most of the time, are also part of the playgroup system. As children of dual-earner families mostly make use of day-care centres, children in playgroups tend to come from lower-income groups and/or from minority backgrounds. The growing capacity of day-care centres has, of course, limited the use of playgroups, although a substantial share of three- and four-year-olds still make use of playgroups. The overall coverage rate of child facilities in that age group is approximately 90%; children who do not make use of childcare tend to make use of playgroups. This specific setting gives the Dutch childcare system for young children a two-tiered appearance. Market forces dominate the care services for dual-earner households, while lower-income or disadvantaged minorities with children aged two to four have the option of public playgroups.

Prices

The net price that parents have to pay for childcare services that are covered by the Child Care Act has a large range. Point of departure is that the financing is on a tripartite basis, with employers paying one-third of actual childcare costs. Parents' share of the childcare costs then ranges between 3.5% for low and 66.6% for high-income households (Plantenga, 2012). The parental contribution is set at a national level and thus standardised. The Child Care Act does not regulate the prices to be set by the providers, yet in practice, there is a 'soft cap' due to the maximum price (€6.36 per hour in 2012) that the parents can receive reimbursements for. It is difficult for providers to push prices above the subsidy cap since any small increase in the hourly gross price translates into a large increase in the net price that parents will have to pay. The cost for low earning families might increase rather rapidly if the hourly price is set above the maximum. In 2008, 70% of the surveyed day-care centres took into account the maximum price that the parents could receive their subsidies for (Berden and Kok, 2009).

For playgroups, the prices are set by the local authorities and may differ between municipalities. Usually parents pay a contribution depending on income. As playgroups are not targeted at working parents, there is no contribution by the employer. The total hourly cost per child of playgroups is about 20% higher than day-care centres, partly because of a lower occupancy rate (Berden et al, 2011).

Quality

The Child Care Act 2005 does not stipulate any quality standards with regards to child-to-staff ratios beyond verbal encouragement, allowing instead for self-regulation through the quality standards agreed on by the (representatives of) childcare providers and parental organisations (OECD, 2006; Brancheorganisatie Kinderopvang, 2012). The stipulated quality standards provide a benchmark for local government, which is charged with registration and inspection. In effect, quality criteria agreed on by the parental organisations and childcare providers are binding.

The actual quality of childcare facilities has been followed by the successive projects of the Dutch Consortium for Child Care Research (NCKO) since 1995. The initial results from the 1995 wave found the quality of Dutch childcare in day-care centres to be above levels found in the UK and US (van Ijzendoorn et al, 1998). A follow-up study from 2001 using a similar methodology in the same project found declines in quality, with some day-care centres scoring particularly low on process quality measures (Deynoot-Schaub and Riksen-Walraven, 2005). The two more recent follow-ups in 2005 and 2008 similarly found declines in process quality. The overall process quality scale that ranges from a maximum of seven to a minimum of one, decreased from about five in 1995 to three in 2008. This translates into a drop from above-average quality childcare in Dutch day-care centres to below-average quality. Already in 2005 the researchers involved in the project concluded that the Netherlands could no longer be ranked among countries with high-quality childcare (Vermeer et al, 2008).

A plausible explanation for the decline in quality in the Netherlands might be the dramatic rise in availability and quantity of childcare since the introduction of the Child Care Act. Potential staff shortages, lack of experience in staff and management as well as difficulties in inspection and quality regulation caused by the rapid expansion in the childcare sector are possible explanations for the drop in quality levels.

Unlike the day-care centre, the quality in playgroups is regulated directly by the state through the Law for Child Care and Quality Requirements for Playgroups (WKO). The most significant difference between the content of the regulations for day-care and playgroups is in the child-to-staff ratios. The child-to-staff ratio in playgroups is at eight to one, while the requirement agreed on by parental organisations and childcare providers for two-year-olds in day-care centres is six to one. Both day-care and playgroup staff in the Netherlands are required to have completed vocational training for childcare. The training programme's level corresponds to intermediate vocational training in the Netherlands.

Comparing day-care services and playgroups with the Pre-COOL database

In order to compare the quality of childcare services and play groups, it is necessary to use a data source that contains the relevant data for both types of services. A useful dataset in this respect is the Pre-COOL survey, which is a longitudinal cohort following several thousand children starting from age two. Pre-COOL is a joint project of Kohnstamm Instituut of Amsterdam, Utrecht University and Nijmegen University. Constructed variables and basic results are made publicly available through the Dutch Data Archiving and Network Services (DANS).[1] The first data wave was collected in 2010 and 2011 and this is the wave used in the remainder of our analysis. The Pre-COOL survey is composed of data collected from three sources. Questionnaires for teachers, centre managers and parents provide information on children's background and centre characteristics. The second part contains process quality observations of the centres done by trained observers according to scales constructed by development psychologists. The third and final part of the Pre-COOL survey is a large assessment of children's development, which is not used in this study. Pre-COOL data is complemented by a parental questionnaire and child assessment on a cohort provided by Dutch Statistics (CBS), ensuring that the dataset also includes children who do not receive formal childcare at all.

Using the teacher questionnaires from the Pre-COOL survey we can get a first idea about the relative quality of childcare centres and playgroups by comparing the average staff qualifications; Table 5.2 provides some details in this respect. Around 350 staff responses are available, more than 200 of which are from playgroups. It appears that staff in playgroups tend to work fewer hours, probably because playgroups are open for fewer hours, and have more experience. The difference in experience levels is striking and seems to support the hypothesis that the rapid expansion in the number of day-care centres has been accompanied by a decline in the staff's experience. Out of the staff working in day-care centres, 25.16% had fewer than five years' experience in the childcare sector as opposed to 14.5% in playgroups.

Table 5.2: Netherlands: Staff qualifications (%)

Staff qualifications	All centres	Day-care	Playgroups
Education level			
Secondary education	18.41	15.23	20.79
Lower vocational education	15.30	18.54	12.87
Intermediate vocational education	61.47	62.25	60.89
Higher vocational education	2.83	3.31	2.48
University	1.98	0.66	2.97
(Years of) experience			
0–5 years	19.15**	25.83	14.36
5–10 years	24.51***	30.46	20.30
More than 10 years	56.34***	43.71	65.35
Working hours			
Less than 25 hours	54.67**	35.76	68.81
24–32 hours	30.59**	40.40	23.27
More than 32 hours	14.73**	23.84	7.92

Notes: ***$p<0.01$, **$p<0.05$, *$p<0.1$: Significance of difference between children in day-care and playgroups.
Source: Pre-COOL 2012

The Pre-COOL survey also allows for a direct measurement of the qualities of childcare facilities used by children aged two. Unlike the previous projects by NCKO, Pre-COOL collects data on the process and structural quality of both day-care centres and playgroups, allowing for a more complete picture of the overall quality of formal childcare services in the Netherlands. The process quality is measured using the Classroom Assessment Scoring System (CLASS) through multiple 20- to 30-minute observations of classrooms. Several groups have been measured in a total of 159 formal childcare services in the current wave. Out of 159, 91 are playgroups and 68 are day-care centres. While groups within the centres are observed individually, for the purposes of this study, multiple measurements of each centre from different classrooms are averaged to generate an overall score for each formal childcare centre. Two domains of the CLASS are available in the Pre-COOL survey: instructional and emotional support (Thomson and La Paro, 2009). Domains are made up of dimensions such as quality of feedback and language modelling for instructional support and positive climate and teacher sensitivity for emotional support (Slot and Leseman, 2012). The instructional support measure is intuitively more likely to predict school readiness later. Equal access to higher instructional support quality may be critical to ensure that all school-age children have a similar starting point.

Table 5.3: Netherlands: Means and standard deviations of structural and process quality in Dutch day-care centres and playgroups

Childcare quality measures	All formal care	Day-care	Playgroups
Process quality			
Emotional support	5.00	5.01	4.99
	(0.64)	(0.61)	(0.66)
Instructional support	3.30**	3.10	3.44
	(0.80)	(0.71)	(0.84)
Structural factors			
Child to staff ratio	5.08*	5.29	4.93
	(1.36)	(1.04)	(1.54)

Notes: ***$p<0.01$, **$p<0.05$, *$p<0.1$: significance of difference between day-care and playgroups.
Source: Pre-COOL 2012

Table 5.3 shows the means and standard deviations for the two process quality domains for 68 day-care centres and 91 playgroups. The domain values shown are simply averages of the dimension scores. Overall, Dutch formal childcare services have above-average quality according to the CLASS scale in the emotional factor measures. For the instructional support measures, the reverse is true, and the mean in both day-care centres and playgroups is only slightly above three. The gap between the scores for emotional and instructional support is in line with previous measures of Dutch day-care centres' quality that use different measurements (Vermeer et al, 2008; NCKO, 2009). As for the structural factor available, child-to-staff ratio, the observed average for day-care is below the prescribed ratio of six to one for two-year-olds. The standard deviation is large, however, meaning that not all centres match this criterion in practice. Finally, any difference between day-care centres and playgroups is socially important given the overrepresentation of low-income and minority children within playgroups. On average, there is no large difference in quality between playgroups and day-care centres. Playgroups even have slightly higher average scores for instructional support. Apparently, the two-tiered system in the Netherlands works well in ensuring that formal childcare services are available to all without generating any inherent gaps in the quality of childcare accessible to different groups.

Compared to a recent study using CLASS to measure childcare quality in Finland (Pakarinen et al, 2010), the scores found show similar patterns. The mean scores for emotional factors are generally higher than the mean scores for instructional support. However, the means for instructional support in the Pre-COOL sample appear to be lower than the findings for Finland. This may be due to exceptional quality in Finnish childcare centres rather than a particularly poor level in Dutch centres. The mean measures in Table 5.3 appear to be equal to or in some cases higher than those found for the US (Mashburn et al, 2008), although this is not very encouraging given the concerns about childcare quality in the US (see Chapter Nine, this volume).

Differences in the use of formal childcare: descriptives

As the focus of this chapter is on equal access to high-quality care, we need to combine the data on quality of the previous section with data on the actual users (children and parents). The Pre-COOL dataset includes data on children aged two and the characteristics of their parents. As the Pre-COOL survey contains information on both children who make use of childcare services and children who do not, the full sample is made up of two sub-samples: one fully and the other partially observed without information about the quality of childcare services used and child development information. It is worth noting that the data on children in the partially observed sub-sample include some missing values since it is based on the parental questionnaires rather than centre surveys.

Table 5.4 provides information on the sample make-up. We limit the analysis to children of parents who are currently residing with a partner. The decision-making process for single parents is more constrained since one partner staying at home to take care of the child is not an option. Out of the full sample, a total of 91 children attend both day-care and playgroups, and for 35 of the 91 there is no centre quality information. These children are included in the final sample, as part of both the playgroup and day-care sub-samples. Although there are more individual playgroups than day-care centres observed within

Table 5.4: Netherlands: Children, aged two, in Pre-COOL sample

	Total	In formal care	Day-care	Playgroups	No formal care
Full sample	1,209	1,096	729	436	113
Fully observed	495	495	266	229	0
Partially observed	714	601	430	184	113

Note: The sum of the observations in day-care and playgroups exceeds the total in formal care since 91 children attend both day care and playgroups. Additionally, we do not know the type of formal childcare for 22 children.

the Pre-COOL survey, there are more children in day-care centres that we have information about.

The control variables of interest are straightforward. Two higher-level education dummies, college and high level vocational training (HBO) are used for both men and women (so the omitted or reference group is the least educated group). For ethnic background, indicator variables are included for Dutch mothers, fathers and families with both parents from the Netherlands and grandmother's nationality (so the reference group is children with parents and grandmothers born abroad). Additional controls are added for household characteristics such as the number of younger and older siblings and father's income. Mother's income is not controlled for due to both multicollinearity and endogeneity issues. Mother's income is likely to be highly correlated with the socio-economic background variables already in the analysis. Additionally, mother's decision to work is more likely to be jointly taken with the decision to use childcare and may be influenced by childcare quality. Table 5.5 presents the percentages of parents in the socio-economic and ethnic categories of interest. Unsurprisingly, there are large differences between the socio-economic characteristics and ethnicities of children in day-care centres and playgroups – children in

Table 5.5: Netherlands: Summary statistics of independent variables (%)

	Full sample	Observed in day-care	Observed in playgroups	No formal care
Mother's education				
College	16.87***	16.17	4.37	8.85
HBO	31.43***	38.35	16.16	32.74
Father's education				
College	16.79***	15.41	3.93	7.96
HBO	23.99***	31.20	17.90	21.24
Demographics				
Dutch mother	82.80***	89.85	78.17	76.11
Dutch father	81.89***	86.84	75.11	72.57
Father's monthly income (€)				
1,000–2,000	42.76	38.72	42.79	56.64
2,000–3,000	31.51***	35.71	20.96	25.66
3,000–4,000	6.87	5.64	4.37	7.96
>4,000	4.14	4.89	3.93	0.88

Notes: The full sample also includes partially observed children in addition to children observed in day-care centres and playgroups.

***$p<0.01$, **$p<0.05$, *$p<0.1$: significance of difference between children in day-care and playgroups.

day-care centres tend to be from more affluent and higher-educated Dutch families.

The dependent variables for the analysis of the use of childcare services and types of centre regressions are binary variables. In the former, a variable is constructed and used with value 1 when formal care is used and 0 otherwise. For the type of care regression, due to the large number of missing data in the parental questionnaire on playgroup and day-care choices, the sample is limited to children observed at their childcare institutions. The variable in this case is 1 if the child was surveyed in a day-care centre and 0 if observed in a playgroup. The choice for dependent variables in estimating the effects of family backgrounds on the quality of care received is more complicated. Three dependent variables are used to measure access to quality. Rather than using the means of the dimensions to measure process quality domains, we use instead summary variables generated through factor analysis. The factor analysis generates variables for emotional support and instructional support domains that better capture variations in each dimension's measurements. Staff-to-child ratio is the only structural quality indicator used.

Differences in the use and quality of formal childcare: multivariate analysis

Use of formal childcare

Appendix 5.1 presents the results from a probit model for the use of formal childcare services in the full sample. A second probit model is fit for the choice between playgroup and day-care, with the sample limited to children in at least one type of formal care from the fully observed dataset. As such, the children in the sample of the second probit regression differ in whether they were in a playgroup or day-care during the survey.

The results in model 1 are similar to what would be expected. Parents with college education tend to be more likely to use formal care once father's income is controlled for. The coefficients are not very large, however. A college degree for the father increases the probability to use formal care by 4.8%. Surprisingly, father's income has a negative effect. This may be due to higher use of private paid childminders among the high-income levels.

Model 2 shows that the effects are much stronger if we restrict the analysis to whether day-care centres are used rather than playgroups. Since day-care centres are used by dual-earner families, children from lower socio-economic and minority backgrounds are much more likely to use playgroups. The divide between the type of childcare chosen by single-earner and dual-earner families leads to a selection effect, with high-income parents using day-care centres. Beyond the significant differences in participation in formal childcare of children from different socio-economic backgrounds, the total hours of formal childcare may be very different since playgroups tend to be used for shorter hours.

Quality of childcare

The main purpose of the analysis in this section is to see whether all children have access to similar quality childcare. When interpreting the results within the two-tiered Dutch childcare system, any differences between socio-economic groups or ethnicities in terms of the quality of care can be attributed to two different reasons. First, quality of care within the day-care market or among playgroups may diverge across socio-economic groups due to differences in neighbourhoods, information levels or demand for high-quality childcare. Second, any effects of lower socio-economic or minority statuses may be the result of inherently lower quality in available playgroups which are used more often by lower-income and minority groups.

A maximum likelihood selection model is used based on Heckman (1979) in estimating the quality of the formal childcare service used. The model estimates two equations simultaneously, a selection equation for whether childcare quality is observed and another equation with the childcare quality measure as the dependent variable. There are two concurrent selection processes in our data. A more straightforward ordinary least squares regression on the sub-sample of children with an observed formal childcare service quality would be biased if parents use formal care based on the quality of care they can get, or if there was sample selection in the data collection procedure for the CLASS observations. The key issue in estimating a selection model is the identification of the selection equation through exclusion restrictions to avoid multicollinearity in the quality regression (Puhani, 2000). For our analysis, the number of younger and older siblings and whether the child was underweight at birth are used as exclusion restrictions and are only included in the selection equation. The reasoning is that parents with more children or a child with health problems may be less likely to use formal care, while these factors are unlikely to affect the quality of the formal childcare services chosen.

Appendix 5.2 shows the effects of family background characteristics on the quality of formal childcare services received in both playgroups and day-care centres. The results suggest that children of parents with higher education and income receive formal childcare with higher-quality emotional support. Most of the effects are insignificant for instructional support with the exception of a negative coefficient for fathers with an HBO diploma. The results do not seem to be the product of an inherent difference in the quality of playgroups and day-care centres. Although children from lower socio-economic backgrounds do use playgroups more, the average quality in playgroups is either equal to or better than the day-care centres. Instead, a better judgement of care quality, willingness to pay prices above the government cap for childcare subsidies, flexibility in choosing care centres further away from the home, could all contribute to inequality in quality with regards to emotional support. Alternatively, children from lower socio-economic backgrounds may be limited in their options if the centres available in lower-income neighbourhoods are of lower quality.

A surprising finding is the negative coefficient on the control for Dutch mothers, which is significant at the 10% level for emotional support. Taken together with the results on the use of childcare, these results suggest that Dutch parents use more childcare but the centres they use tend to be of lower quality.

There are almost no significant effects from any of the factors for the child-to-staff ratio and instructional support. Children with highly educated fathers seem to even get slightly lower quality care in terms of instructional support. The variation by socio-economic background is thus mostly in terms of the emotional support measure. The emphasis on behaviour rather than cognitive development is in line with research by development psychologists about what Dutch parents focus the most on when caring for their children (Harkness et al, 2007). Additionally, factors influencing emotional support such as a positive atmosphere in the classroom may simply be more visible to parents, allowing parents with higher socio-economic backgrounds to either choose better formal childcare services or demand their provider supply higher-quality care.

The same regressions are fitted in a sub-sample that excludes children in playgroup and are presented in Appendix 5.3 to check whether the differences in quality are driven by the two-tiered system of playgroups and day-care centres. Regressions were also fitted in a sub-sample excluding children from day-care centres, but there were few significant variables in that case. The results in Appendix 5.3

show that father's income continues to be significantly correlated with quality of emotional support. Mother's education similarly has a positive effect, although the effects are less significant than the full sample. Surprisingly, instructional support appears to be better for children from lower socio-economic backgrounds in the day-care sub-sample, which might be related to the higher availability of VVE programmes among day-care centres located in disadvantaged areas.

Conclusions

The Dutch childcare system is essentially two-tiered. Childcare subsidies in the day-care market are given directly to parents, meaning that the market should be dominated by demand-side considerations and consumer preferences. In fact, the switch to a demand-side subsidy in 2005 appears to have been successful in terms of improving on the availability of day-care. Although there are still some waiting lists, the market was able to respond to the rise in demand during the last decade, as a result of which the number of children in day-care has increased dramatically. On the other hand, playgroups continue to be the second major form of formal care, especially among the two- and three-year-olds. The challenge for the Dutch childcare sector is to ensure that the day-care market responds to parents' preferences in quality, and that the playgroups at least match the level of childcare quality provided in day-care centres.

The equality of quality of care in playgroups and day-care centres has largely been achieved according to Pre-COOL data. Playgroups appear to do at least as well as day-care centres in both measures, and even score higher in instructional support measures. Although the Dutch system is heavily segmented by background characteristics such as income, education and minority status, at least the system works well in ensuring that formal childcare services are available to all without generating any inherent gaps in the quality of childcare accessible to different groups. Despite the similar levels of childcare quality in day-care and playgroups, there remain differences in the quality of childcare that children with different socio-economic backgrounds receive. Children of parents with more income and higher-education levels appear to attend formal childcare services with higher quality of emotional support. There is no significant difference in the instructional support measure, but these are low across all childcare services anyhow. We may therefore conclude that the switch to a more demand-driven system in the day-care market in 2005 has raised availability and flexibility, while at the same time contributing to inequality if higher-quality childcare is being demanded by parents with a high income. Allowing for parents' preferences to be better represented through the market also allows for the differences in preferences and information asymmetries to be more visible.

The regulatory attempts on the structural quality in both day-care centres and playgroups do not seem to have succeeded in keeping childcare quality in the Netherlands high. In addition, our analyses have demonstrated that there exist some inequalities in access by socio-economic status. The large rise in the availability of day-care centres shows the dramatic effect that consumer preferences can have on a sector. Following the same reasoning, the quality of formal childcare services might increase if only there was a demand for more quality. This presumes, however, that parents have information on the quality of childcare services. Given the difficulty parents have in judging quality, the market would function better if information on the quality of day-care centres was publicly available. In fact, a similar strategy was successful in raising quality in Dutch secondary schools (Koning and van der Wiel, 2010). The challenge continues to be in identifying factors that determine or are indicators of (process) quality that are easily measurable.

Note

[1] More information on DANS can be found at www.dans.knaw.nl/en; details of the Pre-COOL project are available in Dutch at www.pre-cool.nl

References

Berden, C. and Kok, L. (2009) *Ontwikkelingen op de markt voor kinderopvang 2004–2008* [*Developments in the Market for Child Care 2004–2008*], Amsterdam: SEO Economisch Onderzoek.

Berden, C., Kok, L., Koopmans, C. and Dosker, R. (2011) *De waarde van kinderopvang* [*The Value of Child Care*], Amsterdam: SEO Economisch Onderzoek.

Brancheorganisatie Kinderopvang (2012) *Convenant Kwaliteit Kinderopvang* [*Covenant for Child Care Quality*], Utrecht: Brancheorganisatie Kinderopvang.

Dekker, B. and Paulussen-Hoogeboom, M.C. (2010) *Monitor capaciteit kinderopvang 2008–2011* [Monitor for the Capacity of Child Care 2008–2011], *Capaciteitsgegevens in het jaar 2009. Eindrapport,* Amsterdam: Regioplan.

Deynoot-Schaub, G.M.J.J.M. and Riksen-Walraven, J.M.A. (2005) 'Child care under pressure: The quality of Dutch centers in 1995 and 2001', *The Journal of Genetic Psychology*, vol 66, no 3, pp 280–96.

Eurostat (2011) *Income and Living Conditions Database* (based on EU-SILC), Luxembourg: Eurostat.

Gemmeke, M. and Paulussen-Hoogeboom, M. (2007) *Basisgegevens kinderopvang [Basic Child Care Data]*, Amsterdam: Regioplan Beleidsonderzoek.

Heckman, J.J. (1979) 'Sample selection bias as a specification error', *Econometrica*, vol 47, no 1, pp 475–92.

Harkness, S., Johnston, C., Sutherland, M.A., Super, C.M., Hyun, O., Moscardino, U., Rha, J., Axia, G., Palacios, J., Blom, M. and Huitron, B. (2007) 'Cultural models and developmental agendas: Implications for AroUSl and self-regulation in early infancy', *Journal of Developmental Psychology*, vol 2 no 1, pp 5–39.

Koning, P. and van der Wiel, K. (2010) *School Responsiveness to Quality Rankings: An Empirical Analysis of the Secondary Education in the Netherlands*, IZA Working Papers 4969.

Mashburn, A.J., Pianta, R.C., Barbarin, O.A., Bryant, D., Hamre, B.K., Downer, J.T., Burchinal, M., Early, D.M. and Howes, C. (2008) 'Measures of classroom quality in prekindergarten and children's development of academic, language, and social skills', *Child Development*, vol 79, no 3, pp 732–49.

Moss, P. (1990) *Childcare in the European Community. Women of Europe. Supplement No 31*, Brussels: European Commission Childcare Network.

NCKO (Nederlands Consortium Kinderopvang Onderzoek) (2009) *Pedagogische kwaliteit van de opvang voor 0- tot 4- jarigen in Nederlandse Kinderdagblijven in 2008 [Pedagogic Quality of Care for 0 to 4 Year Olds in Dutch Day Care Centres]*, Utrecht: NCKO.

NICHD Early Child Care Research Network (2006) 'Child-care effect sizes for the NICHD Study of Early Child Care and Youth Development', *American Psychologist*, vol 61, no 2, pp 99–116.

Noailly, J. and Visser, S. (2009) 'The impact of market forces on child care provision: Insights from the 2005 Child Care Act in the Netherlands', *Journal of Social Policy*, vol 38, no 3, pp 477–98.

OECD (Organisation for Economic Co-operation and Development) (2006) *Starting Strong II: Early Childhood Education and Care*, Paris: OECD.

Pakarinen, E., Lerkkanen, M., Poikkeus, A., Kiuru, N. and Nurmi, J. (2010) 'A validation of the classroom assessment scoring system in Finnish kindergartens', *Early Education & Development*, vol 21, no 1, pp 95–124.

Plantenga, J. (2012) 'Local providers and loyal parents: Competition and consumer choice in Dutch child care market', in E. Lloyd and H. Penn (eds) *Child Care Markets: Can They Deliver an Equitable Service?*, Bristol: Policy Press.

Plantenga, J. and Remery, C. (2009) 'The Netherlands: bridging labour and care', in S.B. Kamerman and P. Moss (eds) *The Politics of Parental Leave Policies. Children, Parenting, Gender and the Labour Market*, Bristol: Policy Press, pp 175–90.

Plantenga, J., Remery, C. and Takács, J. (2012) 'Public support to young families in the European Union', in T. Knijn (ed) *Work, Family Policies and Transitions to Adulthood in Europe*, Basingstoke: Palgrave, pp 180–201.

Puhani, P.A. (2000) 'The Heckman correction for sample selection and its critique', *Journal of Economic Surveys*, vol 14, no 1, pp 53–68.

Slot, P.L. and Leseman, P. (2012) 'Presented in "Het kind, de opvang en de kwaliteit seminar"' ['The child, the care and the quality seminar'], ECCESS Seminar, 12 December, Utrecht University.

Thomson, A.C. and La Paro, K.M. (2009) 'Measuring the quality of teacher–child interactions in toddler child care', *Early Education and Development*, vol 20, no 2, pp 285–304.

van Ijzendoorn, M.H., Tavecchio, L.W.C., Stams, G.J.J.M., Verhoeven, M.J.E. and Reiling, E.J. (1998) 'Quality of a child-care center and attunement between parents and caregivers: A child-care center in cross-national perspective', *The Journal of Genetic Psychology*, vol 159, no 4, pp 437–54.

Vermeer, H.J., van Ijzendoorn, M.H., de Kruif, R.E.L., Fukkink, R.G., Tavecchio, L.W.C., Riksen-Walraven, J.M. and van Zeijl, J. (2008) 'Child care in the Netherlands: Trends in quality over the years 1995-2005', *The Journal of Genetic Psychology*, vol 169, no 4, pp 360–85.

Appendix 5.1: Netherlands: Marginal effects on formal childcare use for two-year-olds

	Model #			
	(1)		**(2)**	
	Formal care use		**Day-care**	
Mother's education				
College	0.023	(0.023)	0.312***	(0.067)
HBO	−0.014	(0.019)	0.270***	(0.050)
Father's education				
College	0.048**	(0.019)	0.229**	(0.085)
HBO	0.016	(0.018)	0.132**	(0.058)
Demographics				
Dutch mother	0.020	(0.030)	0.006	(0.101)
Dutch father	0.070	(0.048)	−0.043	(0.108)
Both partners Dutch	0.030	(0.028)	0.269***	(0.086)
One Dutch grandmother	−0.047*	(0.028)	−0.025	(0.121)
Both grandmothers Dutch	−0.021	(0.026)	−0.008	(0.092)
Father's monthly income (€)				
1,000–2,000	−0.067**	(0.028)	0.090	(0.066)
2,000–3,000	−0.052	(0.032)	0.159**	(0.067)
3,000–4,000	−0.115*	(0.063)	0.090	(0.126)
<4,000	0.037	(0.041)	0.017	(0.133)
Household characteristics				
# of younger siblings	−0.004	(0.020)	−0.081	(0.062)
# of older siblings	−0.038***	(0.009)	−0.116***	(0.031)
Child health				
Underweight	0.010	(0.024)	−0.058	(0.079)
Observations	1,209		495	

Notes: ***$p<0.01$, **$p<0.05$, *$p<0.1$. Robust standard errors in parentheses.

Appendix 5.2: Netherlands: Access to quality childcare for two-year-olds

	Model #					
	(1)		**(2)**		**(3)**	
	Child-to-staff ratio		**Emotional support**		**Instructional support**	
Mother's education						
College	−0.061	(0.186)	0.614***	(0.185)	−0.113	(0.171)
HBO	0.022	(0.134)	0.330**	(0.131)	−0.052	(0.114)
Father's education						
College	0.252	(0.184)	0.147	(0.202)	−0.274	(0.184)
HBO	0.139	(0.146)	−0.120	(0.137)	−0.264**	(0.112)
Demographics						
Dutch mother	−0.086	(0.253)	−0.490**	(0.225)	−0.160	(0.189)
Dutch father	0.050	(0.244)	−0.049	(0.248)	0.319	(0.199)
Both partners Dutch	0.247	(0.292)	−0.069	(0.196)	−0.100	(0.171)
One Dutch grandmother	0.007	(0.344)	0.583**	(0.280)	0.069	(0.242)
Both grandmothers Dutch	0.208	(0.242)	0.083	(0.197)	−0.024	(0.159)
Father's monthly income (€)						
1,000–2,000	−0.100	(0.178)	0.539***	(0.160)	−0.137	(0.140)
2,000–3,000	−0.162	(0.173)	0.597***	(0.172)	0.009	(0.146)
3,000–4,000	0.293	(0.397)	0.661***	(0.248)	−0.066	(0.232)
>4,000	−0.146	(0.309)	0.295	(0.316)	−0.383	(0.293)
Observations	1,209		1,209		1,209	
Quality observations	495		495		495	

Notes: ***$p<0.01$, **$p<0.05$, *$p<0.1$. Standard errors in parentheses.

# of younger siblings, # of older siblings and underweight at birth used as exclusion restrictions.

Wald test indicates that Heckman selection model should be preferred over OLS for model (2).

Appendix 5.3: Netherlands: Access to quality excluding children in playgroups

	Model #					
	(1)		(2)		(3)	
	Child-to-staff ratio		Emotional support		Instructional support	
Mother's education						
College	−0.388	(0.267)	0.391*	(0.235)	−0.262	(0.182)
HBO	0.030	(0.203)	0.002	(0.186)	−0.262*	(0.140)
Father's education						
College	−0.159	(0.273)	0.027	(0.248)	−0.046	(0.193)
HBO	0.288	(0.213)	−0.176	(0.196)	−0.056	(0.149)
Demographics						
Dutch mother	0.414	(0.367)	−0.683*	(0.353)	−0.393*	(0.214)
Dutch father	0.115	(0.396)	−0.022	(0.348)	0.236	(0.219)
Both partners Dutch	0.180	(0.344)	−0.189	(0.319)	0.092	(0.250)
One Dutch grandmother	−1.108***	(0.427)	0.975**	(0.403)	0.534**	(0.270)
Both grandmothers Dutch	0.382	(0.319)	−0.038	(0.279)	0.031	(0.187)
Father's monthly income (€)						
1,000–2,000	−0.218	(0.273)	0.527**	(0.265)	0.174	(0.177)
2,000–3,000	−0.258	(0.273)	0.579**	(0.267)	0.176	(0.181)
3,000–4,000	−0.168	(0.408)	0.676*	(0.375)	−0.121	(0.258)
>4,000	−0.277	(0.456)	0.624	(0.475)	−0.130	(0.408)
Observations	831		831		831	
Quality observations	266		266		266	

Notes: ***$p<0.01$, **$p<0.05$, *$p<0.1$. Standard errors in parentheses.

# of younger siblings, # of older siblings and underweight at birth used as exclusion restrictions.

Wald test indicates that Heckman selection model should be preferred over OLS for models (1), (2) and (3).

SIX

Access and quality issues in early childhood education and care: The case of Germany

Pamela Oberhuemer

Introduction

The past decade in Germany has witnessed an unprecedented increase in policy initiatives and fast-paced change in the field of early childhood education and care (ECEC). This enhanced prioritisation of the years from birth to the start of compulsory schooling at age six has been stimulated by three main agendas.

The first is a longer-term policy concern regarding the expansion of publicly subsidised early childhood services. Propelled by the issues of gender equity, women's workforce participation and life–work balance, and accompanied by debates around other factors such as the low fertility rate in Germany, the first significant moves towards increasing the levels of early years provision in the Western regions gained momentum during the 1990s. This was considerably later than, for example, in the Nordic countries or in France. A first wave of policies centred on granting legal entitlement to a place in kindergarten for all three-, four- and five-year-olds as from 1996. As one of the challenges that followed, kindergartens in Western Germany found themselves faced with increased demands for extending predominantly half-day provision into longer or full-day options. Currently, a second wave of expansion policies represents a more fundamental and paradigmatic change. In 2007, government legislation pledged to extend legal entitlement to a place in a centre or home-based setting to one- and two-year-olds. August 2013 was set as the target date for providing places for 35% of this age group. After decades of political and cultural resistance towards publicly subsidised education and care for the under threes, an extraordinary transformation is now taking place. The year 2007 marked the starting point of a highly prioritised drive in the Western federal states to increase the very low levels of services outside the larger metropolitan areas. The dynamics associated with this high-speed expansion and the related issues of quality of provision is a constant theme throughout this chapter.

The second is the early education agenda, initiated by the publication of findings from the first round of the international OECD-PISA (Organisation for Economic Co-operation and Development-Programme for International Student Assessment) study at the end of 2001. Besides highlighting unexpectedly low reading performance levels of 15-year-olds, the findings also pinpointed significant achievement gaps between children with and without an immigrant[1] background, suggesting that the former are particularly disadvantaged within the German school system (see also OECD, 2004). Not only did the entire education system come under increased scrutiny as a result, but also the years preceding formal schooling. In terms of policy drives, this culminated, for example, in first-time curricular frameworks for work in early childhood settings and in increasingly regulated collaborations with the primary school sector.

The third is the social inclusion agenda. With its strong links to education issues, this has led to parental fees for five-year-olds being abolished in some of the Western *Länder* (states). Across the country it has precipitated a new policy focus on language assessment and literacy enhancement programmes in the years preceding compulsory schooling. In some federal states it has also led to an explicit broadening of the remit of early childhood centres to cater more specifically for children from disadvantaged families through new forms of integrated services for children and families.

Germany is thus experiencing a period of fundamental change and transition in the field of ECEC, particularly in the Western regions. With these three interconnected policy areas in mind, this chapter attempts to show how children from disadvantaged families fare across the country in their access to and participation in ECEC settings, and how this provision may differ in terms of key quality criteria. At the same time, it must be emphasised that there is no hard and fast definition of 'disadvantaged' families and children, since such definitions depend on the criteria applied. In general, children growing up in 'precarious living conditions' (Walper and Riedel, 2011, p 4) are often those subjected to cumulative risk factors such as family income poverty, parental unemployment, low levels of parents' education, an immigrant background or single-parent family unit. There will be reference to such factors relating to ECEC usage, with a particular focus – for reasons previously mentioned – on children from families with a background of migration.

By way of an introduction to the strongly decentralised face of ECEC in Germany, the chapter starts with a general picture of regional variations in the population size and composition across the country.

Setting the scene: population patterns in a regional perspective

Germany in the second decade of the twenty-first century is a federal republic with a population of 80.5 million (2012). Following the unification of the East and West German states in 1990, the country today comprises 16 federal states or *Länder*, each with its own regional government alongside the federal-level government. Berlin, Bremen and Hamburg are regarded as city-states. The other 13 *Länder* vary in size and demographics, Bavaria being the largest in terms of land area and Northrhine-Westfalia having the highest population density.

Over 4 million children up to the age of six live in Germany, and the majority are located in the Western *Länder*. Only 604,996 live in the five Eastern federal states, whereas over 892,000 live in Northrhine-Westfalia alone (Statistisches Bundesamt, 2012a). Other variations include the distribution of the immigrant population, which is also mainly concentrated in the Western *Länder*. Only 590,000 with a migration background live in the five Eastern federal states, compared with 15.2 million in the Western *Länder* and Berlin (Integrationsbericht, 2012, p 34, data from 2010).

Almost one-fifth of the population are classified as 'people with a migration background'.[2] The 2010 micro-census (a representative 1% sample survey conducted annually by the Federal Statistical Office) shows that people with a Turkish background comprise the largest group, accounting for 15.8% of the immigrant population. Families originating from former Soviet Union states represent the second largest group (Integrationsbericht, 2012, p 31).

Before examining how these population patterns translate into general and more specific patterns of usage of ECEC services in the Eastern and Western *Länder*, the following section outlines some of the defining characteristics of the system of ECEC in Germany.

Key features of the ECEC system

Federalism and subsidiarity are core political concepts underpinning the structures, legislation, regulation and funding of early education and childcare in Germany.

Multi-level governance

At the federal level (*Bund*), the Federal Ministry of Family and Youth Affairs has 'stimulatory competence' (*Anregungskompetenz*) regarding childcare issues. The Child and Youth Services Act 1990 and subsequent amendments provide the legislative framework. Overall, ECEC from birth to age six is part of the child and youth welfare system, and not part of the education system. Significant amendments to the 1990 Act include the legal entitlement to a 'place' in kindergarten or family day-care mentioned earlier. Another key modification is the Childcare Funding Act 2009, which provided the framework for extending entitlement to one- and two-year-olds as from August 2013. Both are federal-level policies to promote needs-based access.

At the regional level (*Länder*), the 16 governments are responsible for adapting federal legislation requirements into state-specific ECEC laws and for providing a regulatory framework for service provision and financing. Each federal state not only has its own legislation, but also policy initiatives regarding access and quality issues in ECEC. While these vary in focus and intensity, there are also common themes across the *Länder*. This will become clearer as the chapter progresses.

At the local level, the municipalities (*Kommunen*) are in charge of organising and securing funding for ECEC provision. However, provider structures are strongly linked to the so-called *subsidiarity principle*. According to this principle, which was first anchored in the Youth Welfare Act 1922, re-endorsed 30 years later in West Germany in the Youth Welfare Act 1952 and again re-authorised in unified Germany in the Child and Youth Services Act 1990, public authorities are only obliged to provide social services if non-governmental agencies are not in a position to do so. Around two-thirds of centre-based childcare provision across the country are run by these voluntary child and youth welfare providers (*Freie Träger der Jugendhilfe*).

In other words, Germany has a strongly decentralised system of ECEC. Responsibility is shared between the federal government, the 16 regional governments and local government bodies, in partnership with a wide range of non-profit agencies and service providers. This can lead to considerable variance at the local level. For example, data collected from child and youth welfare authorities show a marked range (between 7% and 38%) in the participation rates of under threes in the Western *Länder* (Autorengruppe Bildungsberichterstattung, 2012, p 56; Riedel et al, 2011).

Variations in provision profiles

The following tables show the main kinds of centre-based settings attended by the under threes (Table 6.1) and by children aged three up to six (Table 6.2).

Overall, the largest proportion of under threes (over 42%) attends traditional nursery groups, particularly in the Eastern regions (over 60%), where this kind of provision was in place before unification. However, in the Western federal states the majority of under threes are in provision types that also cater for older children. The greater majority of three- to six-year-olds still attend kindergartens, either the 'classical' kindergarten model (over 58%) or one that has extended its admission procedures to include two-year-olds (over 24%).

Diversity of providers

As previously mentioned, childcare services (including those for school-age children after school hours) are organised largely by non-profit agencies. Federal-level statistics for 2012 (see Figure 6.1) indicate that roughly two-thirds of centre-based settings are run by these voluntary or 'free' *Träger* and just over 33% by public authorities.

Table 6.1: Germany: Types of centre-based settings attended by children less than three years of age, according to region, 2012

	Total number of centres	Nursery groups (birth up to age 3) (%)	Kindergarten groups (age 3 up to school entry) extended to 2-year-olds (%)	Mixed-age groups (birth up to school entry age or beyond) (%)	Centres without permanent group structures (%)
Eastern *Länder* (excluding Berlin)	138,837	60.8	4.3	27.7	7.2
Western *Länder* (excluding Berlin)	295,596	34.1	18.0	39.9	8.0
Germany (excluding Berlin)	**434,433**	**42.6**	**13.6**	**36.0**	**7.8**

Source: Bertelsmann Stiftung (2013, Tab 36b, p 207); translated and adapted by author

Table 6.2: Germany: Types of centre-based settings attended by children from three up to six years of age according to region, 2012

	Total number of centres	Kindergarten group (age 3 up to school entry) (%)	Kindergarten group extended to 2-year-olds (%)	Mixed-aged group (birth up to school entry age or beyond) (%)	Centres without permanent group structures (%)
Eastern *Länder* (excluding Berlin)	348,460	65.9	12.9	14.5	6.7
Western *Länder* (excluding Berlin)	1,798,061	56.8	26.8	10.0	6.4
Germany (excluding Berlin)	**2,146,521**	**58.3**	**24.6**	**10.7**	**6.4**

Source: Bertelsmann Stiftung (2013, Tab 36a1, p 308); translated and adapted by author

Figure 6.1: Germany: Providers of children's services (early childhood and out-of-school), 2012

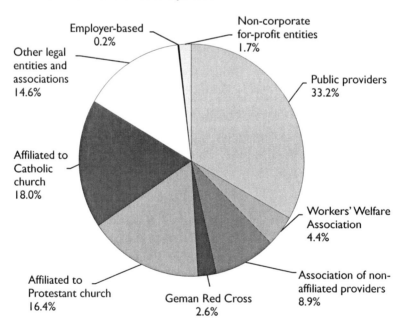

Source: Statistisches Bundesamt (2012a); own calculations

The traditional dominance of the non-governmental sector has even increased in recent years. An independent survey (Schreyer, 2009) of the providers of centre-based services for children in 13 *Länder* registered an increase of almost 42% since 2002. According to this study, the decrease in numbers of public, municipality-run centres is particularly marked in the Eastern part of the country, whereas in the Western *Länder* the absolute number of church-affiliated centres has decreased. However, the proportion of other kinds of voluntary providers has increased significantly in both parts of the country. The 2012 federal statistics show that private, for-profit providers continue to have only a very small share of the market (1.6%).

Having clarified the main organisational features of the system of early childhood services, the following two sections look at variations in usage of ECEC services in the Eastern and Western *Länder*.

East–West disparities in patterns of usage of ECEC services

Table 6.3 illustrates the broad regional disparities relating to usage of centre-based settings and publicly subsidised family day-care. For children under three, the participation levels in centre-based early childhood settings are far lower in the Western (18%) than in the Eastern (44%) federal states, reflecting the historically different childcare cultures, but also the higher availability of provision in the Eastern *Länder*. Similarly, participation rates in Berlin (38%), which since 1990 includes former East Berlin, are way above the national average. These disparities even out when it comes to the older pre-

Table 6.3: Germany: Children in centre-based settings and publicly subsidised family day-care according to age and region, 2012

	Centre-based settings		Family day-care	
	Under 3 (%)	3 to under 6 (%)	Under 3 (%)	3 to under 6 (%)
Eastern *Länder* (excluding Berlin)	43.9	94.9	5.1	0.6
Western *Länder* (excluding Berlin)	18.2	92.3	4.0	0.5
Berlin	38.4	92.8	4.2	1.2
Germany	**23.4**	**92.8**	**4.3**	**0.5**

Source: Bertelsmann Stiftung (2013, adapted); data from Federal Statistical Office (01.03.2012)

school children, with participation rates in the Western *Länder* being only slightly below the national average.

Family day-care is clearly the less preferred option for families in both the Eastern and Western *Länder*. Even for the under threes age group, only approximately 4% are in family day-care, whereas over 23% attend an early childhood centre.

In terms of age-disaggregated data, Table 6.4 illustrates the differences between the Eastern and Western *Länder* very clearly, particularly in terms of the participation rates for one- and two-year-olds. It also indicates that very few children (2.8%) are cared for outside the home before their first birthday, which can be explained by the parental leave benefit that families receive for the 12 months following childbirth. This amounts to 67% of average earnings over the previous year (with a minimum of €300 and a maximum of €1,800 per month), with payments extended to 14 months if the father takes at least two months' leave (Blum and Erler, 2011).

The participation rates of under threes have risen dramatically in recent years, from 9% in 2002 to over 25% in 2011 (BMFSFJ, 2012). Recently published data from the Federal Statistical Office for 2012 show a further increase up to 27.6% (Statistisches Bundesamt, 2012b). Between 2006 and 2011 alone, the number of available places more than doubled. Yet despite this impressive increase, the total still falls seriously short of government targets for August 2013. It is estimated that 174,300 places in centre-based settings and 87,800 in family day-care are still needed in the Western *Länder* (Autorengruppe Bildungsberichterstattung, 2012, p 54) – an enormous challenge for the field.

Having firmly established the differences (participation rates of under threes) and similarities (participation rates of three to under six-year-

Table 6.4: Germany: Participation rates in early childhood centres and publicly subsidised family day-care according to age, 2012

	Under 1 year (%)	1 year (%)	2 years (%)	3 years (%)	4 years (%)	5 years (%)
Eastern *Länder* (excluding Berlin)	4.7	59.4	82.5	93.0	96.9	97.4
Western *Länder* (excluding Berlin)	2.3	20.7	43.4	86.3	96.3	97.6
Berlin	3.0	48.9	76.6	90.5	95.0	97.7
Germany	**2.8**	**28.4**	**51.1**	**87.6**	**96.4**	**97.6**

Source: Bertelsmann Stiftung (2013, adapted); data from Federal Statistical Office (01.03.2012)

olds) in the Eastern and Western regions, the next section goes on to show more differentiated patterns across the 16 *Länder* in terms of the children's background. In particular, it looks at how the incidence of usage among children with a migration background compares with that of children from families without a history of migration.

Equal access? Patterns of usage of ECEC services according to family background

In terms of general rights of access to a place in early education and childcare provision, the legislative framework in Germany can be seen as a significant inequality-reducing feature of the ECEC system. Not only have all children from the age of three up to school entry been eligible, since 1996, to a place in a centre-based setting or in family day-care, but that entitlement has been extended to one- and two-year-olds. Any other entitlement criteria are laid down by the regional government, local government administration, or by the specific service provider. After debates about how a 'place' is to be interpreted in terms of daily hours of attendance, several federal states have made specifications. Some guarantee at least five hours (Hamburg, Saxony-Anhalt) or six hours of access (Brandenburg, Mecklenburg-West Pomerania). Additionally, some have already extended the entitlement to two-year-olds (Berlin, Thuringia), and Rhineland-Palatinate has even introduced full-day entitlement for two-year-olds. However, this basic right to access does not always translate into equitable access.

A longitudinal analysis of usage patterns in the Western *Länder* based on data from 1995–2008 revealed that the group who are profiting most from the expansion of places for under threes are the higher-educated mothers (Krapf and Kreyenfeld, 2010). During this period, roughly three times as many mothers with *Abitur* (the German equivalent of A-levels) were accessing places for their under threes compared with mothers with a lower formal education. According to current procedures, places are generally allocated to parents in employment, and highly qualified mothers are more likely to take up employment when their children are still very young and therefore to seek a place in a day nursery. This suggests that the pattern of distribution of the restricted number of places available for this particular age group appears to be benefiting already privileged groups.

However, other determining factors such as the general economic situation of the family, the number of people and siblings living in the household, migration background and the amount of available time parents have to spend with their children and to complete household and other tasks can also affect children's chances of participation in early education and care services (Alt, 2012). According to the recent German Youth Institute AID:A Survey[3] (Rauschenbach and Bien, 2012), if the household income is below 60% of the average income level (roughly €1,700 per month for a family with two children), only 17% of the children attend some form of childcare, compared with approximately 30% of children from families with a higher-level income. In terms of reaching children from disadvantaged families, data from the AID:A Survey also show a link between the mother's education background and ECEC participation rates. Whereas almost half the mothers with a university degree enrol their under threes in a centre, this is the case for only 17% of those with a secondary school-leaving certificate (Leu, 2012, p 131).

As previously mentioned, the immigrant population is concentrated in the Western federal states. The proportion is highest in Hamburg, where, in 2011, children with a migration background accounted for 51% of the under threes population and 43% of children aged from three up to six (Bock-Famulla and Lange, 2011, p 118). Table 6.5 compares the combined participation levels in centre-based settings and family day-care of children with and without a migration background by age group. They are consistently lower for children with a migration background, particularly for the under threes.

Furthermore, with the important goals of tackling social disadvantage and improving educational chances in mind, it is disconcerting to note that among the three- to six-year-olds in Hamburg and Bavaria, 20% of children with a migration background are *not* attending some form of early education or childcare, compared with only 6% and 4% respectively of children without a family history of migration.

The AID:A survey, focusing on childhood and adolescence and not just early childhood, suggests a so-called middle-class bias in the use of state welfare services in general (Gottschall and Pothmann, 2012, p 8). However, regarding the specific use of kindergartens, the generally high participation rates for the three- to six-year-olds indicate that even for children from disadvantaged families, attending an ECEC centre has become a matter of course for this age group. However, social background at least co-determines the *duration* of time spent in an ECEC setting in terms of years. Also, there continue to be considerable regional differences in the number of hours daily that children spend in ECEC centres and whether a meal is provided at midday. Two examples of these regional variations (Bock-Famulla and Lange, 2011, p 317):

Table 6.5: Germany: Participation rates of children with and without a migration background[a] in early childhood centres and publicly subsidised family day-care according to age-groups and Länder,[b] 2012

Federal state/ region	Under 3			3 to under 6		
		Proportion of age-group:			Proportion of age-group:	
	Total (%)	with migration background (%)	without migration background (%)	Total (%)	with migration background (%)	without migration background (%)
Germany	**28**	**16**	**33**	**93**	**87**	**96**
Western *Länder*	22	15	26	93	89	95
Eastern *Länder*	49	26	53	96	74	100
Hamburg	36	22	46	86	80	94
Bavaria	23	15	26	91	80	96
Schleswig-Holstein	24	14	27	91	86	92
Lower Saxony	22	12	26	93	79	98
Baden-Wuerttemberg	23	17	27	95	95	95
Hesse	24	15	30	86	80	94
Northrhine-Westfalia	18	13	21	93	91	94
Rhineland-Palatinate	27	21	30	97	101	96

Notes: [a] 'Migration background' is defined here as having at least one parent of foreign origin. [b] Two Western *Länder* (Bremen and Saarland) and all Eastern *Länder* are not included in the table, since there are no representative data available on the immigrant child population in these federal states.

Source: Bertelsmann Stiftung (2013, pp 312-13); data from Federal Statistical Office (2013, Sonderauswertung)

- Whereas 73% of children of three- to six-year-olds *without* a migration background in the Eastern *Länder* and 70% in Berlin have contractual agreements for seven or more hours in a centre-based setting, this is the case for only 25% of the same population group in the Western *Länder*.
- For the same age group *with* a migration background, 33% in the Western *Länder* (excluding Berlin) spend seven or more hours in the centre, but this varies between 15% in Baden-Wuerttemberg and 43% in Hesse.

The emerging picture of regional disparities regarding the availability, usage and organisational structures of ECEC is also reflected in the overall funding and funding procedures, and in the costs for families. The next section looks at the way funding is distributed at different levels, and outline some of the issues arising relating to children from disadvantaged families.

Funding disparities: Federal, regional and local-level procedures and issues

The federal level (*Bund*) is not involved in the day-to-day funding of service provision; this is the responsibility of the *Länder* and the municipalities, and parents generally pay towards costs. However, the Federal Ministry of Family and Youth Affairs – in its 'stimulatory role' – may provide incentives for reform initiatives of national priority. In the case of the expansion of childcare places for the under threes, it was agreed that the *Bund* would provide one-third of the €12 billion projected funding, as well as contributing towards the running costs for new places during the expansion phase. A total of €770 million are transferred annually to the *Länder* for this purpose (BMFSFJ, 2012). Initial estimations in 2007 assumed a need for 750,000 additional places, whereas later estimations were based on a projected 780,000 new places before August 2013. In the summer of 2012, the Federal Ministry therefore allocated a further €580,500 million for an additional 30,000 places.[4] This funding is partly earmarked, in the sense that the *Länder* are obliged to report back to the *Bund* every three months as to how the money is being used. However, according to a recent press release by the Federal Statistical Office, the number of additional places needed is currently even higher and now totals 220,000 (Statistisches Bundesamt, 2012b).

The allocation of funding for ECEC services at the regional level (*Länder*) has risen steadily over recent years. However, variations between the federal states are considerable. Whereas in 2010 Berlin allocated €4,645 for each child under six years of age, per capita funding in Bavaria amounted to €2,950 (Bertelsmann Stiftung, 2013, p 298). One reason for these contrasts is the higher rate of full-day places in Berlin; another relates to the overall rate of under threes in centre-based settings, which in Berlin is also high. Differences between the *Länder* in staff-to-child ratios are also an explanation for these discrepancies. Per capita funding is higher in federal states where the public sector (*Land* and *Kommunen*) contributes more towards the total expenditure on ECEC than in those federal states in which parents and non-profit providers contribute proportionately more to overall costs. For example, in Bavaria public expenditure on ECEC services has been consistently lower than average for the Western *Länder*, whereas Brandenburg has consistently provided high level expenditure. In both *Länder*, the exact contribution of the non-profit provider sector towards the running costs of their own childcare services is not known. However, based on an assumed expenditure of €100 million, the estimated distribution of costs in Bavaria would be as follows: municipalities 46.7%, regional government 29.3%, parents 18.8% and the non-profit service providers 5.2%. In Brandenburg the relative funding contribution of the municipalities would be considerably higher: municipalities 58%, regional government 22.3%, parents 17.5% and non-profit service providers 2.2% (Bock-Famulla and Große-Wöhrmann, 2010).

It has been estimated that parents contribute €2.7 billion per year towards the cost of financing ECEC services (Autorengruppe Bildungsberichterstattung, 2012, p 54). Rhineland-Palatinate (RP) was the first federal state to introduce (in 2007) free access for children in the year before school entry, and this is now practised in five other federal states. In the meantime, access in RP is free for all children as from the age of two. Parental fees are mostly income related, conceived as a way of securing access for children from low-income families. However, as can be seen from the AID:A Survey findings in Table 6.6, which are presented in the 2012 National Education Report, the fees are highly variable and range between no costs at all for parents (7.5%, including nearly 3% of fee exemptions for individual children in centres where fees are normally charged) to fees of more than €200 monthly (14.4%). Fees are on average higher in the Eastern *Länder*, where income levels are generally lower; this is presumably related to the longer daily usage times.

The inflexibility of the funding of early education and care in Germany was one of the criticisms in the evaluative report of the OECD review team (OECD, 2004). In recent years several federal states have been reassessing their funding policies. Bavaria was the first to change from supply-side funding for provision regardless of the specific profile such as opening hours and quality of programme, to a supply-side per capita funding, which has since also been introduced in Northrhine-Westfalia (Diekmann et al, 2008). In Bavaria, a so-called 'base value' (*Basiswert*) is calculated according to specific weighting factors, including the number of hours spent at the centre. No state funding is provided in cases of less than three hours' daily attendance. The weighting criteria are calculated for specific groups: children under three (2.0); children from three up to school entry (1.0); school-age children (1.2); children with disabilities (4.5); and children whose

Table 6.6: Germany: Parental fees according to regions, net monthly income and receipt of benefits, 2009

| | Monthly costs for parents for a place in childcare (€) | | | | | | |
| | **0** | | | | | | |
	No fee charged	Fee exemption for specific groups	1–50	51–100	101–150	151–200	Over 200
			%				
Regions							
Germany	4.9	2.6	12.8	32.0	18.6	14.8	14.4
Western *Länder* and Berlin	5.4	2.8	13.6	34.4	16.4	12.5	15.0
Eastern *Länder*	(2.0)	(1.8)	8.3	18.9	30.6	27.2	11.3
Monthly household net income (lowest and highest income groups)							
Up to €1.400	(6.9)	(9.9)	24.3	25.9	(18.4)	(8.6)	(6.0)
€4000 plus	4.3	(0.4)	6.6	22.6	15.5	19.9	30.8
In receipt of social benefits?							
No	4.7	2.0	11.5	32.4	19.0	15.3	15.2
Yes	(7.0)	(9.1)	25.3	27.5	14.5	(10.3)	(6.3)

Note: The items in brackets cannot be interpreted because the case number is too small.
Source: Autorengruppe Bildungsberichterstattung (2012, Table C2–10web, adapted and translated by author); data from AID:A Survey, 2009.

parents are both of non–German speaking origin (1.3). For children in family day-care, the weighting value is uniformly 1.3.

Other federal states have been experimenting with demand-side funding through a voucher system. To date, four have made this move: Baden-Wurttemberg, Berlin, Hamburg and Thuringia (Diekmann et al, 2008). In Hamburg, a voucher system has been in operation since 2003 and in the meantime is a consolidated part of the city-state ECEC provision. The move was highly controversial at the time, and was initially criticised for not helping to ease access for children from disadvantaged families whose parents were workless. The state-regulated eligibility requirements were subsequently linked to social criteria (such as having a migration background) rather than just the employment status of the parent/s. As a consequence, participation rates – particularly among under threes – have risen steadily in recent years. As indicated in Table 6.5, Hamburg now has the highest participation rate among the Western *Länder* for children in this age group with a migrant background. Eligible parents apply for a child-specific voucher through the local authority and can exchange it for a place at an accredited early childhood centre of their choice. The centre provider is then allocated the appropriate funding. In terms of supporting children from disadvantaged families this kind of funding concept needs to fulfil certain key criteria. These include (all of which are in place in Hamburg): transparency of funding and weighting criteria; an overall budget volume which allows for good staffing ratios and regular continuing professional development (CPD) of the staff; and regular procedures for monitoring quality. Parental fees in Hamburg were reduced as from August 2011 and are calculated according to income level, family size, the child's age and the number of hours attended.

In *Länder* that have not switched to a per capita or voucher system, there are mostly practices in place to help ensure that local needs are met through the allocation of additional funding, although specific practices differ starkly (Bock-Famulla and Lange, 2011, p 21). Extra funding tends to be allocated for more staff in centres in disadvantaged areas and for working with children with a migration background, with children with disabilities and for language enhancement programmes.

One of the most controversial issues over the past year or so has been the centre-right Coalition government's intention to introduce a monthly childcare allowance (*Betreuungsgeld*), starting in 2013 at €100 and rising to €150 as from 2014. The stated aim is to give parents the choice of caring for their child at home rather than using an ECEC setting. The proposed legislation had to be debated twice in Parliament and, despite strong resistance at all levels, was finally pushed through on 9 November 2012 (with 310 MPs voting for it, 282 against and 2 abstaining). Critical analyses have pointed out that the move could lead to exactly those children being kept at home who would benefit most from attending ECEC provision, that is, children from low-income, single-parent and low skilled households (Gathmann and Sachs, 2012, p 2). During heated public debates it was also suggested that the allowance was part of a policy move to veil the fact that the government target for under threes provision is unlikely to be met by the envisaged date.

Having looked in detail at the variations in access to ECEC, the final sections now focus on issues of quality, looking in particular at three aspects: programme requirements, staffing and integrated forms of provision.

Three quality-enhancing dimensions of ECEC

The innovative work of a National Quality Initiative from 2000–06, which developed a range of evaluation instruments both for ECEC staff and for providers, with major federal-level funding and support from 10 *Länder*, was unexpectedly overshadowed by the concurrent and highly mediatised debate following the 'PISA shock'. Early childhood education was catapulted into a hitherto unknown public limelight.

Quality programmes: early childhood curricular frameworks and language/literacy enhancement initiatives

As a consequence, between 2003 and 2008, all 16 regional governments issued early childhood curricular frameworks. This represented a major new regulatory step for the Western *Länder*. It was a move to ensure that access to ECEC settings is framed within a set of universally endorsed (across providers) and applicable (for *all* children) principles of educational quality. Also, for the first time, a non-binding Common Framework for Early Education was agreed on by the 16 Ministers for Youth Affairs and the 16 Ministers of Education and Cultural Affairs (Standing Conference, 2004). Whereas most curricular documents are considered to be 'guidelines', in some federal states early childhood centres are obliged by law to include the main principles, aims and areas of learning in their centre-specific philosophy statements. In Berlin, implementing the curriculum is combined with prescribed evaluation procedures. In general, however, specific control measures in terms of compliance are low key and based mainly on agreements with the provider organisations. Neither external evaluations nor written reports are required on an annual basis. Some centres may choose to present evaluation data on their websites, but there is no requirement to do so.

The 16 *Länder*-curricula vary in terms of content, length and age group addressed. Most are aimed at the 0–6 age group, but several go beyond this to include school-age childcare services, and in Hesse, the same principles are valid for both the early childhood and primary school sectors as well as for family day-care services. All frameworks are based on an holistic, participatory and inclusive approach, and not on a narrow 'school readiness' agenda.

At the same time, all federal states are focusing more specifically than before on language and literacy development. Around one-quarter of three- to six-year-olds are considered to be in need of language support, in particular children learning German as an additional language (Autorengruppe Bildungsberichterstattung, 2012, p 66). In a number of *Länder*, it is now a requirement for children to participate in a language screening assessment prior to school entry. In Bavaria, for example, a screening test is not required, but since 2008, the language competence of all children is assessed through a prescribed instrument before the start of their final year in kindergarten. Beyond this, an extensive network of early childhood language coordinators with the task of coaching centre teams has been set up with considerable funding support from the regional government and the Confederation of Bavarian Industry. An evaluation report was published in 2013 (Nicko and Schreyer, 2013). The *Bund* is also currently allocating €400 million to provide language support services up to 2014 in 4,000 early childhood centres across the country – with the aim of increasing the educational chances of all children, particularly those from disadvantaged families (BMFSFJ, 2012).

Quality staffing: qualifications and structural issues

The qualifications and working conditions of staff in early childhood centres are widely recognised as perhaps the most significant contributory factor towards achieving and maintaining high-quality services. Three issues have dominated the discourse in Germany in recent years.

The first is a direct outcome of the PISA debate and the expectations directed towards ECEC centres in terms of high-quality early education as set down in the new curricula. It has long been argued that the current requirement for contact staff with group responsibility (a three-year post-secondary qualification gained at a specialist vocational training college) is not sufficiently theoretically grounded for the challenging work of decision making on a day-to-day basis about appropriate and individualised pedagogical strategies with young children from a wide range of social backgrounds. Whereas in Germany only approximately 4% of staff in children's services have a university-level qualification, in most European countries a Bachelor qualification is the minimum requirement for working with three-to six-year-olds (Oberhuemer et al, 2010). The Bologna process has opened up possibilities for German universities of applied sciences to offer a Bachelor qualification in early childhood education (0–6) or childhood education (0–12). Such degree courses have mushroomed since 2004 and there are now over 80 across the country. This dynamic expansion has been somewhat disrupted by a controversial decision to place the traditional post-secondary qualification on the same level as the Bachelor degree within the National/European Qualifications Framework (Level 6). Whether this will lead to a drop in interest in the Bachelor pathway remains to be seen, particularly since central issues such as parity of remuneration remain unsolved.

The second is the issue of CPD, which in Germany comprises predominantly non-mandatory, one-off, short-term and non-formal activities without an acknowledged system of credit transferability across providers (Oberhuemer, 2012). In order to improve the quality, transparency and formal acknowledgement of CPD, a large-scale, nationwide Early Years Workforce Initiative was set up in 2009 and will continue through to the end of 2014. It is funded by the German Federal Ministry of Education and Research and the European Social Fund, and receives publicity support from the Robert Bosch Foundation. The German Youth Institute (DJI) is responsible for commissioning studies and expert reports, supporting advisory groups and developmental work and generally coordinating the initiative, known in Germany as WiFF (*Weiterbildungsinitiative Frühpädagogische Fachkräfte*).[5] To my knowledge it is the only professionalisation project of its kind in Europe.

The third is the critical issue of staff recruitment and staff-to-child ratios in the wake of the current expansion drive. It has been estimated that in the Western *Länder* approximately 12,400 additional staff will be needed in centre-based settings and between 22,000 and 29,000 in family day-care services if the targets for 2013 are to be achieved (Autorengruppe Bildungsberichterstattung, 2012, p 61; Schilling and Rauschenbach, 2012). A number of *Länder* have recently introduced shorter pathways and part-time studies in order to ameliorate this problem. However, the issue of staff-to-child ratios is an additional problem. Variations across the *Länder* are considerable. For work in day nursery groups for under threes these have been estimated to range from a median of 6.2 children per adult in Brandenburg to 3.1 in Bremen, averaging at 4.5 for Germany overall, excluding Berlin (2012 data); for work in kindergartens which take in two-year-olds the estimated median is 11.8 in the Eastern and 7.9 in the Western *Länder*; for work in age-integrated groups including both children under three and school-age children 8.3 and 4.8 respectively; and for work in kindergartens for three- to six-year-olds 11.8 and 8.6 respectively (Bertelsmann Stiftung, 2013, p 318). Clearly, staffing is one of the central quality issues.

Quality of family inclusion: ECEC centres as family centres

Initially inspired by the first early excellence centres and Sure Start children's centres in England, the establishment of family centres as integrated services for children and families can be seen as a specific policy move towards supporting disadvantaged families. A key goal is to provide easily accessible and low threshold services for families and to network with relevant agencies and organisations in the community (Diller et al, 2008). In most cases an early childhood centre is the hub of such service networks, with the centre head taking responsibility for the provision as a whole. Depending on the preferred approach, the centres provide either targeted services in disadvantaged areas, or follow a more universal concept. Northrhine-Westfalia has been promoting family centres since 2006 and in the meantime almost 2,000 centres have been accredited by an external rating agency. Hamburg supports centres for parents and children under age three (*Eltern-Kind-Zentren*) in disadvantaged areas. Since 2007, funding has been steady and to date there are 41 such centres in the city-state, where quality standards are currently being developed by researchers in close collaboration with the centres. Since September 2011, Hesse has also been providing funding for family centres. An interim evaluation of the centres in Northrhine-Westfalia reports overall positive feedback from the directors, despite noting lack of space and funding for certain services and the need for more investment in the overall management of services (Stöbe-Blossey, 2011; see also Stöbe-Blossey, in press).

Research on quality in the German context

With the tremendous drive towards expansion, many experts are concerned about the quality of the places on offer. A small-scale study in Munich/Bavaria concluded that, for a successful transition to high-quality practices, work with under threes needs to be more strongly represented in initial and continuing professional development and to be well resourced in terms of space and personnel (Wertfein et al, 2009). Another regional study – with a longitudinal focus on ethnic-related inequality in ECEC settings in Hesse – conducted standardised tests with approximately 1,000 children from age three to seven as well as interviews with their parents. Roughly half the children came from a Turkish background (Becker, 2012). The study revealed that not only did the Turkish children start kindergarten somewhat later than their German contemporaries, but they also tended to attend settings where the learning environment quality was less favourable. Although centre attendance had a positive effect on the acquisition of German language skills, the extent of this depended on the quality of the specific conditions in the centres.

With the same basic issue of quality services in mind, the first National Study on Education, Care and Upbringing in Early Childhood (NUBBEK) was initiated in 2009 (Tietze et al, 2013). A multi-methods approach was used to gather data on approximately 2,000 two- and four-year-old children in a variety of settings, including the family, across the country. Approximately one-quarter of the children came from families with a Turkish or Russian background. A preliminary report on the findings (Kalicki and Egert, 2012) shows usage patterns that reflect the national and regional data previously presented in this chapter. New, however, are the findings that show that overall, families with a Turkish migration background start attending ECEC settings later than other families and spend less time daily in the settings. However, in those Turkish families where the mother works outside the home, has a higher level of education and a less traditional role model perception, usage patterns in terms of the starting age of children and length of time spent in the centre do not differ from those in families without a migration background. This turned out to be a consistent pattern across a number of NUBBEK findings: not migration status as such, but social status, education level, maternal employment patterns and normative orientations determine usage patterns.

The NUBBEK study also assessed the quality of 403 centre-based settings and 164 family day-care settings with widely used rating scales.[6] It was found that more than 80% of settings were judged to be 'mediocre' in terms of educational process quality, less than 10% of 'good' quality, and more than 10% of 'below average' quality (Kalicki and Egert, 2012). According to the instruments used, groups in the Eastern *Länder* fared less well than those in the Western federal states. Family day-care settings were also judged to be of predominantly mediocre quality. The NUBBEK study concludes by questioning whether recent quality improvement initiatives such as the curricular frameworks have had the expected effects. It is suggested that a systematic and ongoing monitoring of quality is necessary in order to provide service agencies, local authorities and *Länder* ministries with the information necessary for effective steering.

Conclusions

This chapter has looked at ECEC in Germany with a focus on selected issues of access and quality. On both counts, there is considerable variability across the country.

Access opportunities tend to depend on the child's age, family background and socio-geographical location. The participation rates for older pre-school age children suggest that in general they have good access chances. The basic entitlement to a place is a key contributing factor, and the recent introduction of fee-free attendance for five-year-olds in several federal states will presumably give an added boost to the generally high levels of participation among three- to six-year-olds across the country. For this age group, family background does not appear to be a major factor in preventing participation in ECEC, although it may affect the length of time spent in settings. However, even among the older pre-school children, those with a family background of migration are less likely to attend ECEC provision than those without, although the socio-economic status of immigrant parents plays a significant role here as well.

Younger preschool age children have very varied chances of access. If they live in the Eastern regions, where provision has been part of a historically different childcare tradition, the chances are considerably higher. Children whose families have a low income or are dependent on social benefits are less likely to be in an ECEC setting than those from higher-income or higher-educated families. The same applies to under threes from families with a migrant background. Beyond the seemingly insurmountable task of providing enough places by the stated government target date, ensuring that the current expansion drive with its attendant dynamics does not lead to a heightening of these disparities across the country is a major policy challenge.

In terms of quality, the 16 *Länder* have well developed systems of regulatory practices and requirements, and these probably make it unlikely that private (for-profit) providers will become significant players in the field, despite the desperate need for places at the present time. However, compliance strategies tend not to depend on external evaluation or inspection, but more on consensual self-regulation within the field through agreements between the public authorities and the provider organisations, which also have their own quality assurance systems. This is a defining feature of the German ECEC system.

With regard to staff qualifications, Germany is relatively well resourced compared with, for example, English-speaking countries such as Australia, the UK and the US. Seventy per cent of the workforce in centre-based settings have a specialised, post-secondary qualification (Statistisches Bundesamt, 2012a, own calculations). Also, the number of non-qualified staff is very low (2.5%). On the other hand, the proportion of those with a degree-level qualification (Bachelor or above) is at 4% much lower than in most other countries. Following the controversial placing of the traditional vocational training award at Level 6 on the National and European Qualifications Framework – on a par with a Bachelor degree – this issue will undoubtedly be further debated in the future, not least in terms of the quality of the different training routes and remuneration levels. The most immediate policy challenge in terms of staffing, however, is the recruitment and retention of staff qualified to an acceptable level in the face of the fast-paced expansion, particularly in the metropolitan areas. Another will be to maintain and, particularly in the case of work with under threes, to improve staff-to-child ratios, especially in the Eastern regions.

Although the national evaluation study reported on in the previous section has suggested a need for quality-raising practices across the country, it is perhaps too early as yet to assume that the fairly recently introduced quality initiatives – whether curricular frameworks, self-evaluation procedures or enhanced opportunities for CPD – are not effective in the field. Considerably more research and evaluation studies are needed in order to gain a comprehensive picture, including a wide range of qualitative studies that look closely at process quality on the micro-level of ECEC and parental involvement in ECEC settings.

Notes

[1] In Germany, the term 'immigrant' is not in common usage, although it is applied occasionally in this chapter because of its international currency. Instead, the official terminology is *Personen mit Migrationshintergrund* (people with a migration background).

[2] Federal Statistical Office definition: people not born within the borders of present-day Germany who entered the country in 1950 or later; and/or people who are not German nationals or have not acquired German citizenship. Children who have been granted German citizenship are still considered to have a migration background if one parent fulfils at least one of the previously mentioned criteria (Integrationsbericht, 2012; translated by author).

[3] The AID:A Survey on 'Growing up in Germany' conducted by the German Youth Institute (Deutsches Jugendinstitut, DJI) is planned as a replicative, cross-sectional study, drawing on a new random sample approximately every four years.

[4] www.bmfsfj.de

[5] www.weiterbildungsinitiative.de

[6] These include the German-language versions of ECERS-R (Early Childhood Environment Rating Scale – Revised), ITERS-R (Infant/Toddler Environment Rating Scale – Revised) and FCCERS-R (Family Child Care Environment Rating Scale – Revised), and the CCIS (Child Caregiver Interaction Scale).

References

Alt, C. (2012) Ungleiche Platzvergabe: Wer vom Ausbau der institutionellen Betreuungsangebote für Kinder unter drei Jahren profitiert? [*Unequal Allocation: Who Is Profiting from the Expansion of Institutional Childcare Places for Under-threes?*], Munich: DJI, Deutschen Jugendinstituts, no 4, pp 16–18.

Autorengruppe Bildungsberichterstattung (2012) *Bildung in Deutschland 2012: Ein indikatorengestützter Bericht mit einer Analyse zur kulturellen Bildung im Lebenslauf* [*Education in Germany 2012: An Indicator-led Report with an Analysis of Cultural Education across the Lifespan*], Bielefeld: W. Bertelsmann.

Becker, B. (2012) 'Ethnische Bildungsungleichheit in der frühen Kindheit: Ergebnisse aus dem Projekt ESKOM-V' ['Ethnicity and educational inequality in early childhood: Findings from the ESKOM-V project'], *Frühe Bildung*, vol 1, no 3, pp 150–8.

Bertelsmann Stiftung (ed) 2013 *Ländermonitor Frühkindliche Bildungssysteme 2013* [*Länder Monitor on Early Childhood Education Systems 2013*], Gütersloh: Bertelsmann Stiftung.

Blum, S. and Erler D. (2011) *International Review of Leave Policies and Related Research, Country note: Germany* (www.leavenetwork.org/fileadmin/Leavenetwork/Annual_reviews/Complete_review_2011.pdf).

BMFSFJ (Bundesministerium für Familie, Senioren, Frauen und Jugend) (2012) *Dritter Zwischenbericht zur Evaluation des Kinderförderungsgesetzes* [*Third Interim Evaluation Report on the Childcare Funding Act*], Berlin: BMFSFJ.

Bock-Famulla, K. and Große-Wöhrmann, K. (2010) *Länderreport Frühkindliche Bildungssysteme 2009. Transparenz schaffen: Governance stärken* [*Länder Report on Early Childhood Education Systems 2009. Creating Transparency: Strengthening Governance*], Gütersloh: Bertelsmann Stiftung.

Bock-Famulla, K. and Lange, J. (2011) *Länderreport Frühkindliche Bildungssysteme 2011: Transparenz schaffen – Governance stärken* [*Länder Report on Early Childhood Education Systems 2011: Creating Transparency – Strengthening Governance*], Gütersloh: Bertelsmann Stiftung.

Diekmann, L.C., Enste, D. and Hülskamp, N. (2008) 'Kita-Gutscheine: Für eine verbesserte Betreuung und Bildung' ['Childcare vouchers: Towards improved care and education'], *Wirtschaftsdienst*, vol 10, pp 666–71.

Diller, A., Heitkötter, M. and Rauschenbach, T. (eds) (2008) *Familie im Zentrum* [*Families at the Centre*], München: DJI-Fachforum Bildung und Erziehung, Band 6, München: Verlag Deutsches Jugendinstitut.

Gathmann, C. and Sachs, B. (2012) *Taxing Childcare: Effects on Family Labor Supply and Children*, IZA Discussion Paper No 6440, Mannheim: Institute for the Study of Labor.

Gottschall, K. and Pothmann, J. (2011) *A Question of Justice*, Munich: DJI, Deutschen Jugendinstituts.

Integrationsbericht (2012) *9. Bericht der Beauftragten der Bundesregierung für Migration, Flüchtlinge und Integration über die Lage der Ausländerinnen und Ausländer in Deutschland* [*9th Report of the Federal Government Commissioner for Migration, Refugees and Integration on the Situation of Foreigners in Germany*], Berlin: Bundesregierung für Migration, Flüchtlinge und Integration über die Lage der Ausländerinnen und Ausländer in Deutschland (www.bundesregierung.de/Content/DE/_Anlagen/IB/2012-06-27-neunter-lagebericht.pdf).

Kalicki, B. and Egert, F. (2012) *Effekte der Früh-Erziehung* [*Effects of Early Education*], Munich: DJI, Deutschen Jugendinstituts, no 2, pp 37–40.

Krapf, S. and Kreyenfeld, M. (2010) 'Nur eine Alternative für hoch qualifizierte Frauen? Kleinkindbetreuung in Deutschland: Erhebliche Unterschiede zwischen Ost und West' ['Only an alternative for highly qualified women? Childcare in Germany: significant differences between East and West'], *Demografische Forschung aus erster Hand*, vol 7, no 4, p 3.

Leu, H.R. (2012) 'Betreuungsrendite oder Bildungsrendite? Zum Ertrag der frühkindlichen Bildung, Betreuung und Erziehung' ['Care returns or education returns? On the benefits of early childhood education and care'], in T. Rauschenbach and W. Bien (eds) *Aufwachsen in Deutschland – AID:A: Der neue DJI-Survey* [*Growing up in Germany – AID:A: The New DJI Survey*], Weinheim: Beltz, pp 123–37.

Nicko, O. and Schreyer, I. with Kademann, S. (2013) *Sprachberatung in Kindertageseinrichtungen in Bayern – Evaluationsbericht* [*Language Coaching in Early Childhood Centres in Bavaria – Evaluation Report*], München: Staatsinstitut für Frühpädagogik.

Oberhuemer, P. (2012) *Fort- und Weiterbildung frühpädagogischer Fachkräfte im europäischen Vergleich* [*Continuing Professional Development of Early Years Educators in Europe: A Cross-national Study*], with Denise Hevey, Camilla Hvorth Weber, Maelis Karlsson Lohmander, Marta Korintus, Arianna Lazzari and Tatjana Vonta, WiFF Studie 17, Munich: Deutsches Jugendinstitut (Weiterbildungsinitiative Frühpädagogische Fachkräfte).

Oberhuemer, P., Schreyer, I. and Neuman, M.J. (2010) *Professionals in Early Childhood Education and Care Systems – European Profiles and Perspectives*, Leverkeusen: Barbara Budrich.

OECD (Organisation for Economic Co-operation and Development) (2004) *Early Childhood Education and Care Policy in the Federal Republic of Germany: Country Note*, Paris: OECD Publishing (www.oecd.org/edu/preschoolandschool/33978768.pdf).

OECD (2006) *Where Immigrant Students Succeed. A Comparative Review of Performance and Engagement in PISA 2003*, Paris: OECD Publishing.

Rauschenbach, T. and Bien, W. (eds) (2012) *Aufwachsen in Deutschland – AID:A: Der neue DJI-Survey* [*Growing up in Germany – AID:A: The New DJI Survey*], Weinheim: Beltz.

Riedel, B., Hüsken, K. and Fuchs-Rechlin, K. (2011) 'Kita vor Ort: DJI-Betreuungsatlas nimmt regionale Ungleichheiten unter die Lupe' ['Early childhood centres on the ground: DJI Childcare Atlas takes a close look at regional disparities'], *Forum Jugendhilfe*, no 3, pp 38–41.

Schilling, M. and Rauschenbach, T. (2012) *Zu wenig Fachkräfte für unter Dreijährige* [*Not Enough Personnel for the Under-threes*], Munich: DJI, Deutschen Jugendinstituts, no 2,.

Schreyer, I. (2009) 'Die Kita-Trägerlandschaft in Deutschland' ['Early childhood service providers in Germany'], in M. Hugoth and X. Roth (eds) *Handbuch für Träger von Kindertageseinrichtungen* [*Manual for Providers of Early Childhood Services*], Cronach: Carl Link, pp 1–25.

Standing Conference of the Ministers for Youth Affairs and Standing Conference of the Ministers of Education and Cultural Affairs (2004) 'A common framework for early education', in Pestalozzi-Fröbel-Verband (ed) *Early Childhood Education and Care in Germany*, Weimar, Berlin: Verlag das Netz, pp 14–21.

Statistisches Bundesamt (2012a) *Statistiken der Kinder- und Jugendhilfe: Kinder und tätige Personen in Tageseinrichtungen und in öffentlich geförderter Kindertagespflege* [*Child and Youth Services Statistics: Children and Workers in Centre-based Settings and in Publicly Subsidised Family Day Care*], Wiesbaden: Statistisches Bundesamt (www.destatis.de/DE/Publikationen/Thematisch/Soziales/KinderJugendhilfe/TageseinrichtungenKindertagespflege5225402117004.pdf?__blob=publicationFile).

Statistisches Bundesamt (2012b) 'Pressemitteilung' ['Press notice'], Nr 382, 6 November, Wiesbaden: Statistisches Bundesamt (www.destatis.de/DE/PresseService/Presse/Pressemitteilungen/2012/11/PD12_382_225.html).

Stöbe-Blossey, S. (2011) 'Familienzentren in Nordrhein-Westfalen – eine Zwischenbilanz' ['Family centres in Northrhine-Westfalia – an interim assessment'] (www.iaq.uni-due.de/iaq-report/2011/report2011-06.pdf).

Stöbe-Blossey, S. (in press) 'Governance of integrated services: the example of Family Centres in North Rhine-Westphalia', *Early Years: An International Research Journal*, vol 33, no 4.

Tietze, W., Becker-Stoll, F., Bensel, J., Eckhardt, A.G., Haug-Schnabel, G., Kalicki, B., Keller, H. and Leyendecker, B. (2013) *NUBBEK – Nationale Untersuchung zur Bildung, Betreuung und Erziehung in der frühen Kindheit* [*NUBBEK – A National Study on Early Childhood Education and Care*], Weimar, Berlin: Verlag das Netz.

Walper, S. and Riedel, B. (2011) *How Poverty Matters*, Munich: DJI: Deutschen Jugendinstituts.

Wertfein, M., Spies-Kofler, A. and Becker-Stoll, F. (2009) 'Quality curriculum for under-threes: the impact of structural standards', *Early Years – An International Journal of Research and Development*, vol 29, no 1, pp 33–44.

SEVEN

New Zealand: A narrative of shifting policy directions for early childhood education and care

Helen May

Introduction

Between 1999 and 2008 the centre-left Labour government in New Zealand made radical changes to the provision of early childhood education and care (ECEC). The government introduced funding to support participation in 'high need' centres and services, delivered on a policy of 20 hours' free early childhood education (ECE) per week for three and four-year olds, increased universal subsidies including for children under three and was on target by 2012 to have teacher-led ECEC centres staffed entirely by qualified teachers. These policies were embedded in the Labour government's Strategic Plan, *Pathways to the Future – Ngā Huarahi Arataki 2002–2012*, intended to provide a robust infrastructure for delivering high-quality, affordable, ECEC participation by all children (Ministry of Education, 2002).

The scope of New Zealand's ECEC policy directions attracted international attention. Peter Moss described New Zealand as 'leading the wave' of early childhood innovation, having 'confronted the wicked issues' with the development of an integrated approach to funding, regulation, curriculum and qualifications (Moss, 2007, p 33). Moss pointed to New Zealand's vision of early childhood education as 'a broad and holistic concept that covers, children, families and communities, a concept of "education-in-its-broadest-sense" in which learning and care really are inseparable and connected to many other purposes besides' (2008, pp 7–8). In New Zealand, political commentator Colin James argued that investment in early childhood education may be the most memorable achievement of Labour's period in office: 'Making early childhood systematic … takes us deep into a zone of policy debate: on citizens' access to participation in our economy and society…. Early childhood education is investing in infrastructure, just like building roads. It is arguably Labour's most important initiative, its biggest idea' (*Otago Daily Times*, 19 February 2008).

However, the election of a centre–right government in November 2008 caused a shift in policy direction. Retrenchment was immediate after the election, with the 2010 Budget signalling the changes ahead. Research, training grants and professional development programmes were culled. Labour's target of 100% qualified teachers in ECEC by 2012 was cut to 80%. Instead, new initiatives were announced to improve ECEC participation in 'high need' locations with large populations of indigenous Māori children, or Pasfika children whose families had migrated over several decades from Pacific Island nations. The government argued that previous policies had failed to redress low ECEC participation for these children that in some localities had fallen as low as 59% (Morrison, 2009).

There was wide support for these new initiatives, but the cutbacks around quality were called 'a brutal blow' (NZCA, 2010). The *NZ Herald* (24 May, 2010) summed up more conservative opinion in an editorial, 'Preschool Budget cuts right move':

> Plainly National does not regard specialist teaching of preschool children to be quite as important as Labour did. It is probably right…. Did childcare centres ever need to be fully staffed by trained teachers? Or is this a classic case of "qualification inflation"…. It is easy to insist little children deserve nothing but the best … but "the best" at that level might not require professional training. The Government is right to direct more of its early education support to areas where children are missing out…. Contentious the decision may be but it seems educationally harmless, socially equitable and financially necessary.

The issue remains 'contentious', reflecting political divides between left and right over state interest in the universal funding of quality ECEC for all children versus targeting funding towards those children, families and communities deemed most in need. Anne Tolley (2011), Minister of Education between 2008–11, justified the government's position:

> Taxpayer investment in early childhood services has trebled over the last five years…. Despite this growth in funding, too many children that the evidence tells us would benefit most from ECE are still missing out. They are at a disadvantage

before they even start school. The economic reality is that money will be tight for the foreseeable future, so more than ever we must invest in the areas that will make the biggest difference to children and their families.

This chapter is written as a narrative of change in 2012 while a Ministerial Advisory Group on Early Childhood Funding designs a new ECEC funding model. On the 'cusp of change' it is useful to appraise past and current approaches to ECEC funding and in particular to reflect on the quality and costs of ECEC for disadvantaged families. The current policy approach is shaped by wider social concerns over 'vulnerable' children, families and communities who have become a priority for government policy (Ministry of Social Development, 2011). In its *White Paper for Vulnerable Children* (2012), the government quantified between 20,000 to 30,000 vulnerable children and families (out of a population of 4.4 million) who 'live a life far below the norm' and are 'at significant risk of harm to their well-being now and into the future' (Ministry of Social Development, 2012, p 4). The risk factors include a combination of abuse, neglect, health and poverty issues. ECEC participation policy initiatives are intended for a wider frame, but ensuring access to ECEC for the most vulnerable children is one aspect of a range of new strategies contained in the White Paper's 'Children's Action Plan' to identify and support these children.

Cusp of change

Treasury Briefings in 2011 to the incoming Minister of Education in the re-elected national government recommended a better alignment of policy with the government's social and economic objectives and some 'carefully managed trade-offs' (NZ Treasury, 2012). The 2012 Budget was labelled the 'zero budget', a reflection of straightened financial times where new spending would mean cuts elsewhere. Additional monies were budgeted for early childhood centres in 'high need' areas, to assist solo parents to get back into the workplace, and to improve access to Māori language immersion centres. In justifying the increase in expenditure in a zero budget year, new Minister for Education, Hekia Perata, argued that 'this will support vulnerable children who are not receiving sufficient support to succeed in education.... By targeting resources to these learners we will raise participation to give them a strong platform for their compulsory school years' (Perata, 24 May 2012). The funding is intended to help reach a new target for 2016 of 98% of new entrants to school at age five having participated in early childhood education, part of a strategy of 'raising achievement for all' (Perata, 16 May 2012).

Of concern to the profession is a potential trade-off between quality, affordability and participation. To offset the increase the Minister announced that the 20 hours ECE subsidy for three- and four-year-olds (originally called 20 hours' free ECE) would not have an inflation adjustment. The *NZ Herald* (25 May 2012) reported the 'freeze' as 'cuts by stealth to strained centres.... Thousands of families could pay more for their early childhood education after the budget put a funding freeze on subsidies in favour of targeted spending.' Two-thirds of centres would have a reduction in funding. The Minister justified this shift of resources as a containment of current funding levels and a prioritising of expenditure to 'priority learners'.

Funding for ECEC in New Zealand doubled between 2006/07 and 2010/11 (and trebled compared to 2004/05) (Education Counts, 2012, Table EXP4). While the government seeks to contain rising ECEC expenditure, the counter-argument is that ECEC had been historically under-resourced and that the previous government's policies were redressing the balance. International comparisons indicate that New Zealand government expenditure on ECEC as a percentage of gross domestic product (GDP) was below the average of OECD (Organisation for Economic Co-operation and Development) countries until 2010–11, when the accumulation of increased spending placed the New Zealand figure closer to 0.8% of GDP and slightly above the OECD average of 0.7% (Ministry of Education, 2010). New Zealand has been rated 9th out of 45 countries for affordability of ECEC to parents (Economist Intelligence Unit, 2012). The 2010 and 2012 Budgets herald a philosophical shift by the government, undermining the universal tenets of ECEC funding formulae linked to affordability and access for all children, the costs of quality and investment in the infrastructure of quality such as qualified teachers, professional development, curriculum and research. There has always been targeted funding for selected children, centres and services, but it was on top of rather than in place of universal subsidies.

ECEC in New Zealand

Government-funded ECEC services are available for children from birth until school age, usually when children start school on their fifth birthday, although school is not compulsory until age six. Overall participation rates are high and increase by age. In 2011, around 18% of children under one were enrolled in an ECEC setting, rising to

40% of children aged one, 60% of children aged two, over 90% of three-year-olds and 100% of four-year-olds (although these numbers are overestimates, as they double-count children enrolled in more than one setting) (Ministry of Education, 2011b, Figure 1). Enrolment has increased steadily for all age groups over the last two decades, and most steeply for children aged one, two and three.

Participation rates vary according to children's background. Statistics for 2012 show that if schools are divided into deciles according to students' socio-economic status, just 1% of children arriving at the top decile of schools have not attended any ECE, compared to 17% of children in the bottom decile (Ministry of Education, 2012). Participation rates are also much lower for children from Māori or Pasifika backgrounds, although the gaps have narrowed over the last decade, as shown in Figure 7.1. Even among those who have participated, children from disadvantaged backgrounds are likely to have attended for a shorter duration and for fewer hours per week. For example, 40% of children in the bottom socio-economic decile have attended for one year or less, compared to 21% of children from the top decile (Ministry of Education, 2012).

New Zealand has a diverse range of ECEC services including both centre and home-based programmes, and for some funding streams divided into 'teacher-led' and 'parent-led' services. There is also an unlicensed sector, mainly consisting of playgroups attended by infants and toddlers and run by parents, which receives grants in aid. In New

Figure 7.1: New Zealand: ECE non-participation rate on starting school, by ethnic group

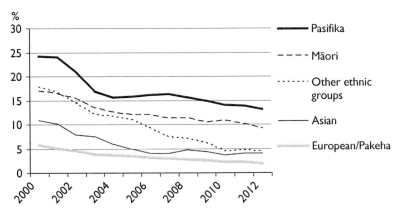

Note: This shows the percentage of children who start school having not attended any early education setting.
Source: Ministry of Education (2012, Table 1)

Zealand the state is not a provider of ECEC. Instead, ECEC services are a mix of private and community-based provision.

Education and care centres are the most common form of provision. These have grown rapidly since the 1970s, and are significantly used by working parents as the services are open all day, although many childcare centres also accept sessional placements (and working parents might use a home-based programme, a kindergarten or *kōhanga reo*). Many centres offer places for children under two. In the education and care sector there is a mix of community and private ownership, including workplace provision, church-run centres, independent Māori immersion or bilingual centres, Montessori centres and some large corporate chains with national or regional coverage (May, 2009). This is a teacher-led sector although not all centres have 100% qualified staff.

Kindergartens traditionally offer part-day sessions for three- and four-year-olds, but more recently many include younger children and offer a range of extended hour options including some full childcare provision. Kindergartens have 100% qualified teachers, except in a few situations where staff are concurrently training to be teachers. Kindergartens are not-for-profit organisations, run by kindergarten associations, first established in the nineteenth century.

Licensed home-based programmes are run by home educators working in their own or a child's home. Home educators themselves are not required to be qualified but are regularly supervised and supported by qualified teachers (coordinators), and must implement the national early childhood curriculum. Coordinators visit home educators at least once a month, observing interactions between adults and children, and some also run playgroups for carers and children. All home-based services offer places for under two-year-olds.

Playcentres are sessional programmes for children from birth to school age, staffed by parents who undergo training. They are run by not-for-profit playcentre associations, first established in the 1940s.

Kōhanga reo (language nests) were established in the 1980s under the umbrella of Te Kōhanga Reo National Trust. They are staffed by trained *kaiako* (educators) who are sometimes qualified teachers and *whānau* (family) speakers of Māori. *Kōhanga reo* include children from birth to school age and generally open for a school day of 9.00am– 3.00pm.

Finally, bilingual Pasifika centres, first established in the 1980s, are registered as education and care centres, representing a range of different island cultures and languages. The centres are often connected to churches and staffed significantly by teachers, although not always at the 100% rate.

All licensed ECEC services fall under the responsibility of the Ministry of Education. Historic divides between care and education were bridged when childcare services relocated from the Department of Social Welfare in 1986 and cemented further when teacher education programmes were integrated and a unified regulatory and funding framework was developed. In 1996 a national early childhood curriculum, *Te Whāriki*, brought pedagogical cohesion to this diverse sector with the metaphor, translated from Māori, of 'a mat for all to stand on' (Ministry of Education, 1996). The curriculum celebrates diversity with 'mats' of many patterns reflecting the ECEC services in the sector (Smith, 2010).

The landscape of the ECEC sector has been shifting (Education Counts, 2012), shaped by new funding policies, the promotion of the benefits of quality ECEC and changing workplace participation. The proportion of preschool children from two-parent families in employment increased from 29.7% in 1998 to 38.2% in 2009, while the proportion in single-parent employed families increased by 2.4 percentage points over the same period (Statistics NZ, 2012). As Table 7.1 shows, there was a 26% increase in ECEC enrolments during the 2000s, and there was also a shift in service type, reflecting parental preference, market availability and new funding drivers. Between 2000 and 2011, there was a 60% rise in education and care centres offering mainly full-day childcare, and a doubling of home-based enrolments for mainly under three-year-olds (although from a low starting point). Enrolments in kindergartens, playcentres and *kōhanga reo* fell.

The median average weekly attendance across all service types was 17 hours in 2009, up from 10 hours in 1998 (Statistics NZ, 2012). By 2011 57% of children attended between 15 and 36 hours per

Table 7.1: New Zealand: Enrolments in licensed early childhood services, by service type

	Number of enrolments			Difference 2000–11	Share of total enrolments		
	2000	**2007**	**2011**	**(%)**	**2000**	**2007**	**2011**
Education and care	71,231	91,733	113,976	60	46	54	59
Kindergarten	45,869	43,695	36,967	–19	30	26	19
Home-based	8,937	11,073	17,955	101	6	6	9
Playcentre	15,808	14,664	15,112	–4	10	9	8
Te kōhanga reo	11,138	9,236	9,631	–14	7	5	5
Total	153,967	171,138	194,101	26	100	100	100

Source: Education Counts (2012, Table 2)

week (Ministry of Education, 2011). This increase in the level of participation per child is a result of policies intended to make ECEC more affordable.

The number of qualified teachers in the sector increased by 150% between 2001 and 2011, with 69% of staff in 2011 in the teacher-led sector holding an ECE teaching qualification (see Table 7.2), and 51% of unqualified staff enrolled in a teaching qualification (Education Counts, 2012). This was an area of significant investment by government. Not included, however, are parent-led services – playcentres, playgroups and *kōhango reo*. Table 7.3 shows a shift towards teacher-led services, in particular education and care centres, between 1998 and 2009 for children from Māori and European backgrounds. There is no evidence of this shift for children from Pasifika households, and the data, which are from the New Zealand Childcare Survey, point to a fall in enrolment in formal care for Pasifika children.

The policy drivers underlying these trends will be elaborated later in the chapter. The statistics, however, reveal that not all children are beneficiaries of past policy initiatives. Government policy has classified some of these children as potentially 'vulnerable', a 'risk' to society and a 'priority' for ECEC. There are 'risks' too for the ECEC sector as a whole if this becomes a dominant political gaze shaping government interest in ECEC.

Funding ECEC

The ECEC funding system, now under review, contains drivers around quality, affordability, equity, access and universality. The success of these drivers, evident in the trends outlined above, is also the cause

Table 7.2: New Zealand: Percentage of staff who are qualified teachers, by sector

	2001	2002	2003	2004	2005	2006	2007	2008	2009	2010	2011
Education and care	39	39	40	42	46	50	54	55	58	62	64
Kindergarten	97	96	95	95	96	96	97	97	97	96	96
Home-based	76	80	88	95	98	99	99	99	98	99	99
Total	49	49	49	51	54	57	60	61	64	67	69

Notes: Data relates to licensed ECE teacher-led services. Excluded are parent-led services, including playcentres, playgroups and *kōhanga reo*. For home-based services, data relates to coordinators (caregivers and educators are excluded).

Source: Education Counts (2012)

Table 7.3: New Zealand: Enrolments in different services, by ethnic background, 1998 and 2009 (%)

	Māori		Pasifika		European		Total	
	1998	2009	1998	2009	1998	2009	1998	2009
Kindergarten	13.8	13.8	18.2	11.7	20.6	16.5	19.2	15.2
Education and care centre	11.4	19.9	10.1	11.1	20.4	29	17.4	24.9
Organised home-based	2.4	4.1	–	–	3.3	4.8	2.9	4.3
Any teacher-led	**27.6**	**37.8**			**44.3**	**50.3**	**39.5**	**44.4**
Playcentre	3.8	5.6	–	–	8.7	8.2	7.2	6.7
Kōhanga reo	14.2	8.1	3.7	–	1.4	0.8	3.4	2.4
Playgroup	2.6	3.1	–	–	6.5	7.9	5.3	6.6
Any parent-led	**20.6**	**16.8**	**3.7**		**16.6**	**16.9**	**15.9**	**15.7**
Any formal care	**46.3**	**50.1**	**42.5**	**30.8**	**55.4**	**58.5**	**51.9**	**53.9**

Notes: No data reported if estimate less than 1,000. Children may be counted in more than one ethnic group, and may attend more than one setting.

Source: Statistics NZ (2012), from the New Zealand Childcare Survey

of the government's desire to contain the rising cost, a task given to a ministerial ECE Taskforce in 2010 (ECE Taskforce, 2011).

The main ECEC funding is a universal subsidy per child paid to centres and services for a maximum of 30 hours a week per child. The level of the subsidy is differentiated between children under two years and over two years and is otherwise the same across services, including licensed home-based programmes. This policy stretches back to reforms in the late 1980s intended to provide equitable levels of funding across the childcare and what had been the sessional preschool sectors. Fees to parents are still charged, although in sessional services the subsidies cover a much higher proportion of costs.

In addition, a childcare subsidy is available to parents using licensed ECEC services, including home-based, who cannot afford fees and/ or are single parents trying to enter the workplace, or where children have special needs. This is a means-tested benefit paid to the centre on behalf of the child and can cover up to 100% of fees. In 2009 the subsidy was used by 28% of children attending ECEC including 43% of children whose parents were government beneficiaries (Statistics NZ, 2012). This subsidy is a significant mechanism for supporting disadvantaged children and families to access ECEC.

In 2000, the Labour government set up an Equity Working Party to develop a funding mechanism to raise participation in groups that were under-represented. Subsequently an Equity Funding 'add on' was paid to community-based providers, both teacher-led and parent-led, to recognise costs associated with low socio-economic communities; children with special needs and non-English-speaking backgrounds; delivery in a language and culture other than English; and rural isolation (Ministry of Education, 2005). The rates vary according to the component being applied for and the Equity Index rating (determined each Census) of the location of the centre. The government intends to extend this mechanism to deliver its new participation programmes. Since 2011, privately owned centres have been able to apply for Equity Funding.

In 2001 the Labour government appointed a working group to develop a ten-year plan for the sector. The vision was for all children to participate in quality ECEC, although recommendations from the working group that children have the 'right to a free ECE' were rejected (May, 2009). In 2002, the government published a ten-year Strategic Plan for early childhood (Ministry of Education, 2002). It was from this point that the sector was divided for funding purposes into parent-led services and teacher-led services. The former included many *kōhanga reo* and all playcentres that children attend because of their parents' commitment to the philosophical principles of these programmes. Broadly, 87% of all enrolments are in teacher-led services, and this share is rising (see Table 7.1 above). The Strategic Plan goal for teacher-led services was to have 100% qualified teachers in the education and care centres to match the kindergartens' long tradition of qualified teachers.

The Strategic Plan created two new funding drivers that significantly increased the cost of ECEC to government. First, to encourage centres to employ qualified teachers 'quality funding bands' were developed linked to the proportion of qualified staff in the centre. The funding bands were calculated around the cost of salaries, recognising the 2002 equal pay settlement by kindergarten teachers (providing equality with primary and secondary teachers) and a pay settlement for teachers in education and care centres leading towards parity with kindergarten (May, 2005). These funding bands were not accessible to *kōhanga reo* unless they were employing qualified teachers, or to playcentres. The organisations providing these services made strategic decisions that they wanted to emphasise *whanau* (family) involvement, and their training programmes were not intended as teaching qualifications.

With increased intakes into colleges and universities, the targets were on track if staff already in training could be counted during the phase in period. However, the 2010 Budget removed the 100% funding band: the required targets became 80% for children over two and 50% for children under two, with no funding for qualified teachers above 80%. Centres that already had 100% qualified staff had their funding cut.

Second, in 2004 there was a surprise announcement that all three- and four-year-olds in community services would have 20 hours' free ECE from 2007 in addition to the universal subsidy. Parents using private centres demanded that the policy be extended (which it was). Private centre owners did not support the policy, not wanting government interference with their fee structures or their profit margins (Mitchell, 2010). Nevertheless, uptake was high and eventually included most private centres and all corporate chains. Despite the initial turmoil the policy was a winner. There was an immediate impact on fees. The Consumer Price Index recorded a 32% drop in the cost of early childhood education, causing a 5.2% drop in the overall price of education in the country (Statistics NZ, 2007). In 2010 the policy was extended to the parent-led *kōhanga reo* and playcentre, but by then the new government had dropped the word 'free', with the policy now called a 20 hours ECE subsidy. This allowed the previously monitored 'optional charges' to become real fees. These are still monitored by government and can only cover 'extras' such as increased staff ratios, outings or meals. Not all centres charge an additional fee, but the cost of keeping 100% qualified staff might, in consultation with parents, be covered this way. There is still a strong perception among parents that this is 20 hours' free ECE.

The government has justified its moratorium on ECEC funding on grounds of a lack of evidence that the 20 hours' free ECE policy increased participation. The Minister for Education pointed out that there had been only a one percentage point increase (from 93.6% in 2007 to 94.7% in 2011) in 'the only real measure we have' of participation, the share of children starting school who have attended an ECE setting (Tolley, 2011). This interpretation of the statistics is disputed. In the timeframe under scrutiny (between mid-2007 and mid-2010) there was little increase in the provision of services in areas of low participation (Froese and Jenkins, 2008). But Figure 7.1 above shows a steady decline nonetheless in non-participation for children from some ethnic groups. Furthermore, there is evidence that between 2007 and 2011 the 20 hours ECE policy led to a 23% increase in attendance *hours* at kindergarten and an 11% increase at education care centres (Education Counts, 2012). A government evaluation showed that 17% of all parents and 30% of low-income parents decided to participate in ECEC because of the 20 hours ECE policy (Mitchell et al, 2011). Linda Mitchell, a key player in getting the policy implemented, has argued that 'the universal investment in ECEC helped to diminish inequalities in access and enabled more children irrespective of their family circumstances to participate' (Mitchell, 2012, p 103). As a member of the ECE Taskforce, Anne Smith strongly argued with ECE Taskforce members intent on changing the funding policy: 'Making these hours free allows some families to use these services in a more sustained and regular way, which is a very favourable outcome for children and families (Smith, November 2010, p 1).

Quality directions

Increasing participation in ECEC has been a policy initiative of successive governments. The Strategic Plan policies of the 2000s made a further commitment to quality participation, acknowledging that participation in poor quality ECEC could be harmful and accepting the research evidence that qualified teachers were a key to delivering quality (Ministry of Education, 2002), alongside measures already covered by regulations such as group size, relationships with parents, resources and physical environment. Improving the minimum adult-to-child ratios was also proposed, but is still lingering at broadly 1:5 for under twos and 1:10 for over twos. Improvements to these ratios were delayed by the national government although the under twos ratio is again under consideration. Many centres improve on these regulated standards.

Implementing the principles of the national early childhood curriculum, *Te Whāriki*, was also deemed a pedagogy for quality. Under *Te Whāriki*, ECEC is about the empowerment of children (*Whakamana*); the involvement of families (*Whānau tangata*); is based on holistic understandings of learning and development (*Kotahitanga*); and cemented through 'reciprocal and responsive relationships with people, places and things' (*Ngā Hononga*) (Ministry of Education, 1996). *Te Whāriki* is theoretically complex and, for unqualified staff, challenging to implement (Nuttall, 2003). *Te Whāriki* resists telling teachers what to teach, requiring them, with their children and their family and *whānau*, to 'weave' their own curriculum patterns through a process of talk, reflection, planning, evaluation and assessment, framed around the five strands of empowerment, each with embedded goals for children:

Mana Atua	Wellbeing
Mana Whenua	Belonging
Mana Tangata	Contribution
Mana Reo	Communication
Mana Aoturoa	Exploration

The strands weave an aspirational vision for children in New Zealand:

> To grow up as competent and confident learners and communicators, healthy in mind, body, and spirit, secure in their sense of belonging and in the knowledge that they make a valued contribution to the world. (Ministry of Education, 1996, p 9)

The implementation of *Te Whāriki* for all children was a driver of the 100% qualification policy, although research evidence indicates that there are still a proportion of centres unable to realise the potential of *Te Whāriki*, particularly in relation to its cultural and social tenets (ERO, 2010, 2011).

With the cut-back to funding for qualified teachers there has been discussion concerning the difference this will make to the quality of ECEC, both for three- and four-year-olds, and for younger children, for whom the target has been reduced from 100% to 50% qualified teachers. Prime Minister John Key declared that, 'It is a matter of personal belief as to whether a high proportion of all centre staff should be qualified' (*NZ Herald*, 3 May 2010). In response, Margaret Carr and Linda Mitchell (2010) argued that:

> It is a matter of an informed and evidence-based educational decision. These questions would never be raised about adults who teach 5–6 (or older) year-olds in school… (p 1)

> We had hoped that 100% qualified teachers for *all* children in ECE made us different to other countries with a high level of income inequality and contribute to the government's aim of equitable and quality outcomes for all children. (p 4)

Minister Tolley claimed there was no research evidence to show 100% qualified teachers were better than 80% qualified teachers. Conversely, Anne Smith, in argument with other ECE Taskforce members and the Minister, claimed that:

> Such research would be hard to do. (There are few countries that employ 100% qualified teachers in ECE.) There isn't any research either which shows that 100% qualified staff *isn't* better than 80%. (Smith, November, 2010, p 2)

Smith pointed to research demonstrating that 'Qualified teachers provide more sensitive and responsive learning opportunities for children.... Logically the more qualified teachers ... the better outcomes there will be for children's well-being and learning' (November 2010, p 2).

Investigating this premise was the focus of the research project 'Early childhood teachers work: practices in centres with different staff profiles' (Meade et al, 2012). Quality indicators in centres with 100% qualified teachers were compared with those from centres with 50–79% qualified teachers. The project identified a number of important effects of having 100% teachers in a centre:

> Compared with children in the centres with 50–79% qualified teachers, children in the 100% centres benefit from more teachers asking more open-ended questions and posing challenges in ways that lead children to use more complex thinking.... Children in the 100% centres had: more interactions with qualified teachers; more conversations with these teachers; more episodes of sustained shared thinking; more teacher mediation of their concept development; and slightly higher scores on indicators to do with independence and concentration.... The research literature tells us that these effects are significant; for example, sustained shared thinking has significant predictive value for children's later success. (Meade et al, 2012, pp xii–xiii)

The report also emphasised that the centres with 100% qualified teachers provided higher-quality care and education than the 50–79% centres for the under twos as well as older children.

There are lessons to be learned about the current political trade-off that shifts funding from qualified teachers to initiatives to 'raise education achievement for all' children, and in particular to children targeted for participation in ECEC. Unless it is quality participation the benefits of ECEC may not be fully realised.

Market-led ECEC

The rise in the private for-profit sector has accompanied increases in government funding. Private ECEC services are intended to make a profit, sometimes for the owner but sometimes as a dividend for shareholders (Mitchell, 2012). The private sector has become a significant player in the provision of childcare. In 2010, 64% of all education and care services and 74% of the home-based services were privately owned. Between 2007 and 2011, community-based services only increased by 2.8% whereas the private sector grew by 47% (Education Counts, 2012). There is no differentiation in government funding between private and community services.

The rise in for-profit provision in the education and care and home-based sectors raises issues about quality and participation. New Zealand studies have shown that privately owned centres are more likely to be sited in high-income areas where parents can pay higher fees (Mitchell and Brooking, 2007). Furthermore, private centres have been tardy in moving towards qualified teacher targets (Mitchell, 2002; Mitchell and Brooking, 2007) and employ staff on poorer conditions of work, both of which have implications for quality outcomes. Studies on process measures of quality such as communication and responsive relationships indicate lower levels of quality in privately owned services, linked mainly to the employment of the regulated minimum numbers of qualified staff (Smith, 1996; Mitchell et al, 2011). However, the Education Review Office, which regularly monitors and publicly reports on all licensed programmes, has found a spread of quality across service types and programmes linked to the quality of leadership as well as qualifications (ERO, 2007a–b, 2009a–d). The 100% qualified teacher policy was intended as a mechanism to redress the differences in quality across the range and types of ECEC provision, but its curtailment still allows centres to operate with as low as 50% qualified teachers.

There have been attempts to curtail private sector profits. When the Early Childhood Council, representing the interests of many private owners, campaigned against the costs of implementing Strategic Plan policies, the press reported the following government response:

> Education Minister Steve Maharey issued a warning to the main commercial chains, telling them that they cannot expect to continue to make profits on the back of heavy government subsidies for childcare ... with the growing emphasis on quality care there would be little scope for private operators to deliver a return to shareholders ... any surplus should be reinvested to deliver quality care and education.... The sector will over time become more and more like compulsory schooling and the chances of making a profit ... almost nil. ('Editorial', *Sunday Star Times*, 6 May 2007)

As a consequence of these strongly worded statements there was an immediate drop in the share prices of corporate childcare companies. The Commerce Commission subsequently reprimanded Maharey for political interference in the market. Politicians were walking a fine line between protecting quality early childhood for children and promoting the interests of business in childcare provision.

The Quality Public Early Childhood Education (QPECE) project was an attempt to redress the balance. This was a coalition of national ECEC organisations that were either providers or advocacy umbrella groups for the community sector (May and Mitchell, 2009). The group proposed an alternative model of provision premised on the idea that ECEC is a public good (Mitchell, 2012) and that provision should be provided and planned as a partnership with government. Traditionally, the kind and location of ECEC services have been determined by the particular interests of private enterprise or community organisations. Although the QPECE group was working 'against the tide' of political opinion, it was also timely to voice the collective aspirations of community ECEC services:

Vision:
- Every child has a right as a citizen to participate in free early childhood education.
- Every family that wishes to can access high quality, community-based early childhood education.

Goals:
- Promotion of community-based ECE services including parent-led services through the development of a national plan for all ECE provision throughout *Aotearoa* New Zealand.
- Provision of appropriate services to ensure every child can participate in free high-quality ECE.
- Robust accountability to government, parents, *whānau* and communities linked to indicators that demonstrate high quality ECE. (May and Mitchell, 2009, p 4)

Realising these aspirations in the current fiscal and political climate may be distant, but is necessary for realising the ideals of full participation in quality ECEC for all. Current policy directions in a 'zero budget' era, to target 'priority children and communities' is delivering a more 'hands-on' approach to provision in some localities, but might have the unintended consequences of reducing overall quality levels, as well as making ECEC less affordable to a significantly greater number of children.

Targeted participation in ECEC

There have been many programmes for increasing ECEC participation in targeted communities (Barney, 1975; May, 2009). During the 1990s and early 2000s this was spearheaded by Early Childhood Development, a government agency charged with the oversight of community ECEC support programmes, and particularly in areas with high numbers of Māori and Pasifika families. The work of this agency was merged into the Ministry of Education in 2004.

The incoming national government in 2008 determined to refocus ECEC policy, away from building the 'big picture' of policy infrastructure, towards targeted initiatives for increasing participation in identified high need areas. This process was assisted by in-depth surveys, demographic and statistical analysis of several suburbs, almost street by street as well as in several rural regions. Information was sought concerning 'the likely reasons for low participation in early childhood'. The general conclusions were that, 'the socio-economic or ethnic make-up of an area is the single most important factor determining its likely level of ECE participation … [but that] the level of service provision and the responsiveness of services to local needs do matter' (Morrison, 2009, pp 20–1). The Ministry of Education subsequently established Intensive Community Participation Projects in areas of high need to run as trials for three years. These are currently based in so-called 'vulnerable' communities where up to a quarter of children are starting school without having attended an early childhood service. The focus is on finding new ways to support families and encourage and ease participation:

> The first step for the intensive community projects is to build a clear understanding of the reasons why families are not or cannot access ECE within a community. The second step is to work out ways to address these barriers. (ECE Lead, 2012)

These programmes, while attracting higher numbers of children from disadvantaged families, are not segregated. The focus is one of community development and supporting cultural identity, with the inclusion of all children in the area whose parents want the particular kind of service offered. These projects run alongside a raft of other initiatives such as increased support to parent-led playgroups in communities with high numbers of children not participating in early childhood; the Engaging Priority Families Initiative which works alongside individual families to provide more intensive learning support and facilitate their child's regular attendance in an ECEC programme; and the Flexible and Responsive Home-based Initiative which caters for families who might prefer a home-based ECEC setting. These initiatives and others are in part a repackaging and renaming of older participation projects but collectively showcase the current government's focus for ECEC towards reaching its 98% participation target by 2016.

The broader agenda of the government's social and economic policy is under increasing critique. In a rare joint statement, 80 organisations with 'a collective voice for New Zealand ... urged the Government not to cut services for better off children in its drive to target the most "vulnerable" children' (UNICEF, 2012). The agencies were concerned at the implications of the *Green Paper on Vulnerable Children* (Ministry of Social Development, 2011) and wanted to influence the government's Action Plan released in August 2012 (National Party, 2012). At issue was the stigmatising of the 15% of children defined as 'vulnerable'. The group asked, 'Who will be categorised as vulnerable, how is it defined, and who decides?' The agencies have urged the government to keep existing universal and free services for children, while tackling the wider policies affecting children such as labour market and welfare policy, adequacy of family income, housing, access to transport and communication systems, access to health providers, the system and so on. This is 'big picture' infrastructure. The arguments are illustrative of the divide between the centre-right and centre-left in New Zealand concerning the role of the state. In September 2012, these issues became more contentious when the government announced the first roll-out of 'social obligations' for beneficiaries with children, the first being that children aged from three years to school age must attend 15 hours a week of early childhood education. Non-compliance could lead to up to 50% reduction in benefit payments. Early childhood organisations raised concern at the practicality and ethics of such compulsion.

ECE Taskforce

The establishment of an ECE Taskforce in 2010 to review and refocus ECEC policy in the aftermath of the Strategic Plan 2002–12 was a worry to many in the ECEC sector. The Taskforce terms of reference reflected government concern over rising ECEC expenditure. The phraseology included 'effectiveness and efficiency of the government's expenditure', 'the value gained from the different types of investment' and determining 'cost effective ways to support children's learning in early childhood.' The government asked the Taskforce to propose a new funding model 'without increasing current government expenditure' (ECE Taskforce, 2011, p 176).

One issue considered was evidence that some centres were performing poorly despite the resources provided. In particular, there were concerns about the quality of ECEC provision for infants and toddlers, as well as that of home-based services. At the same time, there were strong submissions of support from the sector for the *Te Whāriki* curriculum. The Taskforce endorsed the curriculum but recommended an evaluation of its implementation. Broadly, the Taskforce urged a 'stepping up' by the sector, including parents (ECE Taskforce, 2011, pp 14–15); a different emphasis to the Strategic Plan in which government positioned itself as becoming a more 'supportive state' (Ministry of Education, 2002).

The funding recommendations of the Taskforce were the most controversial, resulting in Taskforce member Anne Smith releasing a minority report (Smith, May, 2011). Smith's 40-year career of advocacy and her research on quality, participation and qualifications had given some assurance to the sector. The specifics of the new funding model are not clear at the time of writing, but Smith's report expressed concern at the consequences of targeting funds to 'priority children' if this means cutting the level of universal funding:

> I am concerned that the proposed new funding model may have a negative influence on participation rates in ECE for some groups, most particularly middle income earners.... The argument is that the new funding system will be better for low SES [socio-economic status] and Māori and Pasifika, but there is little information about how the new scheme will be able to accurately seek out and identify targeted groups. (Smith, 2011, pp 2–3)

The Treasury advice to the Taskforce was that middle-income parents would be prepared to pay more although the centre-right government had a balancing act because middle-income families were sometimes their own voters.

The narrative

New Zealand provides a case study of shifting frames of political interest and investment in ECEC. By mid-2012, two ECE Advisory Groups had convened and reported to the Minister with advice on implementing the Taskforce recommendations regarding (i) improving quality of ECE sector-wide, and (ii) improving quality of ECE services for children under two years (ECE Sector Advisory Group, 2012a, 2012b). Neither group backed away from highlighting the costs of quality, and urged regulation for better staff ratios and group sizes for under twos, recommending the regulation of 80% qualified teachers as a step towards 100%. The Minister of Education promised a response during 2012. This is likely to be contingent on the third ECE Advisory Group, convened in mid-2012 and tasked with designing the detail of a new funding model.

The arguments around universal versus targeted approaches to funding in this case study are illustrative of ECEC as a site where deeper and conflicting political agendas are being tested. The issues concern the role of the state in supporting families and children. There are two pathways: one aligning political investment in ECEC with interventionist social strategies intended as a priority to redress the 'risks' created by 'vulnerable families and communities'; the other viewing ECEC as a right for the young child citizen, which in New Zealand would be a continuum of the ideals for children at school famously expressed in 1939:

> The government's objective, broadly expressed, is that every child, whatever his level of ability, whether he be rich or poor, whether he live in town or country, has a right as a citizen, to a free education of the kind for which he is best fitted and to the fullest extent of his powers. (Fraser, 1939, p 2)

This has been rephrased to similarly incorporate aspirations for children under five:

> The government's objective should broadly speaking be that every child, whatever their family circumstances, whether their parents are solo, separated or married, at work or at home, whether they be rich or poor, whether they live in town or country, are Māori or Pakeha, should have a right as a citizen to a free early childhood education that meets

their family needs, recognizes their cultural heritage and provides a rich learning environment in a community of learning that empowers both adults and children to learn and grow as equal participants in a democratic society. (May, 2004, p 88)

This chapter concludes with the pathway ahead not clear and likely to be one of pragmatic compromise by both the government and the sector. With an election looming in 2014 there is a degree of bravado in setting a 98% ECEC participation target with 'zero cost' budgets, amidst the political caution at alienating many voters who have experienced the benefit of recent ECEC policies.

References

Barney, D. (1975) *Who Gets to Preschool?*, Wellington: New Zealand Council for Educational Research (NZCER).

Carr, M. and Mitchell, L. (2010) *Qualified Teachers in Early Childhood Centres: Do We Need Them?*, Occasional Paper, Hamilton: University of Waikato.

ECE Lead (2012) ECE Participation Programmes, Wellington: Ministry of Education (www.lead.ece.govt.nz/ProgrammesAndInitiatives/ECEParticipationProgramme/Overview.aspx).

ECE Sector Advisory Group (2012a) Sector Advisory Group Report – Quality for Under-Twos, Wellington: Ministry of Education.

ECE Sector Advisory Group (2012b) *Sector Advisory Group Report – Quality ECE*, Wellington: Ministry of Education.

ECE Taskforce (2010) *Overview of the Early Childhood Education System*, October, Wellington: New Zealand Government.

ECE Taskforce (2011) *An Agenda for Amazing Children. Final Report of the ECE Taskforce*, Wellington: New Zealand Government.

Economist Intelligence Unit, (2012) *Starting Well: Benchmarking Early Education Across the World*, London and Hong Kong: Economist Intelligence Unit.

Education Counts (2012) *Annual ECE Census Summary Report 2011*, Wellington: Ministry of Education (www.educationcounts.govt.nz/statistics/ece2/annual-ece-summary-reports)

ERO (Education Review Office) (2007a) *The Quality of Education and Care in Pacific Early Childhood Services*, Early Childhood Monograph series, Wellington: ERO.

ERO (2007b) *The Quality of Education and Care in Montessori Early Childhood Services*, Early Childhood Monograph series, Wellington: ERO.

ERO (2009a) *The Quality of Education and Care in Home-Based Early Childhood Services*, Early Childhood Monograph series, Wellington: ERO.

ERO (2009b) *The Quality of Education and Care in Infant and Toddler Centres*, Early Childhood Monograph series, Wellington: ERO.

ERO (2009c) *The Quality of Education and Care in Kindergartens*, Early Childhood Monograph series, Wellington: ERO.

ERO (2009d) *The Quality of Education and Care in Playcentres*, Early Childhood Monograph series, Wellington: ERO.

ERO (2010) *Success for Māori Children in Early Childhood Services*, Wellington: ERO.

ERO (2011) *Positive Foundations for Learning: Confident and Competent Children in Early Childhood Services*, Wellington: ERO.

Fraser, P. (1939) *Appendices to the Journal of the House of Representations, Report of the Minister of Education, Peter Fraser, E 1*, Wellington.

Froese, N. and Jenkins, M. (2008) *Early Effects of Free Early Childhood Education*, Wellington: Ministry of Education.

May, H. (2004) 'Towards citizenry rights in early childhood', *Delta*, vol 56, no 1, pp 75–91.

May, H. (2005) *Twenty Years of Consenting Parties. The Politics of 'Working' and 'Teaching' in Childcare 1985–2005*, Wellington: New Zealand Educational Institute (NZEI) – *Te Riu Roa*.

May, H. (2009) *Politics in the Playground. The World of Early Childhood in New Zealand*, Dunedin: University of Otago Press.

May, H. and Mitchell, L. (2009) *Strengthening Community-based Early Childhood Education in Aotearoa New Zealand*, Wellington: NZEI-*Te Riu Roa*.

Meade, A., Robinson, L., Smorti, S., Stuart, M. and Williamson, J. (2012) *Early Childhood Teachers' Work in Education and Care Centres*, Wellington: Te Tari Puna Ora o Aotearoa – New Zealand Childcare Association (NZCA).

Ministry of Education (1996) *Te Whāriki: He Whāriki Mātauranga mō ngā Mokopuna o Aotearoa: Early Childhood Curriculum*, Wellington: Learning Media.

Ministry of Education (2002) *Pathways to the Future – Ngā Huarahi Arataki 2002–2012*, Wellington: Ministry of Education.

Ministry of Education (2005) *The ECE Funding Handbook*, Wellington: Ministry of Education.

Ministry of Education (2012) *Participation in Early Childhood Education: Evidence Booklet*, Wellington: Ministry of Education.

Ministry of Social Development (2011) *Green Paper on Vulnerable Children. Every Child Thrives, Belongs, Achieves*, Wellington: New Zealand Government (www.childrensactionplan.govt.nz/green-paper).

Ministry of Social Development (2012) *The White Paper for Vulnerable Children*, Wellington: New Zealand Government (www.childrensactionplan.govt.nz/whitepaper).

Mitchell, L. (2002) *Differences Between Community Owned and Privately Owned Early Childhood Education and Care Centres: A Review of Evidence*, Wellington: NZCER.

Mitchell, L. (2012) 'Markets and childcare provision in New Zealand: Towards a fairer solution', in E. Lloyd and H. Penn (eds) *Childcare Markets: Can They Deliver Equitable Outcomes?*, Bristol: Policy Press, pp 97–113.

Mitchell, L. and Brooking, K. (2007) *First NZCER National Survey of Early Childhood Education Services*, Wellington: NZCER.

Mitchell, L., Meagher Lundberg, P., Mara, D., Cubey, P. and Whitford, M. (2011) *Locality-based Evaluation of Pathways to the Future – Nga Huarahi Arataki*, Wellington: Ministry of Education.

Morrison, A. (2009) *Likely Reasons for Low Participation in Early Childhood Education in the Low Participation Areas of County-Manukau*, Wellington: Ministry of Education.

Moss, P. (2007) 'Leading the wave: New Zealand in an international context', in *Travelling Pathways to the Future – Ngā huarahi arataki*, Early Childhood Education Symposium Proceedings, 2–3 May, Wellington: Ministry of Education, pp 27–36.

Moss, P. (2008) 'Beyond childcare, markets and technical practice: Re-politicising early childhood', in *Proceedings of Early Childhood Care and Education Seminar Series 2*, Dublin: Centre for Social and Educational Research, pp 5–14.

National Party (2012) 'Ministers launch action plan to support vulnerable children', 22 August (www.national.org.nz/Article.aspx?articleId=39210).

Nuttall, J. (ed) (2003) *Weaving Te Whāriki. Aotearoa New Zealand's Early Childhood Curriculum Document in Theory and Practice*, Wellington: NZCER.

NZ (New Zealand) Treasury (2012) 'Briefing to the incoming Minister' (www.beehive.govt.nz/sites/all/files/MinEdu_BIM.pdf).

NZCA (New Zealand Childcare Association, *Te Tari Puna Ora o Aotearoa*) (2010) Press release: 'ECE Budget: a brutal blow to children and families', 20 May, Wellington: NZCA.

Perata, H. (2012) 'Speech notes: Raising achievement for all in the budget', 16 May, Wellington: Office of the Minister of Education.

Smith, A.B. (1996) 'The quality of childcare centres for infants in New Zealand', in *State of the Art Monograph No 4*, Palmerston North: Massey University, New Zealand Association for Research in Education.

Smith, A.B. (2010) 'Relationships with people, places and things – *Te Whāriki*', in L. Miller and L. Pound, (eds) *Theories and Approaches to Learning in the Early Years*, London: Sage Publications, pp 149–62.

Smith, A.B. (November 2010) *Position Paper on Early Childhood Education to the ECE Taskforce and the Minister of Education*, Dunedin.

Smith, A.B. (May 2011) *Position Paper on Essay 3: Reforming Funding mechanisms*, Dunedin.

Statistics NZ (New Zealand) (2007) *Consumer Price Index: September 2007 Quarter*, 15 October, Wellington: New Zealand Government.

Statistics NZ (2012) *Childcare Use and Work Arrangements in 1998 and 2009*, Wellington: New Zealand Government.

Tolley, A. (2011) Speech to the Childforum Seminar, 4 April, Wellington: Office of the Minister of Education.

UNICEF (2012) Press release, 'Collective voice for New Zealand's children', 12 July, Auckland: UNICEF.

EIGHT

Early education and care in Australia: Equity in a mixed market-based system?

Deborah Brennan and Marianne Fenech

Introduction

Early childhood education and care (ECEC) is a high-profile political issue in Australia. In 2008, Labor Prime Minister Kevin Rudd promised 'a world-class system of integrated early childhood learning and childcare' designed to 'boost national productivity, lift labour force participation, contribute to social inclusion and be the first step towards an "education revolution"'. A year later, the Council of Australian Governments (COAG), representing the Commonwealth, States, Territories and local government, endorsed an early childhood development strategy encompassing children from birth to eight years. *Investing in the Early Years: A National Childhood Development Strategy* sets out a 'comprehensive response to evidence about the importance of early childhood development and the benefits – and cost-effectiveness – of ensuring all children experience a positive early childhood' (COAG, 2009a).

As part of this new commitment to child wellbeing, the ECEC sector has undergone rapid and far-reaching reform. Again through COAG, governments have adopted consistent standards for both long day-care centres[1] and preschools (COAG, 2009b). The standards apply equally to all mainstream services, whether private for-profit, non-profit or government-run.[2] Governments have also endorsed the goal of universal access to preschool education, meaning that all children will have access to 'a quality early childhood education programme ... delivered by a four-year university trained early childhood teacher, for 15 hours a week, 40 weeks a year, in the year before formal schooling' by 2013 (COAG, 2009d, p 5). Importantly, universal access is about participation in a particular type of *programme* rather than attendance at a particular type of *service*; a preschool programme can be delivered in a long day-care centre, a dedicated preschool/ kindergarten[3] or a mobile service that takes early learning experiences to children in remote communities. Australia's commitment to preschool for all children is not as far-reaching as similar initiatives in other countries. The phrase 'universal access' expresses an official aspiration, but does not establish an entitlement for children. And the 15 hours are not necessarily free; rather, governments have adopted the more nebulous goal of ensuring that 'cost is not a barrier to access' (COAG, 2009d, p 6).

An important aspect of the quality agenda is the endorsement of a national early childhood curriculum, the Early Years Learning Framework (EYLF) (COAG, 2009c). The EYLF sets out the principles, practices and outcomes required to support children's learning from birth, and to ensure a smooth transition to school. It has a strong emphasis on play-based learning and recognises the importance of communication and language, including early literacy and numeracy, social and emotional development.

How far has this agenda progressed, and what are its implications for children from low-income families and those experiencing other forms of disadvantage? We begin by describing current patterns of participation in ECEC, highlighting the situation of low-income children, indigenous children, children with language backgrounds other than English, including refugee and migrant children, and children with disabilities. Next, we outline the institutional and policy context that frames Australian ECEC, noting the different roles of the Commonwealth and the States[4] and the entrenched division between education and care that reflects Australian federalism. We then describe Australia's reform agenda in more detail, outlining the EYLF, regulatory requirements and measures to strengthen the early childhood workforce. We conclude with some reflections on the prospects for universal access to high-quality ECEC within Australia's current policy settings and constraints.

Participation in Australian ECEC: a blurred snapshot

Multiple institutions and organisations are involved in funding and delivering ECEC services in Australia. The lines of responsibility between them are not always clear and data are sometimes inadequate – which is why we describe this as a 'blurred' snapshot. Policy responsibility for ECEC is shared between the Commonwealth, State and Territory governments.[5] Services are delivered through a mixed market that includes government, for-profit, non-profit and community-based providers (PWC, 2011, p 14). A longstanding division persists between services perceived to offer 'care' and those deemed 'educational'. Most Commonwealth funds are targeted towards services that support paid work or other forms of economic and social participation. The main Commonwealth-supported services for children below school age are long day-care centres, family day-care[6] and in-home care.[7] Such services typically cater for children from birth to school age and are open or available for at least eight hours care per day throughout the year. Educational services such as preschool or kindergarten generally cater for children in the year or two before school and offer half-day sessions or short days (9.00am–3.00pm) during school terms. These are mainly funded by State governments. In several States, preschool is offered free or at negligible cost, and is often co-located with primary schools. Family day-care provides a service for families who prefer home-based care; it also operates as a complement to preschool, with 46% of family day-care schemes providing 'wrap-around' services (Productivity Commission, 2011, p 117). Formal, regulated services are complemented by the informal care provided by grandparents and other relatives, friends and nannies.

Just over half (55%) of all children below school age participate in either formal or informal childcare, or both. This proportion has not changed greatly since 1996, but participation in formal, regulated services has increased markedly. Attendance at long day-care has grown strongly, with 31% of children below school age participating in 2011, compared with 13% in 1996. In the same period, the proportion of children using informal care has declined from 30% to 22% (see Table 8.1). Thus, it seems, formal services are increasingly replacing informal and family care.

Participation in childcare varies according to parents' employment status. In comparison with similar countries, Australia has a low level of labour force participation: 52% of mothers of children below school age are workforce participants, many working part time (ABS, 2008). In couple families where both parents are employed, 63% of children usually attend childcare; where only one parent in a couple is employed, 31%; and where neither parent is employed, just 25%. Similar patterns are evident in sole-parent households – 82% of children in sole-parent families where the parent is employed participate in ECEC, compared with 49% where the parent is not employed (ABS, 2012a). Access to ECEC also varies with the age of the child.[8] The highest level of participation is among two- and three-year-olds: 54% of children in this age group usually attend formal care and 40% participate in informal care. Average weekly hours of attendance vary by service type; children in long day-care centres typically attend for just under

Table 8.1: Australia: Children aged 0–4 yrs, type of care attended, 1996–2011

	1996 (%)	1999 (%)	2002 (%)	2005 (%)	2008 (%)	2011 (%)
Children who attend childcare	54	59	56	60	59	55
Formal care						
Long day care	13	18	23	24	28	31
Family day care	6	6	6	7	4	4
Occasional care	4	3	3	4	2	2
Before and after school care	4	2	4	2	2	0
Other formal care	1	1	1	1	1	0
Total formal care	24	27	32	35	34	37
Informal care						
Grandparent	n/a	30	25	28	29	22
Brother/sister	2	1	1	0	0	1
Non-resident parent	n/a	2	2	3	3	3
Other relative	30	5	5	4	5	4
Other person	10	8	7	5	5	4
Total informal care	40	43	37	38	38	31
Children in formal care only	14	16	19	22	21	24
Children in informal care only	30	32	24	25	26	18
Children in formal *and* informal care	10	11	13	14	13	12
Children who did not attend childcare	46	41	44	40	41	45

Note: Children may be attending more than one form of care, hence totals do not add up.
Source: ABS (2012a, Table 1)

26 hours, and those participating in family day-care around 20 hours per week (Productivity Commission, 2012, 3.27).

Family income plays a crucial role in mediating access to childcare. In families with a combined weekly income of AUD$2,000 or more, 52% of 0- to 14-year-old children regularly participate in childcare, compared with 25% in families with a weekly income of AUD$800 or less. Family income also affects the types of care used. Children whose parents' weekly income exceeds AUD$2,000 are more likely than those earning less than AUD$800 to use both formal care (18% and 11% respectively) and informal care (24% and 13% respectively). Families earning AUD$800–999 per week are the least likely to use either formal or informal childcare (see Table 8.2).

Although the Australian government has identified participation by children from particular target groups as a key objective for services

Table 8.2: Australia: Children aged 0–14 yrs in couple families, type of care usually[a] attended, by weekly income of parents, 2008 (%) (AUD$)

Type of care	Less than 800	800– 999	1,000– 1,199	1,200– 1,399	1,400– 1,999	2,000 or more	Total
Children with usual childcare arrangements	25	30	37	40	45	52	41
Children in formal care only	11	12	14	17	16	18	15
Children in informal care only	13	16	18	17	21	24	20
Children in both informal and formal care	2[b]	2[b]	5	6	7	10	6
Children with no usual childcare arrangements	75	70	63	60	55	48	59

Notes: [a] 'Usually' refers to a child's typical attendance at childcare, including hours and costs. [b] Estimate has a relative standard error of 25% to 50% and should be used with caution. Children with more than one source of childcare are only counted once. Percentages may not sum to 100 due to rounding.

Source: ABS (2009)

such as long day-care, family day-care and in-home care, children from most of these groups are under-represented. Children from non-English-speaking backgrounds make up almost 19% of three- to five-year-old children in the community, for example, but just over 12% of enrolments in childcare services. Children from Aboriginal and Torres Strait Islander (ATSI) backgrounds represent 4.7% of this age group, but only 2% of children in approved care. Children with disabilities make up 6.3% of three- to five-year-olds, but only 5.4% of those attending Commonwealth approved care. Children from both regional and remote parts of Australia are under-represented (see Table 8.3).

Participation in state-funded preschool services is measured separately from participation in Commonwealth-funded childcare. Although there is a major effort underway to improve data collection, it is not yet possible to present a comprehensive picture of participation in all ECEC services. For example, there is no unique 'child identifier' that would overcome the problem of double-counting of children enrolled in both state-funded preschools and Australian government-funded childcare services. Recently, the Australian Bureau of Statistics (ABS) has published 'experimental estimates' of participation in preschool. These adopt a relatively strict view of preschool participation: a child must be three to six years old and attend a preschool programme

Table 8.3: Australia: Proportion of children aged 0–5 yrs from special groups attending Australian government-approved childcare services, 2011 (%)

	In approved childcare services	In the community
Children from non-English-speaking backgrounds	15.0	20.1
Indigenous children	2.0	4.7
Children from low-income families	24.8	27.1
Children with a disability	2.5	4.0
Children from regional areas	28.7	31.5
Children from remote areas	1.0	3.1

Source: Productivity Commission (2012), Indigenous Compendium, Table 3A.14

(defined as 'a structured, play-based learning programme, usually provided… on a sessional basis') by a four-year university qualified teacher. These estimates suggest that almost 81% of children aged four and five years, including 75% of ATSI children, are enrolled in preschool programmes (ABS, 2012b).

The engagement of ATSI children in early childhood services is of particular importance given the levels of disadvantage in their communities. Most ATSI children who participate in ECEC services are enrolled in mainstream services that cater for both non-indigenous and indigenous children (Productivity Commission, 2012, p 349). Across Australia, there are some 270 indigenous-focused services, including multifunctional Aboriginal children's services, crèches, playgroups, outside school hours care and mobile services designed to meet the needs of local indigenous families. Some mainstream services work closely and productively with indigenous families and communities, but this cannot be said of all. The position of the Secretariat of National Aboriginal and Islander Child Care (SNAICC) is that *all* ECEC services should engage in effective and respectful partnerships with indigenous communities (SNAICC, 2012).

The Australian Early Development Index (AEDI), a population measure of children's health and development, provides a valuable source of data for understanding children's development when they start school. This is particularly useful given the lack of data linking socio-economic status to the quality of children's ECEC experiences. The AEDI is based on a checklist completed by teachers during children's first year of schooling. It measures development in five domains: physical health and wellbeing; social competence; emotional maturity; language and cognitive skills; and communication skills and general knowledge.

The first round of the AEDI, completed in 2009, revealed that almost one-quarter of Australia's children are developmentally vulnerable in one or more of the specified domains. Almost twice as many indigenous children – 48% – were considered vulnerable, as were 32% of children from language backgrounds other than English. AEDI data suggest that participation in high-quality early childhood education is skewed towards more advantaged populations (AIHW, 2012).

Policy context

Divided responsibilities and a mixed market

The Australian government and the State and Territory governments have distinct but overlapping responsibilities in ECEC. Historically, most States have funded educationally focused preschool services, but done little to support forms of provision that meet the needs of working parents. The Australian government entered the early childhood field in a significant way in 1972 with the passage of the Child Care Act, authorising grants to non-profit childcare centres (Spearritt, 1974). The Act was designed to facilitate the labour force participation of mothers of young children and to complement preschool services funded by the States. The Whitlam government (1972–75) expanded federal involvement in ECEC, increasing its financial commitment and supporting new service types such as family day-care and outside school hours care. Over the ensuing years, the Commonwealth came to dominate both expenditure and policy making. The fact that its focus has predominantly been on supporting parental labour force participation has contributed to the perception that state-funded services are about 'education', while Commonwealth-funded services provide 'childcare'. This characterisation does not do justice to the complexities of policy making or provision at either level, but it is a frequently used shorthand for the division that has emerged between the two levels of government (Brennan, 2010).

The mix of ECEC providers varies significantly between States and between service types. Approximately two-thirds of centre-based childcare services operate as private, for-profit businesses (DEEWR, 2010); almost all home-based services, such as family day-care, are run by community-based and non-profit organisations. Non-profit organisations deliver the majority of preschool services along the east coast, while State governments are the predominant providers in Western Australia, South Australia and Tasmania.

In recent years, governments have taken steps to establish a more integrated approach to ECEC. Within the Australian government, an Office of Early Childhood Education and Child Care, located in the Department of Education, Employment and Workplace Relations, has responsibility for children's services. Previously, this function was based in an Office of Child Care located in the Social Welfare Department. Similar changes have occurred in most States. Almost half of all long day-care centres now offer preschool programmes and some preschools offer extended hours or 'wrap-around' care to accommodate employed parents. At least 40% of children who attend preschool do so within childcare services (ABS, 2012a). Despite these advances towards greater integration, differences between education and care remain embedded in the funding for different service types. Most State governments directly fund the capital and operational costs of preschools (a supply-side approach) while, with some exceptions,[9] the Commonwealth employs demand-side strategies to reduce the costs to parents of purchasing care in a mixed market. Wages and industrial conditions differ between the sectors (Brennan, 1998; Productivity Commission, 2011).

Privatisation and the growth of corporate childcare

In the late 1980s, following sustained lobbying by private providers, the federal Labor government amended the Child Care Act, allowing subsidies to be paid to users of for-profit as well as non-profit long day-care centres – a move that was bitterly divisive within the party. Those who supported it argued that families in similar circumstances should receive equal access to subsidies whether or not the childcare service they used was run on a for-profit basis. Opponents countered that the care of children should be a public responsibility rather than an opportunity for profit making. Concerns were also expressed about the standard of care in for-profit centres. In response, the federal government introduced a Quality Improvement and Accreditation Scheme (QIAS). Australia thus had a double regulatory system: the States and Territories regulated measurable inputs such as staff numbers and qualifications, while the Commonwealth, through its QIAS system, assessed 'process' factors such as the quality of interactions between staff, children and parents, the adequacy of individualised learning plans and evidence of management and record-keeping practices that support health, nutrition and learning. Parents could access Commonwealth subsidies only if the long day-care services they used met State/Territory regulations *and* participated in the QIAS.

The centre-right government of Prime Minister John Howard (1996–2007) intensified the marketisation of long day-care. Howard removed the small operational subsidies that had been paid to non-profit services under Labor, making clear that the private sector would be the preferred provider of services for young children. Business responded accordingly (Brennan, 2007a, 2007b). In 2001, ABC Learning became Australia's first publicly listed childcare corporation. Other companies followed suit and, within a few years, Australia had experienced not merely an expansion of for-profit childcare at the expense of non-profit provision, but a shift towards *corporate* care – that is, care provided by companies whose shares are traded on the stock exchange (Sumsion, 2012). By listing on the exchange, ABC gained access to significant amounts of capital, enabling it to expand far more rapidly than non-profit services (Newberry and Brennan, 2013).

ABC adopted an aggressive expansion strategy. It quickly absorbed most of its corporate rivals and took over hundreds of independent centres, becoming the dominant player in Australian long day-care (Ellis, 2009). At the height of its success, ABC's chief executive officer (CEO) was Australia's richest person under 40, his personal wealth estimated at AUD$272 million (Farouque, 2006). Despite its meteoric rise on the share market, ABC's business model of continuous growth and expansion was unsustainable, and in 2008 the company went into receivership. At the time of its collapse, ABC owned approximately 25% of long day-care services in Australia. These catered for 120,000 children and employed 16,000 staff (Ellis, 2009). When the company went into receivership, 55 centres closed immediately and the government spent AUD$24 million keeping the remainder open while their viability was assessed. In December 2009, four of Australia's largest charities, working in conjunction with Social Ventures Australia, formed a new consortium called GoodStart in order to purchase more than 650 former ABC centres from the receivers. Operating as a non-profit organisation, GoodStart is committed to reinvesting its surplus into improvements in the quality of services across the sector. As a result of the GoodStart purchase, the proportion of services run by for-profit organisations fell from 88% to 66% (DEEWR, 2010).

Funding and subsidies

In 2010–11, the Commonwealth provided AUD$4.2 billion to help families purchase childcare from approved providers (which can be for-profit, non-profit or government-run). The States collectively spent approximately AUD$1 billion on preschool education and

AUD$149 million on childcare (Productivity Commission, 2012, Tables 3A.3, 3A.5). State and Territory governments vary markedly in the scale of their investment in preschool and other children's services. New South Wales spends AUD$190 per child per year, for example, compared with the Northern Territory's AUD$1,033 (see Table 8.4). The cost of preschool to families reflects these differences. In 2008, preschool was free or virtually free in Western Australia, South Australia, Tasmania and both Territories, while the median cost was AUD$27 per day in New South Wales.

The Australian government helps families with the costs of childcare through two mechanisms: Child Care Benefit (CCB), which is means-tested and available to families regardless of their workforce status, and Child Care Rebate (CCR), which is not means-tested but is only available to parents who are working, studying or training, and who use approved care.

The rate of CCB varies according to family income and the number of children enrolled in approved care. Working parents using approved services such as long day-care, family day-care or in-home care are eligible for up to 50 hours CCB for each child below school age. Low-income families can claim up to AUD$3.90 per hour, or AUD$195 per week. Families using registered care such as nannies can claim only six cents per hour or AUD$32 per week, regardless of income. CCB is usually paid directly to the service provider, thus reducing upfront fees and obviating the need to make claims and wait for reimbursement. Parents who are not working, studying or training can claim up to 24 hours' CCB per week for approved care, but are required to pay the gap between CCB and the actual fee charged by the service. An important exception is that parents receiving Income Support (Unemployment Benefits or Parenting Payment, for example) who are seeking work, studying, training or undertaking rehabilitation in order to enter the workforce are eligible for additional assistance. Jobs, Education and Training (JET) Child Care Fee Assistance pays most

Table 8.4: Australia: Total State and Territory government real expenditure on children's services per child in the community aged 0–12 yrs ($/child), 2010–11 (AUD$)

NSW	Vic	Qld	WA	SA	Tas	ACT	NT	Aust
190	266	204	556	499	395	489	1,033	291

Notes: NSW – New South Wales; Vic – Victoria; Qld – Queensland; WA – Western Australia; SA – South Australia; Tas – Tasmania; ACT – Australian Capital Territory; NT – Northern Territory; Aust – Australia.

Source: Productivity Commission (2012, Table 3A.37)

Table 8.5: Australia: Differences between approved care and registered care

	Approved care	Registered care
What is it?	Services that meet ACECQA standards *and* open at least 8 hours per day, 48 weeks per year may be approved by the Australian government. Most long day-care, family day-care and in-home care services are approved. Most preschools are not approved, even if they meet ACECQA standards, because of their short opening hours	Grandparents and other relatives, friends and nannies can register with the Australian Government as carers. Individuals working in preschools or private schools may register in some circumstances
Can parents claim CCB?	Parents using approved care may claim up to 50 hours per week CCB if they meet the 'work, study, training' test. They may claim up to 24 hours CCB if they do not meet this test. The amount of CCB depends on family income, number of children in approved care and hours of care used. The maximum is AUD$195 per week	Parents using registered care may claim the *minimum* rate of CCB (AUD$32 per week) if they meet the 'work, study, training test'
Can parents claim CCR?	Parents who meet the work, study, training test may claim CCR in addition to CCB. CCR pays 50% of out-of-pocket expenses up to a maximum of AUD$15,000 per child per year	Parents using registered care are not eligible to claim CCR

of the 'gap fee' for these parents, at least for a limited time, requiring them to make a co-contribution of AUD$1 for each hour of care (DHS, 2012).

On top of CCB, CCR helps working parents by rebating 50% of their out-of-pocket childcare expenses up to a maximum of AUD$15,000 per year per child. CCR is not means-tested, and families do not need to apply for CCR; it is paid automatically if they are eligible. Since high-income families are the most likely to use long hours of high-cost, approved childcare, the effect of CCR is twofold: first, it delivers large benefits to high-income families; and second, it reduces the incentive for providers to keep a lid on fees. Some lobby groups representing professional women have campaigned to have the cap on CCR removed so that parents with out-of-pocket expenses exceeding AUD$15,000 per child can claim additional benefits. These groups have also called for CCR to be extended to nannies and *au pairs* – currently excluded because they are not 'approved' for CCB purposes (Karvelas, 2012a). Although the opposition parties have expressed sympathy with this position, they have not committed to introducing subsidies for nanny care.

Almost all (98%) of families using approved care receive either CCB or CCR; close to three-quarters (72%) of these receive both subsidies. About half the remainder receive only CCB (probably because they use registered rather than approved care and are thus not eligible for CCR) and the other half receive only CCR (most likely because their combined family income renders them ineligible for CCB) (DEEWR, 2012, p 26).

How effective are Commonwealth subsidies at reducing childcare costs? Modelling suggests that they are very effective. Across a wide range of incomes, families require 7–8% of their disposable income to pay for 50 hours of care, after subsidies are taken into account (see Table 8.6). This very positive picture is, however, tempered by the fact that the full rate of CCB is only available in respect of 'approved' services and, in order to be approved, services must not only meet minimum quality standards (discussed in the next section) but also be open for at least eight hours per day for 48 weeks per year. State-funded preschools are not approved for CCB purposes because of their limited opening hours.

The rules governing Commonwealth childcare subsidies result in hardship for families using registered care for work-related purposes. As noted above, the most CCB that can be claimed by a family using a registered service is six cents per hour or AUD$32 per week, and users of registered care are not eligible for CCR, regardless of income or workforce status. The distinction between 'approved' and 'registered' care can be confusing – especially for parents who assume that a service that meets regulatory standards will be 'approved' and thus eligible to attract CCB.

Table 8.6: Australia: National Quality Standard (NQS) ratios and year these come into effect, grandfathered ratios and ratios recommended by Early Childhood Australia

Age of child	NQS ratios and year these come into effect	Grandfathered ratios	Early Childhood Australia's recommended ratios
Birth–12 months	1:4 (2012)	N/A	1:3
13–24 months	1:4 (2012)	N/A	1:4
25–35 months	1:5 (2016)	VIC = 1:4	1:5
3 years	1:11 (2016)	NSW, SA, Tas, WA = 1:10	1:8
≥4 years	1:11 (2016)	NSW, SA, Tas, WA = 1:10	1:10

Source: Productivity Commission (2011)

Despite its strengths, the fact that the Australian childcare system is based in market principles is a major limitation to inclusivity and equity. Parents are expected to be active consumers and to compare services, prices and standards in order to obtain an optimal service. They are presumed to have equal access to information and to be prepared to discipline providers by switching services if they are inadequate or unsuitable. Other than the existence of subsidies, there are few measures that actively support or encourage the enrolment and participation of low-income and disadvantaged children in early childhood services. Parents need to find out about the subsidies, understand them, access them, and to pay any gap that remains.

ECEC quality agenda

Australia's national agenda has a number of elements designed to work together to improve quality (see Figure 8.1). The National Quality Framework (NQF) involves a new quality assurance system that replaces the disparate licensing systems previously operated by the various States and Territories. Its implementation is overseen by a newly established statutory authority, the Australian Children's Education and Care Quality Authority (ACECQA).

Figure 8.1: Australia: National Quality Agenda for early childhood education and care

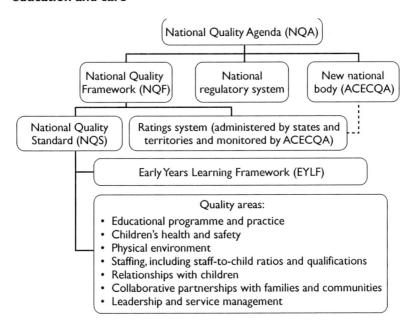

The NQF started to come into effect in 2012. It introduces nationally consistent staff-to-child ratios and staff qualifications that will be phased in over eight years. From January 2014, a university-qualified early childhood teacher will be required in all mainstream long day-care centres and preschools licensed for 25 or more children. (Many indigenous-focused services were initially excluded from NQF, however, as we discuss below.) Half the staff employed in preschools and long day-care services will be required to have, or be working towards, a two-year vocational diploma in children's services; the remaining staff will be required to have, or be working towards, a vocational Certificate III Level ECEC qualification (a six-month entry-level qualification) or equivalent. Achieving these targets and attracting and retaining qualified professional staff will be critical challenges for the sector, especially given that it is characterised by low pay, poor promotion prospects and arduous working conditions. A high proportion of the staff in long day-care are currently paid at minimum award rates, have limited opportunities for career progression and do not benefit financially from upgrading their qualifications (Tarrant, 2008).

The National Quality Standard (NQS) encompasses structural, process, management and leadership factors that contribute to early learning and care and promote children's development (Sylva et al, 2004; Myers, 2006). It is closely linked to the national curriculum or EYLF; indeed, this framework must underpin a programme for each child that enhances learning and development. The quality areas covered by the NQS are: educational programme and practice; children's health and safety; physical environment; staffing arrangements (including staff-to-child ratios and staff qualifications); relationships with children; collaborative partnerships with families and communities; and leadership and service management (ACECQA, 2011). Each area has two or three outcome standards that services must demonstrate during the assessment and rating process. Services are rated on each quality area and given an overall quality rating. Assessors' ratings are based on the compliance and rating history of each centre, examination of its annual quality improvement plan, discussions with staff, sighting of supporting evidence such as centre policies and programme planning and evaluation, and observations of centre practices. The available ratings are:

- Significant improvement required
- Working towards National Quality Standard
- Meeting the National Quality Standard

- Exceeding the National Quality Standard (services that receive this rating will be able to apply to be rated as 'Excellent').

The NQS is premised on the principle of 'earned autonomy': the higher the quality rating, the less frequent will be further formal and informal assessment visits ('spot checks') by the regulatory authority. Services rated as 'working towards the national quality standard', for example, will be subject to at least one formal assessment per year, and liable for spot checks. In contrast, services rated as 'exceeding the national quality standard' will be formally assessed every three years, as well as being subject to spot checks. It is notable, however, that while equity and inclusion are underlying principles of the NQS, evidence of providing equitable access for children from disadvantaged communities is not a requirement of gaining a rating that exceeds minimum standards. Since only a small number of centres will be rated as 'exceeding the national quality standard', it will be critical to monitor the locations of these centres, their fees and the proportion of their users who are from disadvantaged communities.

In most States and Territories the new quality standards represent a significant upgrading of the skills and qualifications required in ECEC settings and will potentially establish the groundwork for greater recognition and remuneration (Fenech et al, 2012). However, although the federal government has provided additional funding to help educators upgrade their qualifications, it has not provided services with the additional funding needed to raise salaries in line with these enhanced qualifications. Thus, the sector faces staff losses and possible shortages of qualified staff in future years. Commenting on the federal government's workforce initiatives, a major trade union in the sector observed that 'these measures fall short of addressing the lack of career structures and wage incentives needed to encourage workers to remain in the sector and to undertake further study or training' (UnitedVoice, 2012, p 8).

A large number of indigenous-focused services have been excluded from the NQF, at least initially, due to their poor level of infrastructure and resources. Many of these are in remote or very remote areas of Australia and additional time and resources will be required to enable them to meet the NQF. The Australian government has allocated almost AUD$60 million for this task, and it is expected that these services will come under the NQF by 2014 (Productivity Commission, 2011, p 363). A major challenge for these services will be attracting and retaining staff (particularly indigenous staff).

The NQF, and indeed the whole quality reform agenda, is characterised by its emphasis on lifting the quality of *individual* services rather than the quality of the *system* as a whole (Myers, 2006). This 'quality-through-regulation' approach means, in practice, that the onus is on services to find ways to meet the new standards and improve the quality of the education and care they provide. Inevitably, the capacity of services to do this will depend upon their resources, including the fees they are able to charge. Thus, unless governments contribute substantially to the costs of improved quality, access for disadvantaged children to the best programmes may be compromised. An approach that focused on the quality of the system as a whole would ensure that adequate funds were provided to support quality standards and pay appropriate wages to ECEC educators.

A further possible limitation on participation in high-quality ECEC by disadvantaged children is the existence of regulatory inconsistencies. Despite the intention that the NQF deliver national quality standards, it has not proved possible to reach agreement across the eight States and Territories on structural standards. Thus, jurisdictions that had already achieved more stringent staff-to-child ratios than those coming in under the NQS will retain the higher standard. As Table 8.6 illustrates, the protection (or 'grandfathering') of state-based staff-to-child ratios that are tougher than the new national standards means that some states and territories will have more robust provisions than others (Fenech et al, 2012).

Another inconsistency is that regulations concerning the employment of university-qualified teachers vary according to the size of the service. The requirement that services employ at least one early childhood teacher only applies to centres licensed to enrol 25 or more children. Centres licensed for fewer than 25 children are only required to have access to an early childhood teacher for 20% of their operating hours. Additionally, teacher requirements will vary across States and Territories due to protected standards that reflect past regulations. In New South Wales, for example, due to these 'grandfathering' provisions, centres licensed for 40–59 children require two teachers, centres licensed for 60–79 children require three teachers, and centres licensed for 80 or more children require four teachers. Given the difference university-qualified teachers can make to the quality of early learning programmes (Siraj-Blatchford and Manni, 2007), it is highly problematic that children's access to a quality centre will remain tied, at least for a period, to where they live and the licensed capacity of the service they attend.

As noted earlier, by 2014, at least 50% of staff in ECEC centres will be required to have or be actively working towards a diploma or higher-level qualification. The remaining staff will be required to hold or be actively working towards a certificate in childcare. While these requirements represent substantial improvement in some States, evidence suggests that the employment of a core of university-qualified staff would be more likely to facilitate higher quality than a general requirement for all staff to have minimum qualifications (Siraj-Blatchford and Manni, 2007; Fenech et al, 2010). Given the teacher requirements noted above, access to quality ECEC services by children from disadvantaged families may, in practice, be more effectively supported by individual centre practices than by government policies.

The rules governing access to CCB may also limit the access of low-income and disadvantaged children to quality ECEC services. As noted above, families can access CCB only for services 'approved' by the Commonwealth government (this is not the same as meeting quality standards). State-funded preschools, although they may meet quality standards, are almost never approved by the Commonwealth for CCB purposes due to their limited hours of operation. From the Commonwealth perspective, this is a way of limiting its liability for taking on State government financial responsibilities. However, in States such as New South Wales where preschool is expensive, the lack of access to CCB causes substantial hardship and undermines the goal of universal access. In other jurisdictions, it should be noted, parents whose children attend long day-care face substantial gap fees and out-of-pocket expenses, while those using preschool may not be required to pay any fees at all (Productivity Commission, 2011, p xxxvii).

Management structures, budgeting and governance are relatively unexplored but potentially critical factors in determining the access of disadvantaged children to quality ECEC. A recent Australian study of the factors contributing to six long day-care centres receiving sustained high-quality ratings on three measures found that, on average, almost 85% of their budgets was allocated to staffing, including the employment of a core group of teachers. All six centres were non-profit. Given that at least two-thirds of long day-care centres in Australia are run on a private, for-profit basis (DEEWR, 2010), the correlation between profit status and quality requires further investigation.

Integrated services

In line with the National Early Childhood Reform Agenda, Australian governments have committed to promoting access to ECEC for disadvantaged families through a strategy of integrated service provision. Integrated services comprise a mix of education, health and welfare services, the make-up and model of provision varying depending on the governing body and the needs of the specific target community.

For indigenous children, whose health and education outcomes are significantly lower than those of non-indigenous children, COAG's National Partnership for Indigenous Early Childhood Development (also referred to as the 'Closing the Gap' initiative) includes the establishment of 38 integrated or child and family centres targeting – but not restricted to – indigenous families in 23 rural and remote and 15 urban areas by mid-2014. This will require an investment of AUD$292.6 million federal funding over six years. As well as this, 38 integrated early learning and care services have been established for special populations. Six of these are for children with autism spectrum disorder and 32 are for families in areas of high disadvantage (Productivity Commission, 2011). Systematic evaluations of the quality of these integrated services, and assessments of the utilisation rates of disadvantaged families, will be undertaken.

Conclusions

Australian governments have taken many positive steps to improve the quality of early education and care, improve affordability and increase access as part of an overarching early childhood development strategy linked to human capital development, labour force participation and social inclusion. The reforms, together with substantially increased investment, should bear fruit in coming decades. Almost 40% of children aged nought to four now participate in formal, regulated ECEC, and solid progress has been made towards the goal of ensuring that all children have access to at least a year's preschool education. The EYLF and nationally consistent regulatory standards now apply to most preschool and childcare services.

Despite these advances, the long-term effectiveness and sustainability of Australia's reform agenda is not yet assured. A particular concern is that governments have not committed the additional funds that will required to meet higher staffing standards without putting undue pressure on fees. Even with the relatively flat-wage structures that prevail in ECEC, the employment of a more highly skilled and credentialed workforce will involve substantial extra costs. It is widely agreed that most ECEC staff are significantly underpaid already. If governments do not meet the additional costs of a more qualified workforce, services will have to raise fees or cut other costs. This could potentially result in children from low-income families – that is, those who have most to gain from high-quality ECEC – being priced out of the system. Some private, for-profit providers have already claimed that the quality agenda is excessively burdensome for them and too expensive for parents (Karvelas, 2012b). They have sought to ally themselves with the Liberal Party, which has expressed concern about 'over-regulation' and interference in the market.

Another issue for the Australian ECEC system is that, beneath the integrated superstructure of curriculum, quality ratings and standards, significant differences and tensions remain – between the Commonwealth and the States, between education and care, and between the workforce and child-oriented goals of the ECEC system. These are apparent in the contrast between the supply-side funding model that operates in respect of preschools and the demand-side market model that characterises the Commonwealth's approach to childcare. Differences in wages and working conditions remain obstinately divided between education and care settings.

The goal of ensuring that every child has access to 15 hours' preschool is a major step forward for Australia, but as noted above, 'universal access' is a political aspiration, not an entitlement. In any case, 15 hours per week preschool for four-year-olds is an extremely modest goal in comparison with the entitlements and service guarantees of some other countries. Most indigenous-specific services are outside the new quality agenda until at least 2014, and it is unclear whether, by then, they will have been able to reach appropriate levels of quality, at least as measured by mainstream ratings and tools. Australia has no access targets for age groups other than children in the year before school, and no clear vision of how parents are expected to manage the transition from maternity or parental leave back to work.

Taken together, these gaps and omissions in Australian ECEC suggest that there is fundamental uncertainty at the political and policy level about the balance between government investment and private or family responsibility. They also suggest a lack of clarity about the emphasis that should be given to the (sometimes competing) goals of the system, including promoting children's development and learning, supporting adult workforce participation and enhancing gender equality.

Notes

[1] 'Long day-care' is the term used in Australia for a childcare centre or crèche.

[2] As discussed later, many indigenous-specific services have been excluded from the new quality agenda, at least initially.

[3] Both terms are used in Australia. We use them interchangeably here.

[4] Australia is a federation with six States and two Territories as well as a national government. From time to time in this chapter we use the term 'States' to cover both types of sub-national jurisdiction.

[5] In Victoria, local government also plays a significant role.

[6] Family day-care involves caregivers providing care and development activities in the caregiver's own home. Schemes are administered and supported by central coordination units.

[7] The In-Home Care programme provides for a carer to be employed in the child's home. Support for in-home care is limited and it is available only to certain types of families, such as those living in remote parts of Australia, families where there are three or more children below school age, and families where either the child or parent has a disability.

[8] A national paid parental scheme was introduced in Australia in 2011. It provides 18 weeks' leave paid at the minimum wage and an additional two weeks if partners take leave. Most Australian parents are entitled to one year of unpaid parental leave.

[9] The most important exceptions are the 269 'budget-based' services that cater mainly to ATSI children and their families.

References

ABS (Australian Bureau of Statistics) (2008) *Social Trends, Cat No 4102.0*, Canberra: ABS.

ABS (2009) *Social Trends*, Cat No 4102.0, Canberra: ABS.

ABS (2011) *Childhood Education and Care*, Cat No 4402.0.55.003, Canberra: ABS.

ABS (2012a) *Childhood Education and Care, Australia, June 2011, Cat No 4402.2*, Camberra: ABS.

ABS (2012b) *Experimental Estimates of Preschool Education, Australia, 2011, Cat No 4240.0*, Canberra: ABS.

ACECQA (Australian Children's Education and Care Quality Authority) (2012) *ACECQA Strategic Plan 2012–2016*, Sydney: ACECQA.

AIHW (2012) *A Picture of Australia's Children, Cat. no. PHE 167*, Canberra: AIHW.

Brennan, D. (1998) *The Politics of Australian Child Care: Philanthropy to Feminism*, Cambridge: Cambridge University Press.

Brennan, D. (2007a) 'Babies, budgets and birthrates: Work/family policy in Australia 1996–2006', *Social Politics: International Studies in Gender, State and Society*, vol 14, no 1, pp 31–57.

Brennan, D. (2007b) 'The ABC of child care politics', *Australian Journal of Social Issues*, vol 42, no 2, pp 213–25.

Brennan, D. (2010) 'Federalism, feminism and multilevel governance', in M. Haussman, M. Sawer and J. Vickers (eds) *Federalism, Feminism and Multilevel Governance*, Farhmah: Ashgate, pp 37–50.

COAG (Council of Australian Governments) (2009a) *Investing in the Early Years: A National Childhood Development Strategy, July* (http://acecqa.gov.au/storage/national_ECD_strategy.pdf).

COAG (2009b) *National Partnership Agreement on the National Quality Agenda for Early Childhood Education and Care* (www.eduweb.vic.gov.au/edulibrary/public/earlychildhood/nqf/nationalpartnershipagreementnqa.pdf).

COAG (2009c) *Belonging, Being and Becoming: The Early Years Learning Framework for Australia* (www.deewr.gov.au/EarlyChildhood/Policy_Agenda/Quality/Documents/Final%20EYLF%20Framework%20Report%20-%20WEB.pdf).

COAG (2009d) *National Partnership Agreement on Early Childhood Education*, Canberra: COAG (www.federalfinancialrelations.gov.au/content/npa/education/early_childhood/national_partnership.pdf).

COAG (2009e) *National Indigenous Reform Agreement (Closing the Gap)*, Canberra: COAG (www.federalfinancialrelations.gov.au/content/npa/health_indigenous/indigenous-reform/national-agreement_sept_12.pdf).

DEEWR (Department of Education Employment and Workplace Relations) (2010) *State of Child Care in Australia*, Canberra: Office of Early Childhood Education and Child Care.

DEEWR (2012a) *Annual Report 2011–2012*, Canberra: DEEWR.

DEEWR (2012b) *Child Care Update*, Canberra: DEEWR.

DHS (Department of Human Services) (2012) *Budget 2012–13: Jobs, Education and Training Child Care Fee Assistance Program*, Canberra: DHS.

Ellis, K. (2009) 'Ministerial Statement – The future of ABC learning', 15 September.

Farouque, F. (2006) 'The other Eddy everywhere', *The Age, 8 April.*

Fenech, M., Giugni, M. and Bown, K. (2012) 'A critical analysis of the National Quality Framework: Mobilising for a vision for children beyond minimum standards', *Australasian Journal of Early Childhood*. vol 37, no 4, pp 5–14.

Fenech, M., Harrison, L., Press, F. and Sumsion, J. (2010) *Contributors to Quality Long Day Care: Findings from Six Case Study Centres*, Bathurst: Charles Sturt University.

Karvelas, P. (2012a) 'Widening gap "a reason" to raise child care cap', *The Australian*, 23 May.

Karvelas, P. (2012b) 'Costly baby rooms go out with the bathwater', *The Australian*, 18 December.

Myers, R.G. (2006) *Quality in Program of Early Childhood Care and Education* (http://unesdoc.unesco.org/images/0014/001474/147473e.pdf).

Newberry, S. and Brennan, D. (2013) 'Economic and social policy tensions: Early childhood education and care in a marketised environment', *Accounting, Auditing and Accountability*, vol 29, no 3, pp 227–45.

Productivity Commission (2011) *Early Childhood Development Workforce, Research Report* (www.pc.gov.au/__data/assets/pdf_file/0003/113907/early-childhood-report.pdf).

Productivity Commission (2012) *Report on Government Services*, Canberra: Productivity Commission.

PWC (PriceWaterhouseCoopers) (2012) *A Practical Vision for Early Childhood Education and Care*, Melbourne: PWC.

Siraj-Blatchford, I. and Manni, L. (2007) *Effective Leadership in the Early Years Sector (ELEYS) Study*, London: Institute of Education, University of London.

SNAICC (2012) *Opening Doors Through partnerships: Practical approaches to developing genuine partnerships that address Aboriginal and Torres Strait Islander community needs*, Melbourne: SNAICC.

Spearritt, P. (1974) 'The kindergarten movement: tradition and change', in D. Edgar (ed) *Social Change in Australia: Readings in Sociology*, Melbourne: Cheshire, pp 583–96.

Sumsion, J. (2012) 'ABC Learning and Australian early childhood education and care: a retrospective audit of a radical experiment', in E. Lloyd and H. Penn (eds) *Childcare Markets: Can They Deliver an Equitable Service?*, Bristol: Policy Press.

Sylva, K., Melhuish, E.C., Sammons, P., Siraj-Blatchford, I. and Taggart, B. (2004) *The Effective Provision of Pre-school Education (EPPE) Project: Technical Paper 12 – The Final Report: Effective Pre-school education*, London: Department for Education and Skills, Institute of Education, University of London.

Tarrant, L. (2008) 'Taking big steps in child care', *Every Child*, vol 14, no 3, p 3.

United Voice (2012) 'Professional wages proposal for early childhood education and care', United Voice 2013 ECC Federal Budget Submission.

NINE

Delivering high-quality early childhood education and care to low-income children: How well is the US doing?

Katherine Magnuson and Jane Waldfogel

Introduction

Early childhood education and care (ECEC) researchers and policy makers have used the metaphor of the 'childcare triangle' – reflecting the connection, and tension, between the goals of advancing access, quality and affordability. The tension between these competing goals has never been so acute as it is today. The high share of children with working mothers makes increasing access an imperative for social policy (Fox et al, 2012). But at the same time, we know more than ever before about the crucial importance of the quality of care for child wellbeing (Shonkoff and Phillips, 2000), suggesting that simply expanding access without attention to quality may be inefficient or even counterproductive. Yet expanding access and improving quality are both costly at a time when budgets are exceptionally tight at both the state and federal level in the wake of the recent economic downturn.

It is within this context that this chapter asks how effectively, and through what mechanisms, the US attempts to ensure access to high-quality ECEC for children of all backgrounds. The chapter focuses on three types of policy – regulation, subsidy and direct public provision – and explores to what extent these mechanisms operate (and interact) to ensure that ECEC is both high quality and accessible to all, with particular attention to access, quality and cost of care for children from low-income families.

Terminology: in line with current US practice, we sometimes use the term 'childcare' as shorthand for the array of programmes and arrangements that make up the ECEC sector. We sometimes use the term 'preschool' to refer to school- or centre-based arrangements that serve three- and four-year-old children (in the year or two before school entry).

The challenge

In the US, most mothers are back at work before their child's first birthday (Han et al, 2008), and children do not start school until about age five.[1] So that leaves a substantial amount of time that preschool age children need care if their parents are working, a situation that is made even more complicated given that many parents (and particularly those who are low-income) work non-standard or irregular hours. But ECEC is more than just a work support – if it is of high quality, it can also play an important developmental role, particularly for low-income children who benefit the most from high-quality education and care but whose parents are least able to afford it on their own.

Evidence on the potentially beneficial effects of high-quality ECEC on child wellbeing comes from several sources. First, there have been a small number of randomised controlled trials of small-scale high-quality childcare programmes. The evidence from these studies is invaluable in showing what the effects of high-quality programmes can be, but is less informative about the effects of the types of childcare generally available today for children in the US. Second, there have been numerous observational studies of associations between various types of childcare and child outcomes. These studies provide very useful descriptive information, but of course are possibly biased due to the selection of particular types of children into particular types of care. Third, there are some studies of the effects of childcare policies on child wellbeing. These studies are important in showing what the likely effects of future policies might be.

The random assignment studies of high-quality childcare programmes (see the reviews in Karoly et al, 1998; Waldfogel, 2006a; Almond and Currie, 2011) show conclusively that high-quality childcare, even at a young age, can have strong positive benefits for children's health and development, with particularly large effects for children from socio-economically disadvantaged backgrounds. But, as noted earlier, these programmes are typically small-scale, and represent much higher quality than what is on offer in larger-scale programmes. The recent random assignment studies of the federal government's largest compensatory childcare programme, Head Start, serving disadvantaged three- to five-year-olds (and the smaller Early Head Start programme, serving a small number of disadvantaged nought- to two-year-olds), also showed some positive impacts on child health and development, but these were generally much smaller in magnitude than those found in the model programmes. However, it is important to keep in mind that the counterfactual conditions of these recent studies are different than those of earlier studies. It is both the case that children in THE control condition are more likely now to experience centre-based childcare, although it is of varying quality, and THAT their mothers are much more highly educated than in prior studies (Duncan and Magnuson, 2013).

A large number of observational studies have estimated the effects of features of childcare arrangements (in particular, its quality, type and duration) on various child outcomes. As mentioned, such studies are confounded by the fact that children who attend particular types of ECEC are not a random group, but rather may be positively or negatively selected. In addition, the effects of childcare features may vary depending on what the care entails, who is receiving the care and what the counterfactual is (that is, what type of care the child would have received in the absence of the childcare). It is therefore not surprising that studies have produced a range of estimates. Among the most consistent findings is that attending school- or centre-based care is generally associated with better academic achievement and cognitive outcomes at school entry, but may also be associated with more externalising behaviour problems (particularly if that care is for long hours and/or of poor quality) (see the review in Waldfogel, 2006a). Another consistent finding is that preschool and prekindergarten programmes generally produce larger gains for more disadvantaged children than for more advantaged peers (see, for example, Magnuson and Waldfogel, 2005).

The issue of *quality* as it pertains to ECEC has received particular attention. Development proceeds at an astonishingly rapid rate during the first few years of life, and children's day-to-day experiences play an important role in these developmental processes. Recognising the importance of such early experiences, researchers have sought to describe the quality of ECEC settings, both in terms of the extent to which these settings conform to basic health practices, as well as the extent to which they provide warm, responsive interactions with staff, and offer enriching opportunities for learning.

Given this multidimensional conceptual model of quality, it is not surprising that most measurement strategies involve several components. There are two common ways to measure quality in ECEC. The first is to consider structural aspects of the programme, such as the child-to-teacher ratio or level of teacher education. Structural markers have the advantage of being easy to measure and regulate. These factors are expected to indirectly affect children by shaping their day-to-day experiences in classrooms (NICHD ECCRN, 2002). The second set of quality indicators, process measures or global quality measures are designed to directly describe children's day-to-day experiences and interactions. These measures typically involve observing children in the classroom and rating several dimensions of their experience. A common measure of process quality is the Early Childhood Environment Rating Scale –Revised (ECERS-R). It includes 43 items, with seven sub-scales measuring the quality of space and furnishings, personal care routines, language and reasoning opportunities, activities, interaction, programme structure and parents/staff (Harms et al, 1998). A more recently created observational measure of classroom quality used frequently in research, the Classroom Assessment Scoring System (CLASS), focuses entirely on teacher–child interactions in early education settings (Pianta et al, 2007).

Data on the quality of care in the US are limited. Data from recent national studies, however, suggest that assessed by these global measures of care, only a small percentage of care is of high quality (typically 10–12%), and the bulk of care is of moderate quality (Ruzek et al, 2012). Data on structural indicators of quality, such as teacher education and pay, point to improvements over the past 20 years. Research by Daphna Bassok and colleagues (2012) finds that the early childhood education and care labour market is still characterised by 'low-education, low-compensation and high-turnover', but that, since the early 1990s, compensation and education have been rising and turnover decreasing. Overall, the proportion of early childhood workers with at least some college education rose from 46% in 1990 to about 62% in 2009, while the mean average wage rose from US$8.80 to US$11.70 over the same period.

Evidence suggests that, in general, both structural and process aspects of quality predict children's school readiness, but the associations are modest. Because more advantaged children are more likely to experience higher-quality care, the most convincing studies use analytic strategies that attempt to account for these selection processes. For example, NICHD ECCRN and Duncan (2003) found that observed childcare quality and caregiver education predicted children's cognitive outcomes, using a range of rigorous methods. In addition, evidence also suggests that the associations between specific dimensions of process quality are more strongly predictive when they are closely aligned with the outcomes they are predicting. For example, process measures of the extent to which the setting is language-rich are more strongly predictive of children's language outcomes than they are of other child outcomes, and are also more predictive of language outcomes than are more general measures of quality (Burchinal et al, 2011).

Moreover, recent evidence on the importance of structural measures of quality suggests that associations with children's outcomes may be more selective than is generally appreciated. Research generally finds that levels of teacher qualifications are correlated with programme quality (Tout et al, 2005), but efforts to identify the unique effect of teacher qualifications suggest that the association might not be robust. For example, in Early and colleagues' (2007) study of seven centre-based early childhood programme datasets, including prekindergarten and Head Start, they found that there was not a consistent association between caregiver education and measures of programme quality or children's outcomes. The authors are careful to make clear that the fact that credentials do not consistently predict children's learning does not mean that caregiver's skills do not matter. All of the programmes considered were structured early learning programmes with performance standards and goals, including Head Start or prekindergarten programmes, and caregiver education may be more predictive in less structured settings or those with lower levels of regulation (Raikes et al, 2005). One review of evidence from US studies finds that adult-to-child ratio is the most consistent feature of ECEC settings that is associated with children's outcomes (Burchinal, 2012). This finding may reflect the fact that there is such wide variation in ratios across the US (for example, some states require one staff member for every three or four toddlers, while other states allow one staff member to care for as many as 8 or 12 toddlers; see Hotz and Xiao, 2011). There is also recognition among policy makers and practitioners that leadership and management matters and that, in particular, it is difficult to have a good programme in absence of good management (Smith, 2012).

Studies of the effects of ECEC *policies* on child outcomes are more rare, and it is often quite complicated to identify causal effects. Several recent studies in the US, using econometric methods, have examined the effect of childcare subsidies on child development and have reported negative effects (Herbst and Tekin, 2010a, 2010b). These results echo the findings of a Canadian study (Baker et al, 2008a) that analysed the effects on a range of child and family outcomes of the introduction of a universal CAD$5-a-day childcare subsidy programme in Québec, and found significant negative effects of the subsidy on socio-emotional and health outcomes of children under the age of five. But other US studies have found neutral overall effects of childcare subsidies on child outcomes (Johnson et al, 2013; Washbrook et al, 2011). More work is needed to reconcile these discrepancies in findings, and to determine whether such differences are due to differing analytic assumptions or other study characteristics.

Recent international research suggests that the effects of ECEC policies likely depend both on the design of those policies and the groups that receive them. For instance, studies from Norway have found positive overall effects of childcare subsidies on long-term outcomes for participants (Havnes and Mogstad, 2011) and have also shown that effects are much larger for those at the bottom and middle of the earnings distribution (Havnes and Mogstad, 2012).

The policy framework

The landscape with regard to federal and state policy involvement in the ECEC arena has changed quite a bit over the past several decades. However, one constant is that the US relies heavily on the private market (Kamerman and Waldfogel, 2005). Thus, although public funding for childcare subsidies as well as public provision of early childhood education has been expanded over the past two decades, it still remains fairly limited relative to levels of public support for ECEC in other peer countries (Gornick and Meyers, 2003; Waldfogel, 2006b; OECD, 2012; Ruhm, 2012).

Middle-income families with working parents receive some support through the federal child and dependent care tax credit as well as the dependent care assistance plan, and, in many states, through supplemental state childcare tax credits (Donahue and Campbell, 2002; Smolensky and Gootman, 2003).

Low-income families typically do not benefit from these tax credits (as most are not refundable), but may be eligible for assistance through childcare subsidies (funded with both federal and state dollars) or through Head Start (a public programme for low-income or disabled children funded primarily with federal dollars). But neither childcare subsidies nor Head Start are entitlements, in that not all eligible children are served (instead, a fixed amount of slots are available regardless of the number of qualifying children). Childcare subsidies, although greatly expanded during the welfare reforms of the 1990s, are used by less than a third of eligible families (Johnson, 2010), but such low levels of take-up are in large part explained by the use of other publicly funded childcare programmes such as Head Start. (Estimates indicate that only 20% of families with eligible children do not receive any assistance; see Johnson, 2010.) Funding for Head Start, which grew tremendously during the 1990s, has stagnated in recent years and, with increases in child poverty, now reaches only about half of eligible three- and four-year-olds (Gibbs et al, 2011). (A very small Early Head Start programme reaches fewer than 5% of eligible children under age three.)

A newer type of public provision is free prekindergarten funded and administered by local public schools, and offered either onsite or through other cooperating agencies. Prekindergarten programmes are subject to state-specific education standards and tend to employ more highly qualified teachers (like those who teach in primary schools) and meet learning standards. These programmes, largely funded directly by states and local communities, expanded rapidly through the 1990s and early 2000s, and now serve about 28% of four-year-olds, although often in part-day programmes (Barnett et al, 2011). In a handful of states, provision is universal in that there are no restrictions on participation, but even in these states the goal is not to supplant other existing programmes such as Head Start. In other states, provision is universal in particular communities or provision is targeted to disadvantaged children. Prekindergarten programmes are facing limited budgets at the current time as states continue to cope with the aftermath of the recent economic downturn, and inflation-adjusted spending has been declining for these programmes (Barnett et al, 2011).

In addition to funding some ECEC, states also play a role in establishing regulations and providing information to families. States regulate a variety of dimensions of childcare quality. For example, states set minimum levels of educational credentials, child-to-staff ratios and professional development experiences for staff, and also mandate safety practices such as the provision of fire extinguishers and other factors related to the safety of the child's environment. However, states differ in the stringency of such regulations and the rigour with which regulations are enforced.

Employer involvement in the ECEC domain remains relatively uncommon, with only about 15% of employers providing any type of assistance, and as with other employee benefits this assistance is more likely to be provided to higher-income workers than to their low-income counterparts (Waldfogel, 2007, 2009). Most of the assistance that is provided by employers takes the form of programmes allowing employees to pay for ECEC with pre-tax dollars or programmes providing information and referral; direct provision of ECEC or assistance paying for ECEC is rare (Waldfogel, 2007, 2009).

Children who are not enrolled in school- or centre-based care may be at home with their parents or in informal childcare settings.

Estimates suggest that over 50% of children in non-parental care under age six experience informal care, which includes care by a relative, babysitter or nanny (in the child's home or another's home), as well as with a family childcare provider (Iruka and Carver, 2005). Many parents prefer informal care, particularly for younger children, because of its lower cost, individual or family-like orientation and flexibility. However, as children approach school age, most transition into some form of school- or centre-based care. Whereas only 28% of infants who experience non-parental care are in centre-based care, this proportion increases to nearly 78% for children aged three to five who experience non-parental care (Iruka and Carver, 2005). Given that participation in centre-based early education programmes in the year or two before formal schooling begins has been found to improve low-income children's school readiness, policy makers and practitioners worry that without such experiences they are missing an important opportunity to build children's learning capacity. Efforts to address disparities in attendance of early education programmes include programmes such as Head Start and pre-kindergarten, as well as childcare subsidies.

Access, quality and affordability for low-income families

Given the limited public funding available to offset the costs of ECEC, the minimal role of employers and the heavy reliance on the private market, it should not be surprising that low-income families do less well than others on all three dimensions of the 'childcare triangle'.

Access

Increasingly, in advanced industrialised countries, children are enrolled in some form of school- or centre-based 'preschool' programme in the year or two before they start school, and often this preschool is publicly provided (OECD, 2012). However, this is not the case in the US. Enrolment in preschool among three- and four-year-olds is not universal, and a persistent finding is that low-income children are less likely than more affluent children to be enrolled (see, for example, Bainbridge et al, 2005).

In recent work (Magnuson and Waldfogel, 2012), we tracked enrolment trends from 1968 to 2010 for three- and four-year-old children, using nationally representative data from the October Current Population Survey and dividing families into five groups based on income quintiles. We found that, while enrolment in preschool has grown for three- and four-year-olds from all income groups over time, enrolment rates are consistently higher for the top two income groups than for the middle- and lower-income groups (see Figures 9.1–9.3). (The fact that enrolment is not consistently lower for the bottom-income quintile than for the next to bottom or middle quintile reflects the lowest quintile's greater access to help paying for the cost of preschool through childcare subsidies and programmes such as Head Start and prekindergarten.)

Public policy clearly plays a role here. Earlier research found that as kindergarten programmes for five-year-olds were expanded in the 1960s and 1970s, income-related gaps in enrolment for that age group disappeared (Bainbridge et al, 2005). Our analyses of trends for three- and four-year-olds indicated that in years when funding for subsidies, Head Start or prekindergarten has been more generous, a greater share of low-income children have been enrolled (Magnuson et al, 2007; Magnuson and Waldfogel, 2012).

Hispanic children and children of immigrants also have lower levels of preschool enrolment than other children, in large part because their families tend to have lower incomes; but African-American children, in contrast, are if anything more likely than comparable white children

Figure 9.1: US: Percentage of children enrolled in preschool by family income quintile

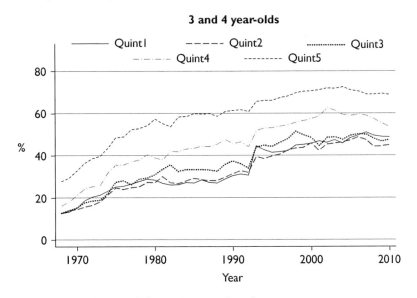

Note: Data from October CPS; data shown are from 3-year moving averages

Figure 9.2: US: Percentage of children enrolled in preschool by family income quintile

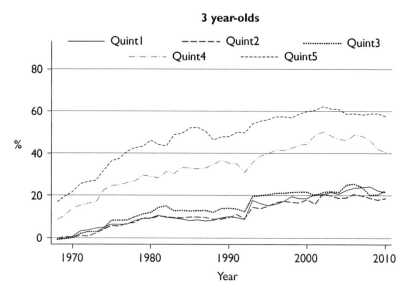

Note: Data from October CPS; data shown are from 3-year moving averages

Figure 9.3: US: Percentage of children enrolled in preschool by family income quintile

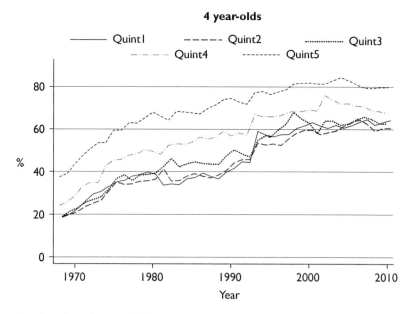

Note: Data from October CPS; data shown are from 3-year moving averages

to be enrolled in school- or centre-based care (Meyers et al, 2004; Magnuson and Waldfogel, 2005; Magnuson et al, 2006).

We know less about gaps in access to ECEC among children younger than three. But the analyses that do exist point to disparities for children in this age group as well. For example, Greenberg (2011), analysing four waves of data on nought- to two-year-olds from the National Household Education Survey from 1995 to 2005, finds that children of more highly educated mothers are more likely to be in any form of non-parental childcare (60% of children of college-educated mothers compared to only 35% of children of mothers with less than a high school education) and are much more likely to be enrolled in school- or centre-based care (21% of children of college-educated mothers compared to only 7% of children of mothers with less than high school education). And, as is the case for older children, holding education and other characteristics constant, both low income and being Hispanic are associated with lower likelihood of enrolment in school- or centre-based care for nought to two-year-olds, while being African-American is associated with higher enrolment (Greenberg, 2011).

Quality

Low-income children also attend ECEC that is of lower quality, on average, than that attended by other children (Waldfogel, 2006a). Tracking national information on ECEC quality, especially process quality, is uncommon. What data exist indicate that poor children are disproportionately likely to experience low-quality care. For example, Ruzek and colleagues (2011) found that, at age 24 months, 43% of poor children in the Early Childhood Longitudinal Study – Birth Cohort (ECLS-B) experience low-quality ECEC, as measured by global process measures of quality, whereas the share of more affluent children that experience low quality is only 16%. At the other end of the continuum, only 9% of poor children experience high-quality ECEC compared with 15% of non-poor children (Ruzek et al, 2011). These differences are also found in children's experiences within other forms of programmes. For example, studies report that prekindergarten programmes that serve a larger proportion of low-income children are more likely to be of lower quality (LoCasale-Couch et al, 2007).

Affordability

Finally, although they are more likely to use informal and lower quality arrangements, low-income families, when they pay for care, tend to pay more for ECEC as a share of their income than more affluent families (Meyers et al, 2004; Rosenbaum and Ruhm, 2007). In addition, single mother families tend to pay more as a share of income than married couple families (Rosenbaum and Ruhm, 2007).

School- or centre-based ECEC programmes, considered to offer the best preparation in terms of boosting school readiness, are generally out of reach for low-income families. The average cost of school- or centre-based ECEC for an infant (US$9,520) is roughly half the average income of a family of three with income at the poverty line (US$18,530), while the average cost of school- or centre-based ECEC for a four-year-old (US$7,705) represents roughly 40% of the poverty line (Child Care Aware of America, 2012). Even families with incomes at twice the poverty line (US$37,060) would have trouble affording a school- or centre-based programme, which on average would cost a quarter of their income (for an infant) or a fifth (for a four-year-old) (Child Care Aware of America, 2012). Moreover, since these cost figures refer to the price for a single child, the cost for a family with more than one young child would be even higher.

Families who receive subsidies, or have access to Head Start or prekindergarten, pay less, but it is important to recall that not all low-income families receive subsidised ECEC. In addition, research has found that there is considerably instability in subsidy receipt, with the median spell of receipt lasting about six months, and a large proportion of children experiencing multiple subsidy spells (Meyers et al, 2002; Ha, 2009). This pattern of subsidy churning has been linked to instability in care providers (Ha et al, 2012).

Efforts to improve access, quality and affordability: federal level

Childcare policy at the federal level is housed in the Department of Health and Human Services (but with linkages established during the first Obama administration to the Department of Education). The primary policy levers available to the federal government are childcare subsidies/tax credits and the Head Start programme (since the federal government plays little role in regulating quality or in providing or funding prekindergarten). As discussed in the following section, the federal government also provides leadership and incentives for the states to take steps to improve quality. We also note that the federal government provides some childcare as an employer; in recent years, the military childcare system administered by the Department of Defense has become a model system in terms of access, quality, and affordability (Floyd and Phillips, 2013).

As mentioned earlier, childcare subsidies were greatly expanded as part of the welfare reforms of the 1990s, but subsidies still reach only a minority of eligible families. Moreover, the type and quality of ECEC subsidised varies widely. While to some extent this is intentional, to allow families flexibility so that rigid rules do not interfere with employment, it is of concern that, as discussed earlier, research on childcare subsidies finds that they have neutral or even negative effects on children and families. Clearly more research is needed to better understand whether the childcare subsidy system can be improved to meet the dual needs of supporting parental work and meeting children's developmental needs.

Proposed reforms to the subsidy system include: guaranteeing childcare subsidy assistance to families with incomes below 200% of poverty; instituting mechanisms to improve the quality of care, coordinating childcare with other early childhood programmes, and ensuring that payment rates are high enough to cover quality care; and making the federal-dependent care tax credit refundable (Greenberg, 2007).

The other policy lever available to the federal government is Head Start. Experts tend to agree that Head Start is beneficial for low-income children, at least in the short term, and many point to non-experimental studies showing important long-term benefits, arguing that the programme should be expanded to serve more children (see, for example, Ludwig and Phillips, 2007; Deming, 2009; Almond and Currie, 2011; Gibbs et al, 2011). The Obama administration has maintained funding for Head Start (following increases as part of the American Recovery and Reinvestment Act of 2009), and there continues to be a good deal of interest in academic and policy communities in improving the quality of Head Start, although there are differing perspectives on how best to accomplish this. Some argue for better aligning Head Start and prekindergarten programmes, typically by giving states control of Head Start monies, and implicitly for blending state prekindergarten and Head Start programmes (Haskins and Barnett, 2010). Others argue that there are unlikely to be greater efficiencies gained, and some may well be lost, if Head Start's focus on the 'whole child' is abandoned in favour of a greater focus on academic skills, which they fear will occur if Head Start funding is handed over to the states (Gibbs et al, 2011).

The Obama administration has taken a pragmatic approach by making the lowest performing Head Start grantees, as measured on several administrative indicators of programme quality, compete for their funding. In the past, grantees have not had to compete for funding, and programme funding was ended in only very rare circumstances. This market-based approach to quality improvement is motivated by the observation that some organisations seem to be better able to deliver high-quality programmes than others, and the hope that competition would improve the chance that funding is going to the auspices that can best meet Head Start's goal of providing high-quality education. The success of such an approach assumes both that the selected criteria that trigger competition accurately identify low-quality programmes, and that, even without increased resources, the competition process can spur programmes into improving and/or that other early childhood organisations will have the capacity to run higher-quality Head Start programmes.

The federal government has taken several other steps to improve the quality of Head Start programmes (Lombardi, 2011). For example, all Head Start programmes in the country are now required to use the CLASS to monitor the quality of their programme and to inform quality improvements. There are also efforts underway to improve the capacity of Head Start programmes to work effectively with second language learners.

The Obama administration has recently sought to elevate the visibility of childcare policy, and its links with education, by creating an interagency working group on ECEC. Joan Lombardi, who served as the first interagency liaison for childcare in the Obama administration (linking the federal Departments of Health and Human Services, and Education), argues that both Head Start and Early Head Start are serving as laboratories for learning, as they try out and develop new approaches that can then be applied in other settings (Lombardi, 2012). She also stresses the role being played by national research and training centres focused on improving practice in both Head Start and other childcare settings on issues such as cultural diversity (in particular, serving second language learners) and better ways to involve and engage families.

Efforts to improve access, quality and affordability: state level

States have a greater number of policy instruments to affect childcare access, quality and affordability: regulation, subsidies and tax credits, and direct public provision, particularly through prekindergarten.

All states now regulate ECEC, although they do so with varying degrees of standards, reach and oversight. Regulations are typically designed to guarantee a minimal threshold of safety and quality in school- or centre-based programmes and, in most states, in family-based providers as well, although family providers serving only a small number of unrelated children are typically exempt. The general trend has been towards increasing the requirements and oversight in licensing ECEC, but increasingly regulation and licensing requirements are viewed as the foundation for quality improvement initiatives, necessary but not sufficient for generating large improvements in programme quality that are needed to improve children's wellbeing (Rigby et al, 2007). Moreover, strict regulation and enforcement of regulation has been demonstrated to have the unintended consequences of increasing the cost and limiting the availability of centre-based care (Hotz and Xiao, 2011).

The most recent state initiative in quality improvement is the implementation of Tiered Quality Rating and Improvement Systems (TQRIS), which have been promoted at the federal level by Early Learning Challenge Grants (federal funds provided to the states provided they meet certain conditions). Although the Early Learning Challenge Grants currently reach only 14 states, the vision is that the kinds of reforms they are supporting could eventually influence practice in all 50 states (Lombardi, 2012).

TQRIS systems are designed to assign ECEC providers a rating level, along a quality continuum, and typically serve two functions. First, they provide a standard way of rating programme quality, based on multiple criteria, and making the rating information available to parents. Nearly all states include staff training and education and the classroom or learning environment (although the latter is only measured at higher levels of quality in some states). States differ on whether and to what extent they include parent involvement activities, business practices, child-to-staff ratios or national accreditation status. The assumption underlying this function of TQRIS is that parents often lack good information about programme quality and if such information was available, they would be more likely to choose higher-rated settings. As a result, lower quality providers would be given an incentive to either improve the quality of their programme or to leave the market (Zellman and Perlman, 2008).

Second, most systems provide a range of technical assistance, resources and incentives for programmes to improve programme quality. Such efforts include consultation around quality improvement (including providing guidance on curriculum and coaching for teachers), increased investments for professional development scholarships, micro grants for other targeted quality improvement efforts, and, in some instances, higher levels of subsidy payments for more highly rated programmes. The goal of these efforts is to foster and support providers' efforts to improve the quality of care they provide.

Thus TQRIS programmes attempt to improve quality by affecting both the demand for high-quality care and the supply of such care. Of course, the success of such efforts rest on the ability of rating systems to accurately identify and measure key aspects of quality, and the willingness of providers to participate in a rating system (Zellman and Perlman, 2008).

Given the relative infancy of most state TQRIS programmes, it is not surprising that conclusions about the effectiveness of such approaches are premature. To date, most research has been focused around issues of implementation and has been descriptive in nature. Moreover, the difference in system designs across states makes it difficult to draw any general conclusions from an evaluation of any one state's system. The emphasis on using research to validate that rating scales effectively differentiate programme quality in recent Early Learning Challenge Grants is providing a strong impetus for states to undertake much needed research (Zellman and Fiene, 2012). Studies that involve child outcomes are rare, and so far provide mixed results, which is not surprising given the diversity of rating systems and related policies. A small study in Missouri found that low-income children in higher-rated programmes learned more than their peers in lower rated programmes (Thornberg et al, 2009). However, a large study of Colorado's rating system did not find that children's gains in school readiness differed systematically as a function of star-rating level (Zellman et al, 2008). The Colorado report highlighted how difficult it is to study children in a system with such high levels of turnover (and thus low levels of exposure to a particular programme).

A few other state quality improvement innovations have garnered attention and been scrutinised. Most prominent is North Carolina's Smart Start programme, which began as a pilot programme in 1993 and expanded to state-wide implementation by the late 1990s. The programme established funding for local, typically county-level partnerships to improve quality of ECEC, as well as other efforts to promote children's healthy development such as home visiting and parenting programmes. Discretion for how Smart Start funds should be spent was given to local boards, but with the goal of improving school readiness and ensuring that more low-income children attended high-quality care. Early reports suggested that almost 30% of funds were spent on quality improvement efforts, and documented that following Smart Start implementation, the proportion of centres rated as 'high quality' improved dramatically (Bryant et al, 2003; US DHHS, 2011). Moreover, recent rigorous work has found that when combined with specific funding for four-year-olds to attend preschool, the programme improved children's test scores in third grade (Ladd et al, 2012).

Indeed, federal officials point to North Carolina as an example of a successful effort to improve quality incrementally, by first using incentives to get providers to raise quality and then, once sufficient numbers of providers had improved, making that higher standard of quality mandatory for all providers (Rudisill, 2012; Smith, 2012). The process took nearly ten years in North Carolina, but their success shows it can be achieved.

There is also a good deal of interest at the state level in universal provision of prekindergarten for three- and four-year-olds (Kirp, 2007). As discussed, this is the model used in most OECD (Organisation for Economic Co-operation and Development) countries, where universal public provision of preschool in the year or two prior to school entry is the norm, but is a relatively new development in the US. Proponents of universal provision argue that it is the only way to ensure strong public support for preschool programmes and to ensure that lower income children are not isolated in separate and poorer quality programmes (Esping-Andersen, 2004, 2009; Waldfogel, 2006a). However, universal provision is costly, and for this reason, some have argued instead for programmes that are more targeted to low-income children (see, for example, Duncan et al, 2007). As mentioned, prekindergarten programmes have expanded and now serve just under 30% of four-year-olds. Yet only a handful of states have truly universal coverage. Compared with peer countries, the US remains very far behind in the provision of universal preschool (OECD, 2012).

Rigorous empirical studies of US prekindergarten programmes have documented that such programmes lead to enhanced school readiness, consistent with the evidence from studies of prekindergarten expansions in other countries (see the review in Ruhm and Waldfogel, 2012). Most recently, Weiland and Yoshikawa (in press) evaluated Boston's prekindergarten programme, a full-day programme with both standardised language and literacy curriculum as well as a maths curriculum and effective coaching and professional development to implement the curricula and manage children's behaviour. Their results suggested that the programme produced substantial improvements in children's maths and vocabulary skills, and smaller, although still meaningful, improvements in children's executive function and emotional development.

Conclusions

As we have seen, the US faces challenges with regard to all three legs of the 'childcare triangle'. Low-income families are less likely than their higher-income peers to access ECEC, and when they do, that care is of lower quality and when they pay out of pocket, represents a larger share of their income.

If the priority is to support parental employment *and* to promote child development, then the most important reforms to pursue are those that would make high-quality ECEC more affordable for low-income families. The challenge is how to do so. One route would be to directly provide more high-quality programmes, such as prekindergarten and Head Start; another would be to use regulations and other tools to improve quality in the vast array of ECEC programmes that children attend. But of course, the two approaches are not incompatible. Ideally, one could envision federal and state systems that both offered more direct provision and worked with existing providers to improve quality by building a culture of continuous programme improvement, such that higher-quality programmes were rewarded and encouraged, but with providers motivated rather than penalised. Tiered quality rating systems were designed with this latter goal in mind, and have succeeded in states like North Carolina, but as of now it is unclear whether they will be effective in all 50 states.

Finally, the fundamental challenge for the US is how to pay for a system that provides high-quality care. Linda Smith, current Deputy Assistant Secretary for Early Childhood at the Administration for Children and Families, eloquently makes this point:

> We haven't figured out how to finance this. When it costs more to produce a product than the consumer can afford to pay, you have a broken market. What we have done is pretty much financed the system on the backs of parents. But the cost of doing it right is more than families can afford to pay – even middle income families are struggling to find quality at a rate they can pay. So how do you then build a structure? (Smith, 2012)

The financial challenges make it all the more important to be sure that the funds that are going into ECEC are being used wisely. We simply cannot afford the status quo, where public (and private) funds are being used to purchase care that is all too often not of good quality. Thus, limited funds do not mean we must set aside the quality agenda; indeed, the financial challenges make the quality improvement agenda all the more urgent.

Note

[1] The US is distinct from other peer countries in not having a national policy providing a period of paid leave to new mothers. Under the federal Family and Medical Leave Act, qualifying parents are able to take up to 12 weeks of job-protected leave after a birth, but the leave is unpaid

References

Almond, D. and Currie, J. (2011) 'Human Capital Development before Age Five', in O. Ashenfelter and D. Card (eds) *Handbook of Labor Economics, Volume 4b*, Amsterdam: Elsevier, pp 1315–486.

Bainbridge, J., Meyers, M., Tanaka, S. and Waldfogel, J. (2005) 'Who gets an early education? Family income and the gaps in enrolment of 3-5 year olds from 1968–2000', *Social Science Quarterly*, vol 86, no 3, pp 724–45.

Baker, M., Gruber, J. and Milligan, K. (2008) 'Universal child care, maternal labor supply, and family well-being', *Journal of Political Economy*, vol 116, no 4, pp 709-45.

Barnett, W.S., Megan, E., Carolan, J.F. and Squires, J.H. (2011) *The State of Preschool 2011: State Preschool Yearbook*, New Brunswick, NJ: National Institute for Early Education Research.

Bassok, D., Fitzpatrick, M., Loeb, S. and Paglaynan, A. (2012) *The Early Childhood Care and Education Workforce from 1990 through 2010: Changing Dynamics and Persistent Concerns*, Center on Education Policy and Workforce Competitiveness University of Virginia, CEPWC Working Paper Series No 5 (http://curry.virginia.edu/research/centers/cepwc/publications).

Bryant, D., Maxwell, K., Taylor, K., Poe, M., Peisner-Feinberg, E. and Bernier, K. (2003) *Smart Start and Preschool Child Care Quality in NC: Change Over Time and Relation to Children's Readiness*, Chapel Hill, NC: FPG Child Development Institute.

Burchinal, M. (2012) Presentation to the Office of Planning and Research Evaluation INQUIRE Meeting, 30 July.

Burchinal, M., Kainz, K. and Cai, Y. (2011) 'How well do our measures of quality predict child outcomes? A meta-analysis and coordinated analysis of data from large-scale studies of early childhood settings', in M. Zaslow, I. Martinez-Beck and K. Tout (eds) *Quality Measurement in Early Childhood Settings*, Baltimore, MD: Paul H. Brookes Publishing, pp 11–31.

Child Care Aware of America (2012) *Parents and the High Cost of Child Care*, Arlington, TX: Child Care Aware of America (www.naccrra.org/sites/default/files/default_site_pages/2012/cost_report_2012_final_081012_0.pdf).

Deming, D. (2009) 'Early childhood intervention and life-cycle skill development: Evidence from Head Start', *American Economic Journal: Applied Economics*, vol 1, no 3, pp 111–34.

Donahue, E. and Campbell, N.D. (2002) *Making Care Less Taxing: Improving State Child and Dependent Care Tax Provisions*, Washington, DC: National Women's Law Center.

Duncan, G., Ludwig, J. and Magnuson, K. (2007) 'Reducing poverty through preschool interventions', *The Future of Children*, vol 17, no 2, pp 143–60.

Duncan, G.J. and Magnuson, K. (2013) 'Investing in preschool programs', *Journal of Economic Perspectives*, vol 27, no 2, pp 109-31.

Early, D.M., Maxwell, K.L., Burchinal, M., Alva, S., Bender, R.H., Bryant, D., Cai, K., Clifford, R.M., Ebanks, C., Griffin, J.A., Henry, G.T., Howes, C., Iriondo-Perez, J., Jeon, H.-J., Mashburn, A.J., Peisner-Feinberg, E., Pianta, R.C., Vandergrift, N. and Zill, N. (2007) 'Teachers' education, classroom quality, and young children's academic skills: Results from seven studies of preschool programs', *Child Development*, vol 78, pp 558–80.

Esping-Andersen, G. (2004) 'Untying the Gordian knot of social inheritance', *Research in Social Stratification and Mobility*, vol 21, pp 115–38.

Esping-Andersen, G. (2009) *The Incomplete Revolution*, Cambridge: Polity Press.

Floyd, L. and Phillips, D. (2013) 'Child care and other support programs', *Future of Children*, vol 23, no 2, pp 79-97.

Fox, L., Han, W.-J., Ruhm, C. and Waldfogel, J. (2013) 'Time for children: Trends in the employment patterns of parents, 1967–2009', *Demography*, vol 50, no 1, pp 25–49.

Gibbs, C., Ludwig, J. and Miller, D.L. (2011) *Does Head Start Do Any Lasting Good?*, NBER Working Paper No 17452, Cambridge, MA: NBER.

Gornick, J. and Meyers, M. (2003) *Families that Work: Policies for Reconciling Parenthood and Employment*, New York: Russell Sage Foundation.

Greenberg, J.P. (2011) 'The impact of maternal education on children's enrolment in early childhood education and care', *Children and Youth Services Review*, vol 33, pp 1049–57.

Greenberg, M. (2007) 'Next steps for federal child care policy', *The Future of Children*, vol 17, no 2, pp 73–96.

Ha, Y. (2009) 'Stability of child-care subsidy use and earnings of low-income families', *Social Service Review*, vol 83, pp 495–523.

Ha, Y., Magnuson, K. and Ybarra, M. (2012) 'The association between child care subsidies and stability of care', *Children and Youth Services Review*, vol 34, pp 1834–44.

Han, W.-J., Ruhm, C., Waldfogel, J. and Washbrook, E. (2008) 'The timing of mothers' employment after childbirth', *Monthly Labor Review*, vol 131, no 6, pp 15–27.

Harms, T., Clifford, R.M. and Cryer, D. (1998) *Early Childhood Environment Rating Scale-Revised*, New York: Teachers College Press.

Haskins, R. and Barnett, W.S. (2010) 'New directions for America's early childhood policies', in R. Haskins and W.S. Barnett (eds) *Investing in Young Children: New Directions in Federal Preschool and Early Childhood Policy*, Washington, DC: Brookings Institution, pp 1–28.

Havnes, T. and Mogstad, M. (2011) 'No child left behind: subsidized child care and children's long-run outcomes', *American Economic Journal: Economic Policy*, vol 3, no 2, pp 97-129.

Havnes, T. and Mogstad, M. (2012) *Is Universal Child Care Leveling the Playing Field?*, CESifo Working Paper Series 4014, Munich: CESifo Group.

Hotz, V.J. and Xiao, M. (2011) 'The impact of regulations on the supply and quality of care in child care markets', *American Economic Review*, vol 101, pp 1775–805.

Iruka, I.U. and Carver, P.R. (2006) *National Household Education Surveys Program of 2005: Initial Results from the 2005 NHES Early Childhood Program Participation Survey, Nces*. Washington, DC: National Center for Education Statistics, Institute of Education Sciences, US Dept of Education.

Johnson, A. (2010) 'Child care subsidies: Who uses them and what do they buy low-income families and children?', Unpublished doctoral dissertation, Columbia University Teachers College.

Johnson, A., Martin, A. and Brooks-Gunn, J. (2013) 'Child-care subsidies and school readiness in kindergarten', *Child Development*, vol 84, no 5, pp 1806–22.

Kamerman, S. and Waldfogel, J. (2005) 'Market and non-market institutions in early childhood education and care', in R. Nelson (ed) *Market and Non-Market Institutions*, New York: Russell Sage Foundation, pp 185–212.

Karoly, L.A., California Wellness Foundation, Criminal Justice Program (Rand Corporation), and Labor and Population Program (1998) *Investing in Our Children: What We Know and Don't Know About the Costs and Benefits of Early Childhood Interventions*. Santa Monica, CA: Rand.

Kirp, D. (2007) *The Sandbox Investment: The Preschool Movement and Kids First Politics*, Cambridge, MA: Harvard University Press.

Ladd, H., Muschkin, C. and Dodge, K. (2012) *From Birth to School: Early Childhood Initiatives and Third Grade Outcomes in North Carolina*. Working Paper, Durham, NC: Sanford School of Public Policy, Duke University.

Lombardi, J. (2011) 'Going to scale: Lessons from Head Start', *Early Childhood Matters*, vol 117, pp 21–7.

Lombardi, J. (2012) Personal communication.

LoCasale-Crouch, J., Konold, T., Pianta, R., Howes, C., Burchinal, M., Bryant, D., Clifford, R., Early, D. and Barbarin, O. (2007) 'Observed classroom quality profiles in state-funded pre-kindergarten programs and associations with teacher, program, and classroom characteristics', *Early Childhood Research Quarterly*, vol 22, pp 3–17.

Ludwig, J. and Phillips, D. (2007) 'The benefits and costs of Head Start', *Social Policy Report*, vol 21, no 3, pp 1–18.

Magnuson, K. and Waldfogel, J. (2005) 'Child care, early education, and racial/ethnic test score gaps at the beginning of school', *The Future of Children*, vol 15, no 1, pp 169–96.

Magnuson, K. and Waldfogel, J. (2012) *The Role of Early Childhood Education in Changing SES Gaps in Achievement*, Working paper. NY: Columbia School of Social Work.

Magnuson, K., Lahaie, C. and Waldfogel, J. (2006) 'Preschool and school readiness of children of immigrants', *Social Science Quarterly*, vol 87, pp 1241–62.

Magnuson, K., Meyers, M. and Waldfogel, J. (2007) 'The effects of expanded public funding for early education and child care on enrolment in formal child care in the 1990s', *Social Service Review*, vol 81, no 1, pp 47–83.

Meyers, M., Rosenbaum, D., Ruhm, C. and Waldfogel, J. (2004) 'Inequality in early childhood education and care: What do we know?', in K. Neckerman (ed) *Social Inequality*, New York: Russell Sage Foundation Press, pp 223–69.

Meyers, M., Peck, L.R. Davis, E.E. Collins, A., Kreader, J.L., Georges, A., Weber, R., Schexnayder, D.T., Schroeder, D.G. and Olson, J.A. (2002) *The Dynamics of Child Care Subsidy Use: A Collaborative Study of Five States*, New York: National Center for Children in Poverty.

NICHD ECCRN (Early Child Care Research Network) (2002) 'Early child care and children's development prior to school entry: Results from the NICHD Study of Early Child Care', *American Educational Research Journal*, vol 39, pp 133–64.

NICHD ECCRN and Duncan, G. (2003) 'Modeling the impacts of child care quality on children's preschool cognitive development', *Child Development*, vol 74, pp 1454–75.

OECD (Organisation for Economic Co-operation and Development) (2012) *Education at a Glance 2012*, Paris: OECD (www.oecd.org/edu/EAG%202012_e-book_EN_200912.pdf).

Pianta, R., Paro, K.L. and Hamre, B. (2007) *Classroom Assessment Scoring System – CLASS*, Baltimore, MD: Brookes.

Raikes, A.H., Raikes, H.H. and Wilcox, B. (2005) 'Regulation, subsidy receipt and provider characteristics: What predicts quality in child care homes?', *Early Childhood Research Quarterly*, vol 20, pp 164–84.

Rigby, E., Ryan, R. and Brooks-Gunn, J. (2007) 'Child care quality in different state policy contexts', *Journal Of Policy Analysis & Management*, vol 26, pp 887–907.

Rosenbaum, D. and Ruhm, C. (2007) 'Family expenditures on child care', *The B.E. Journal of Economic Analysis and Policy*, article 34, vol 7, no 1 (www.bepress.com/bejeap/vol7/iss1/art34).

Rudisill, S. (Director, Office of Child Care, Administration for Children and Families, US Department of Health and Human Services) (2012) Personal communication.

Ruhm, C. (2011) 'Policies to assist parents with young children', *Future of Children,* vol 21, no 2, pp 37–68.

Ruhm, C. and Waldfogel, J. (2012) 'Long-term effects of early childhood care and education', *Nordic Economic Policy Review,* vol 1, pp 23–51.

Ruzek, E., Burchinal, M., Farkas, G. and Duncan, G. (2012) *The Quality of Toddler Child Care and Cognitive Outcomes at 24 Months: Propensity Score Analysis Results from the ECLS-B*, University of California, Irvine, Working Paper.

Ruzek, E., Burchinal, M., Farkas, G., Duncan, G., Dang, T. and Weilin, L. (2011) 'Does high quality childcare narrow the achievement gap at two years of age?', Paper presented at the Society for Research in Educational Effectiveness, March.

Shonkoff, J.P. and Phillips, D. (2000) *From Neurons to Neighborhoods: The Science of Early Childhood Development*, Washington, DC: National Academy Press.

Smith, L. (Deputy Assistant Secretary for Early Childhood, Administration for Children and Families, US Department of Health and Human Services) (2012) Personal communication.

Smolensky, E. and Gootman, J. (eds) (2003) *Working Families and Growing Kids: Caring for Children and Adolescents*, Washington, DC: National Academy Press.

Thornburg, K.R., Mayfield, W.A., Hawks, J.S. and Fuger, K.L. (2009) *The Missouri Quality Rating System School Readiness Study*, Columbia, MO: Center for Family Policy & Research.

Tout, K., Zaslow, M. and Berry, D. (2005) 'Quality and qualifications: Links between professional development and quality in early care and education settings', in M. Zaslow and I. Martinez-Beck (eds) *Critical Issues in Early Childhood Professional Development*, Baltimore, MD: Paul H. Brookes Publishing Co, pp 77–110.

US DHHS (Department of Health and Human Services) (2011) *State Issues and Innovation in Creating Integrated Early Learning and Development Systems*, Rockville, MD: US DHHS.

Waldfogel, J. (2006a) *What Children Need*, Cambridge, MA: Harvard University Press.

Waldfogel, J. (2006b) 'Early childhood policy: A comparative perspective', in K. McCartney and D. Phillips (eds) *The Handbook of Early Childhood Development*, London: Blackwell, pp 576–94.

Waldfogel, J. (2007) 'Work-family policies', in H. Holzer and D. Nightingale (eds) *Reshaping the American Workforce in a Changing Economy*, Washington, DC: Urban Institute Press, pp 273–92.

Waldfogel, J. (2009) 'The role of family policies in anti-poverty policy', in M. Cancian and S. Danziger (eds) *Changing Poverty, Changing Policies*, New York: Russell Sage Foundation, pp 242–65.

Washbrook, E., Ruhm, C. Waldfogel, J. and Han, W.-J. (2011) 'Public policies, women's employment after childbirth, and child well-being', *B.E. Journal of Economic Analysis and Policy*, vol 11, no 1, Article 43. DOI: 10.2202/1935-1682.2938

Weiland, C. and Yoshikawa, H. (in press) 'Impacts of a prekindergarten program on children's mathematics, language, literacy, executive function, and emotional skills', *Child Development*.

Zellman, G.L. and Fiene, R. (2012) *Validation of Quality Rating and Improvement Systems for Early Care and Education and School-Age Care*, Research-to-Policy, Research-to-Practice Brief OPRE 2012-29, Washington, DC: Office of Planning, Research and Evaluation, Administration for Children and Families, US Department of Health and Human Services (www.acf.hhs.gov/programs/opre/cc/childcare_technical/reports/val_qual_early.pdf).

Zellman, G.L. and Perlman, M. (2008) *Child-Care Quality Rating and Improvement Systems in Five Pioneer States: Implementation Issues and Lessons Learned*, Santa Monica, CA: RAND Corporation (www.rand.org/pubs/monographs/MG795).

Zellman, G.L., Perlman, M., Le, V.-N. and Setodji, C.M. (2008) *Assessing the Validity of the Qualistar Early Learning Quality Rating and Improvement System as a Tool for Improving Child-Care Quality*, Santa Monica, CA: RAND Corporation (www.rand.org/pubs/monographs/MG650).

TEN

Common challenges, lessons for policy

Kitty Stewart, Ludovica Gambaro, Jane Waldfogel and Jill Rutter

Although national contexts are different, countries face similar challenges in attempting to ensure that all children have access to high-quality early childhood education and care (ECEC) provision. There are inevitable tensions in trying to deliver on all three corners of what Katherine Magnuson and Jane Waldfogel refer to in their chapter on the US as the 'childcare triangle' – access, quality and affordability. In this concluding chapter we draw together the evidence from our eight country case studies to examine how different countries have best addressed these common challenges.

We begin by asking how disadvantaged children can be encouraged and enabled to access formal ECEC. Second, we ask what can be done to make sure that this provision is of the highest possible quality. We then explore how countries have addressed the trade-off between expanding access to include more children (or including them from an earlier age) and improving the quality of what is on offer. We go on to look at issues of delivery, including decentralised provision and the role of different sectors, including private for-profit providers. Finally, we come back to the bottom line: extending provision costs money, and so does improving quality. Do governments simply need to find more resources or are there ways to spend money more effectively?

Policies, of course, emerge and are implemented against a specific political and institutional context, and scholars of comparative social policy, pointing to the breadth of countries' dissimilarities, warn against the dangers of simple 'policy borrowing' (Mahon, 2006). As the individual chapters illustrate, national approaches to ECEC are underpinned by different social and cultural norms regarding gender equality and childhood, by differences between policy makers as to whether parental employment or child development is the prime focus of concern, and by differences in the length of time that childcare and early education have had a place on the policy agenda (see also, among others, Kremer, 2007; Lewis et al, 2008; Saraceno, 2011). Our aim in this chapter is not to advocate for importing particular policies into any one country, but to identify common themes and highlight insights from good practice which might be useful in thinking about the way ECEC is organised, funded and delivered. We also try not to focus too heavily on contemporary policy debates in any one country: our aim is to draw out broader lessons that will stand the test of time.

1. How can disadvantaged children be encouraged to access formal ECEC?

Consistently across countries, our chapters show that children from low-income and immigrant backgrounds are less likely to access ECEC services. The divide is much sharper for children under than over three, but universal enrolment even among over threes has not been achieved in many places. What can be done to address this?

Free services

One clear message is that free and universal services have much higher enrolment rates than services with a fee. In the UK and France, despite very different traditions of service organisation, universal free preschool for children aged three plus has resulted in near universal take-up.[1] In New Zealand, a policy of 20 hours' free ECEC has also been effective, with enrolment rates above 90% and a narrowing of enrolment gaps between children from different ethnic backgrounds. In the US, Magnuson and Waldfogel argue that extending state schooling downwards to include younger children in prekindergarten programmes is the way to close enrolment gaps; currently, private preschool and centre-based provision is expensive and low-income children, Hispanic and immigrant children are less likely to attend.

While universal policies appear to be most effective at reaching the disadvantaged, they are clearly expensive for government: in order to reach a relatively small group of children, the state pays for provision for many others who would attend anyway. Thus in England, increasing enrolment from around 60% to more than 90% of three-year-olds has been achieved at the cost of extending funding to cover all 90%.[2] There are both instrumental and intrinsic arguments in favour of a universal approach to providing ECEC. In instrumental terms, if early education leads to long-term gains in improved educational and social-behavioural outcomes, subsidising children from richer backgrounds in order to reach all children may be seen as a sensible social investment that will deliver a pay-off in the long run. The intrinsic value of a universal approach is underlined by Helen May in her chapter on

New Zealand, where the idea of early education as a right of the young child, whatever his or her background, has been central to the debate about how services are funded and delivered. Under this line of thought, free universal services are not just an expensive but effective way to reach the most vulnerable, but are part of government responsibility to all children.

Nevertheless, the high cost of a universal approach raises the question of whether it is *necessary* in order to ensure full enrolment: can targeted policies achieve the same goal? The most well-developed example of a targeted early education policy among our case study countries is the Head Start programme in the US, which serves only children below the poverty line or with disabilities. Magnuson and Waldfogel argue that a greater share of low-income children have been enrolled in preschool programmes in years when funding for Head Start and other targeted programmes have been more generous. But enrolment of three-year-olds remains below 20% for the bottom two quintiles of the population, and indeed below 50% for all but the richest quintile, raising questions about whether targeting is appropriate if full enrolment is the aim. Furthermore, some commentators have raised concerns about the lack of social mix in Head Start centres, especially in light of research that suggests that peer effects are important. England has now introduced targeted free provision for the 40% most disadvantaged two-year-olds, alongside universal provision for three- and four-year-olds. This has been cautiously welcomed amid concerns that outreach to draw in families for a targeted service will be harder than it has been for the universal entitlement, both because of the need to identify eligible families and because of potential stigma. The effectiveness of the strategy in comparison to the free universal offer will provide an interesting comparison of the two approaches.

A second question is whether making provision free and universal is *sufficient* to draw in the most disadvantaged groups. In England, the last 7–8% of three-year-olds have proved difficult to reach, despite considerable focus on outreach: central government issues guidance on good practice and requires local authorities to collect and publish data on uptake by disadvantaged groups. In New Zealand, while enrolment gaps have narrowed under the universal strategy, participation remains considerably lower for Pasifika and Māori children. New Zealand has responded in two ways: first, with a greater focus on targeted initiatives, funded by a shift to subsidised rather than free universal hours. Helen May raises concerns about this change, arguing that the most effective strategy is universal access *plus* outreach to vulnerable groups, not one or the other. In a second and still more controversial move, New Zealand is experimenting with compulsion as a way to bring some targeted groups into early education: since July 2013, 15 hours' ECEC attendance has been obligatory for children of benefit recipients from the age of three. The New Zealand Early Childhood Council, representing community and private early childhood centres, has lent this policy its support, but critics are concerned that the threat of benefit sanctions can only add further stress to families already in difficult circumstances, thereby undermining rather than supporting child development.[3]

One final question that arises in relation to free provision is how effectively it fits into a system of childcare for working parents. If many settings delivering the free entitlement operate half-day sessions only, as in the UK, there is the danger of a split between settings that cater part time for children of non-working parents, and those that cater full time for children whose parents work. This is a concern for two reasons: it increases the likelihood of social segregation between settings, and it creates an extra barrier to employment for parents who get their children started with a part-time provider. An effective system of wrap-around care – such as childminders – can prevent both problems, but at the cost of the child experiencing an additional transition between carers each day. Where free provision covers the full school day (as in France) the divide does not arise. Likewise, where settings have the flexibility to offer both sessional and full-day placements (as in New Zealand), part-time free provision appears to reduce the cost of ECEC across the board and increase the number of hours children attend without reinforcing segregation.

Fees and charges

Where there are fees or charges, a number of aspects of funding design appear to help increase participation among disadvantaged groups. One is to have place guarantees and subsidy systems that apply to all families, not just those where parents are working. In Norway, the legal right to a kindergarten place extends to all children from the age of one regardless of their parents' employment status (something that marks Norway out even from some other Scandinavian countries, such as Sweden). State subsidies also extend to all children in Norway, as in New Zealand, Australia, the Netherlands (playgroups only), France (*crèches* only) and some German *Länder* (for example, Hamburg, after initial criticism of its voucher system). In contrast, in the UK and the US, children of non-working parents can routinely access subsidised services only when they reach the age of three, although England has now extended free provision to disadvantaged two-year-olds, as noted before.

Second, the extent to which costs vary with income is clearly important. Almost all the countries in our study operate some sort of income-based charging policy, whether this is a sliding fee paid at the point of access (as in Norway, Germany, New Zealand, the US, playgroups in the Netherlands and *crèches* in France), or an income-related reimbursement paid later to eligible parents through the tax system (the UK, Australia, some US states, working parents in the Netherlands and parents opting for childminders in France). However, the extent of support varies considerably, and a system can be income related without being very generous to those at the bottom of the income distribution. In the UK, tax credit subsidies are tightly targeted on working families on low incomes, but even families receiving the maximum level of support still pay at least 30% of the cost of a childcare place. In the Netherlands, in contrast, all families receive some reimbursement, and those receiving the most support pay just 3.5% of fees, while the highest-income households pay two-thirds. Designing subsidies to be both income related and generous to those most in need raises a basic conundrum which is common to all means-tested systems: if support is withdrawn steeply as income rises, this can create disincentives to increase hours or earnings. To minimise this problem, systems that operate very low or no-fee systems for the lowest-income families need to offer some support to all.

In Norway, very high participation among younger children from disadvantaged backgrounds has been achieved by a combination of policies: the legal guarantee to a place for all children alongside fees that are both low overall and income related. Anne Lise Ellingsæter points to significant growth in the numbers accessing formal care between 2000 and 2011, a period in which services were expanding and parental fees were reduced. Attendance remains higher among higher-income parents, but rates increased fastest between 2004–08 for families on lower incomes. Some 60% of one- to two-year-olds living with a single parent with no employment income are enrolled in kindergarten, as are 31% of those with two non-working parents; these rates are far higher than those for equivalent groups in any of the other countries in our study.

However, it is worth emphasising that even low fees appear to deter access compared to free provision. Pilot projects in Oslo offering free childcare for all four- and five-year-olds found almost all children participating, but when a fee of €80 a month was introduced, one-third of children failed to appear. In France, sliding income-related fees for under threes do not appear to be sufficient to solve the access problem: attendance among low-income families is low in *crèches* despite the high value placed on this type of care in French society, and despite priority access being given to lone mothers. Low-income families make use of extended parental leave, use informal provision or work in shifts to avoid the need to pay for care outside the home. In Germany, fees are income related but take-up is still low among families with a migration background. In Australia, Deb Brennan and Marianne Fenech point to non-working families' eligibility for 24 hours a week of Child Care Benefit (CCB) as a positive feature of the system there, but note that the need to make a part-payment (known in Australia as the 'gap fee') appears to be a major obstacle to participation among families without work.

A third point is that subsidies should be transparent and stable – unlike in the US, where the median spell of receipt of childcare subsidies is about six months, which in turn is linked to instability in care providers. Means-tested support may operate as a barrier to access if it is difficult for parents to calculate how much they will be required to pay: upfront income-related fees may be preferable for this reason to reimbursement through the tax credit system, as in the UK. Income-related fees have the additional advantage for low-income parents that payment is made directly to providers, rather than parents meeting the cost and then claiming a reimbursement, although intermediate options are possible, as in Australia, where families can choose to have CCB paid directly to their service provider. Avoiding the need for reimbursement is likely to be particularly important where subsidies extend to include the children of non-working parents, for whom upfront payment would be most difficult. It is probably no coincidence that countries that subsidise provision for non-working families tend to operate income-related fees rather than reimbursement systems. Income-related fees are much easier to implement in publicly provided systems, such as France, but the experiences of Norway and Germany suggest that they can also work where private providers are involved.

2. How can disadvantaged children be assured high-quality provision?

The second major challenge is how to ensure that the provision on offer is high quality, and in particular, that where disadvantaged children are participating in ECEC they are accessing the highest quality services available. There are two aspects to this: the quality of provision in a country overall, and fair access to that quality. We look at these issues in turn.

Overall quality of provision

Our eight countries use similar policy levers to promote quality – curriculum, staff qualifications, child-to-staff ratios and inspection and monitoring – but they combine and design them differently, placing varying degrees of emphasis on particular levers.

For one thing, there is a broad divide between an approach that mandates a detailed curriculum, which is roughly the way the UK has moved, and a looser arrangement in which highly qualified staff are given more freedom. Norway represents the latter model: as Anne Lise Ellingsæter describes, kindergartens in Norway are charged with laying a sound foundation for the child's development, lifelong learning and active participation in a democratic society. There are few standard requirements, and supervision is up to the municipality. But graduate-level teachers are required in all kindergartens, and heads and pedagogical leaders must also be graduates (with exemptions when no qualified candidates are available). The New Zealand model also fits this mould, with a broad curriculum, *Te Whāriki*, which was itself a key driver of the attempt to move towards a policy of 100% qualified teachers in all early childhood provision, because the curriculum requires practitioners to be reflective, research-oriented and equipped with relevant knowledge. Rather than telling teachers what to cover, *Te Whāriki* requires them to 'weave' their own curriculum patterns around five strands of empowerment: wellbeing, belonging, contribution, communication and exploration.

In England, in contrast, the Early Years Foundation Stage (EYFS) curriculum is detailed and specific. There have been significant increases in the last 15 years in the proportion of staff with vocational qualifications, and investment in a new graduate qualification, but the proportion of graduates among ECEC staff remains relatively low. Germany is following a similar pattern: attempts to improve the quality of provision during the last decade have largely focused on the development of early childhood curricula frameworks. In both England and Germany, curricula are holistic, participatory, play-based and child-centred, not narrowly focused on cognitive achievement, and they have been welcomed by early childhood experts, but in both countries there are concerns about whether they can be effectively delivered without more educated staff. Pamela Oberhuemer points out that, in Germany, only 4% of staff are educated to degree level, which is particularly low given that the system covers children up to the age of six.

A second contrast is in the emphasis placed on monitoring and inspection: this is carried out in a much more systematic and centralised way in all four UK nations, with their official ratings by the education (or care) inspectorate, than in any of the other seven countries. In the Netherlands and Norway, local governments are in charge of monitoring. In Norway, municipalities must develop a plan for supervision, but what form this takes, and how often it happens, is left up to the municipality; the use of the word 'supervision' instead of 'inspection' is interesting in itself. In Germany, *Länder* governments take different approaches, but Pamela Oberhuemer describes the control measures to ensure compliance with the curriculum as generally low key and mainly based on agreements with provider organisations. The US case is difficult to characterise – on the whole, the system relies more heavily on regulations and inspections to ensure quality than it does on curricula, but the strength of those regulations and of inspection systems varies widely by state.

A third area of difference across countries concerns approaches to child-to-staff ratios and qualifications. On the surface, there is some evidence of a trade-off between ratios and qualifications. Both New Zealand and France have more highly trained staff than the UK, for example, alongside a higher ratio of children to each staff member, certainly for younger children. In New Zealand the ratio is 5:1 for children under two and 10:1 for those two plus, and in French *crèches* 5:1 for children who are not yet walking and 8:1 for other children. At the time of writing, a ratio of 3:1 was required for under twos in England and 4:1 for two-year-olds.

This raises the possibility that countries with low ratios might consider raising them to fund higher-qualified staff, but a little nuance is needed.[4] First, in New Zealand there are concerns that ratios are too high, and proposals to bring them down have been mooted. Second, Norway, another country where qualification requirements are very high, operates with ratios very similar to those in the UK, although this is disguised by the fact that municipalities make the decision, with the national requirement simply to ensure that ratios are 'adequate'. Anne Lise Ellingsæter reports that the average ratio in practice in Norway is 3.4 children per adult for under threes. A third point is that cultural differences in the way education is perceived may affect the appropriate ratio in particular countries. High child-to-staff ratios require more focus on groups and less individual attention, and this may fit better with some national models of learning than others.

Other countries in our study currently operate with relatively high ratios alongside relatively low-qualified staff. In Germany, ratios vary across *Länder* from a high of just over 6:1 for under threes in Brandenburg, to a low of just over 3:1 in Saarland. In the Netherlands, where all staff must have completed 'intermediate' vocational training (but just 5% have higher qualifications than this), ratios average 5:1 in both playgroups and day-care centres. However, while this model may help to deliver childcare at lower cost, in both these countries measures of process quality are low, so the combination of high ratios and low qualifications does not look a promising model to follow in terms of quality.

A fourth issue worth highlighting here is the difference in national approaches to the requirements of staff working with younger and older children. Only Norway and New Zealand have the same professional figure working across all age groups – pedagogues in Norway, specifically trained to work with children under six, and teachers in New Zealand. In Germany, staff also work across age groups, but at a lower professional level. Elsewhere a divide is common between the staff employed for three- and four-year-olds and those for younger children. In France, staff in *crèches* (including *crèche* directors) have a background in health rather than education, while in *écoles maternelles* staff are trained teachers. In the UK it is widely accepted in principle that three- and four-year-olds should have access to a teacher, but there is much less consensus about whether this is necessary for younger children.

Finally, across countries centre-based provision is consistently more stringently regulated and has higher staff requirements than home-based arrangements, although several countries have introduced recent reforms to improve childminding quality. In France, initial training has been extended to 12 months, and there has been an expansion of centres offering childminders support and advice. In New Zealand and England, home-based providers must implement the national curriculum, and in England childminders are inspected and rated by the national inspectorate. In New Zealand, home-based providers are coordinated by teachers who visit them monthly and support their practice. It is also worth noting in relation to home-based services that, in almost all countries, only a small percentage of children attend. The exception to this pattern is France, where childminding is the most common mode of provision for children under three. However, Jeanne Fagnani explains that patterns of usage seem to reflect the availability of services rather than preference, as the high demand for *crèches* suggests. This echoes what Ellingsæter and Guldbransen (2007) describe for

Norway, where family-based provision declined rapidly once centre-based places became available.

To some extent, the discussion so far suggests that high-quality ECEC provision might take several different forms. Indeed, what quality looks like will depend in some respects on national preferences and priorities (see, for example, Dahlberg and Moss, 1997). Equally, however – and especially given our focus in this book on child development – too much relativism would be misplaced. Measures of process quality, such as those captured by the Early Childhood Environment Rating Scale (ECERS), Infant/Toddler Environment Rating Scale (ITERS) and Classroom Assessment Scoring System (CLASS), or those developed within individual countries, point to some national arrangements as being more satisfactory than others. Recent national studies in Germany and the US find that only around 10% of settings are of high quality, with the bulk of provision judged as mediocre. The analysis presented by Emre Akgündüz and Janneke Plantenga offers a similar picture for the Netherlands, with fairly low scores for instructional support. Further, structural indicators, and in particular highly qualified staff, have been found to predict higher process quality, and Norway, New Zealand and France (for over threes) are our frontrunners on these indicators. For New Zealand, Helen May reports that the variations in process quality across types of services were found to be related to the quality of leadership and staff qualifications, echoing findings from the Effective Provision of Preschool Education (EPPE) study in England, and lending support to an approach to quality that is centred on well-qualified staff.

Equal access to quality

We turn now to consider mechanisms that ensure that access to higher-quality provision is fair, and that children who are disadvantaged at home are not also disadvantaged in early education. Having high-quality provision on average is one of the key factors, of course, but the way that settings are organised and funded can make a difference to how far the highest quality settings in a country are accessible to the most disadvantaged children.

In general, where chapters provided evidence of the relationship between children's background and ECEC quality, they showed that disadvantaged children were more likely to attend lower quality settings, but the relationship was less clear-cut than might have been expected. In the US, children from low-income families attend lower quality services on average, and this seems true of prekindergarten as well as other programmes. Similarly, in Germany, evidence suggests that Turkish children attend settings with a less favourable learning environment than German children. In England, *within* sectors (focusing on either the private, voluntary and independent sector, PVI, or on state nursery classes) quality is lower in more disadvantaged areas, although the gradient is not steep.

On the other hand, staff qualification requirements are higher in the state sector than the PVI in England, and this works to protect disadvantaged children, as state settings are predominantly found in disadvantaged areas. In the Netherlands, ECEC is characterised by a striking degree of social segregation, with children from dual-income families attending full day-care settings and those from lower-income and minority backgrounds attending playgroups, but the quality of provision is fairly equal (although low) for all. Playgroup staff are similarly qualified to day-care staff, and no large difference in process quality was identified between the two sectors: children from higher socio-economic backgrounds experience better support for emotional but not cognitive development. In Norway, high staff qualification requirements ensure that all provision appears to be of relatively high quality, although Ellingsæter notes that in Oslo – where most immigrants are – there are more difficulties in teacher recruitment.

The absence of a sharper relationship between background and quality is surprising given that all the countries in our study operate a childcare market, to a greater or lesser extent. A market would be expected to deliver sorting, with higher-income parents purchasing higher-quality provision. The fact that this happens less than expected is welcome, but also poses something of a puzzle. A possible explanation is that quality is either not very important or (more likely) not very visible to parents. As has been observed in the healthcare field (for example, Propper, 1996; Propper et al, 2006), and as David Blau and Naci Mocan have argued with regard to childcare (Blau and Mocan, 2002; Mocan, 2007), if a market operates on both price and quality, and consumers do not observe quality clearly, they make decisions based on price, which in turn discourages providers from investing in quality: why spend more when the main observed effect will be higher prices? In the Netherlands, this phenomenon is visible in the way the reimbursement limit operates in effect as a soft cap on fees: centres that charge a higher fee than that covered by the subsidy appear to get priced out. On the surface, this is encouraging from an equity but not a quality perspective: it suggests that the free market does not bid up quality, as is sometimes expected. On reflection, low-quality provision across the board is not good for equity either, as disadvantaged children have most to gain from high-quality provision, and therefore most to lose from mediocre settings.

What conclusions can we draw about how countries might look to improve quality with an eye on disadvantaged children in particular?

First, while competition does not appear to bid up quality automatically, it might do so with more information – but this is likely to have negative effects for equality of access. Increasingly, countries are taking this route, with the publication, for example, of quality ratings in Australia, Ofsted ratings in the UK, and Tiered Quality Rating and Improvement Systems (TQRIS) and star ratings in the US; both the latter are countries in which a relationship between social background and ECEC quality has been identified. In the Netherlands, Akgündüz and Plantenga suggest that higher emotional support identified for children of richer parents may be because this aspect of provision is easier for parents to observe (and perhaps more highly valued in the Dutch context), while no other ratings data are available; ratings systems reflecting wider aspects of quality might therefore shift parental behaviour in the Netherlands. Choice may lead to a social gradient even where the state pays the full cost of provision, as the literature on school choice testifies, but where subsidies are partial or parents are able to top up a state contribution, the challenges to equity increase.

The obvious way to minimise this problem is for the state to set sufficiently high minimum standards for all settings over key drivers of quality such as staff qualifications, so that choice is exercised over less crucial aspects of provision, as, for example, in Norway – where further limits are imposed by a maximum fee. But this is expensive, and the state must meet the costs or risk pricing lower and middle-income families out of formal provision altogether, a danger Brennan and Fenech's chapter underlines sharply for Australia. There are also practical questions about a sudden shift to new mandatory requirements in the absence of sufficient numbers of appropriately trained staff.

An intermediate option is for the state to be more explicit in using subsidies to promote quality, so rather than paying a flat subsidy to settings which is topped up by parental fees, centres which invest in quality receive higher levels of funding, allowing them to improve without pricing out lower-income families. Examples of this are surprisingly rare, but New Zealand provides a model: quality funding bands ensure that centres which employ more qualified staff receive higher levels of funding from government. In England, local authorities can give providers quality supplements in their funding for the three- and four-year-old entitlement, but as authorities themselves receive a fixed budget, few make use of this possibility as it would mean other settings would suffer. On the other hand, dedicated funding streams (such as the Graduate Leader Fund, which ran in England from 2006 to 2011) have proved effective. In the US, TQRIS in some instances provide higher levels of subsidy payments for more highly rated programmes; in North Carolina, for example, settings are financially supported to train and employ more highly qualified staff, with a view to mandating higher qualifications in the long run.

An alternative mechanism for ensuring that the settings accessed by disadvantaged children are high quality is to promote the quality of part-time provision. This has happened in England by historical accident: state nursery classes and schools have higher staff qualification requirements and are located in inner-city areas, where there are high concentrations of low-income and minority ethnic families, and as a result more disadvantaged three- and four-year-olds are much *more* likely to access a setting with a teacher than their better-off peers. The development of *écoles maternelles* for two-year-olds in urban France might be a similar story, although it is not clear that they provide higher-quality provision for this age group than the French *crèches*. In the Netherlands, investing in the quality of playgroups would be a way to target quality improvements on the most disadvantaged groups.

On the other hand, while this is a pragmatic approach, certainly in the short run, it is also a strategy with limitations. First, it ignores the situation of children of low-income working parents in full-time settings. Second, it does nothing to tackle social segregation, and if peer group effects exist (as research by Mathers et al, 2007, for England, and Shager, 2012, for the US, suggests they do), or simply if social mixing has intrinsic value as a part of education, policy needs to be breaking down the distinction between part-time and full-time settings, rather than working with it. Third, part-time provision does little to support an easy transition to work. A part-time place in a state nursery school in England is a good thing from a child development perspective, but logistically complicated for a working parent, and probably means non-working mothers postponing looking for work until a child starts full-time school. This in turn means these places are not doing a good job of supporting poverty reduction during early childhood. Increased funding for *all* settings in disadvantaged areas – similar to the school-level pupil premium in England and Wales – may be a less divisive and more productive strategy.

3. The trade-off between expanding access and improving quality

Several of our countries have seen rapid labour market, demographic and behavioural change in recent years, with significant increases in demand for ECEC provision, particularly for younger children. Ellingsæter points to the 'toddler invasion' in Norway, in which the share of one- to two-year-olds attending kindergarten increased from 37% in 2000 to 80% in 2011. In Germany, participation rates for under threes rose from 9% in 2002 to over 25% in 2011. France has been focused on increasing formal childcare places in the face of a rising birth rate and an increasing reliance on two incomes, while in the Netherlands demand for institutionalised childcare has also grown rapidly since the 1990s with growing female labour force participation. While expanding access, countries have also been trying to improve quality in response to a better understanding of the role of ECEC in child development. Has this led to trade-offs between the two?

Certainly, some countries have expanded provision by compromising on quality. In France, low-qualified women in disadvantaged areas have been encouraged to become childminders, both to increase places in the absence of sufficient *crèche* capacity and to increase female employment directly. Ratios have also been relaxed so that registered childminders can look after four children instead of three. Jeanne Fagnani argues that recent reforms have been driven more by labour market pressure than by the best interest of the child, although there have been simultaneous attempts to improve the training and support available to childminders. On the other hand, direct regulation of childminders' wages has pushed up prices, so this form of care is no longer accessible to the poorest families who instead rely on informal care or shift working; this resonates with debates in England around tighter regulations for childminders which have improved quality, but increased prices. A system which prices lower-income families out of formal provision is clearly not helpful for disadvantaged children, but nor is cheap but low-quality formal care.

In the Netherlands, the government met rising demand with a radical switch from supply-side to demand-side financing in 2005, intended to stimulate an expansion of private sector places. The switch did succeed in increasing places, but indicators of process quality fell markedly. Akgündüz and Plantenga suggest that this fall in quality is not a direct result of the change in funding itself, but may be due to the speed of expansion, with staff shortages, a lack of management experience and difficulties in inspecting and regulating quality during such rapid expansion.

On the other hand, in Norway quality has increased alongside places, indicating that it is possible to act on both fronts at once with sufficient state funding. A survey of kindergartens in 2008 showed that structural quality had improved in parallel with sector expansion, with the share of staff in private kindergartens who are qualified teachers rising from 2004.

However, first, short-term problems of staffing are likely to be inevitable during periods of rapid expansion, and countries have to find ways to address this, perhaps by weakening training requirements in the short run and providing in-post training and support. In France, *crèche* requirements have been reduced so that only 40% rather than 50% of staff need hold a specialised qualification. In Germany, some *Länder* have introduced faster pathways to qualifications to meet the rapid rise in demand for staff.

Second, where resources are short, trade-offs are unavoidable, and there are no obvious answers except to keep both quality and access goals in mind. Very high-quality provision is not much good for disadvantaged children if they cannot access it, and this may justify, for example, the dilution of the New Zealand government's 100% teacher policy to a goal of 80% if funds are used as pledged to improve participation among Māori and Pasifika children. In Australia, recent ambitious moves to improve quality by guaranteeing all four-year-olds access to a trained teacher have been widely welcomed, but have raised concerns that without sufficient funding the result may be better-off children receiving high-quality provision and the less well-off not accessing formal care at all; Australia has opted to make the provision high quality, but not free (somewhat in contrast to the entitlement in England). On the other hand, easy access to low-quality provision is a cause for concern, as highlighted by research in the US and Canada which has identified a negative association between childcare subsidies and child outcomes.

In light of these tensions, some countries are attempting to improve quality without spending (much) more money. For example, the US is pursuing federal competition for Head Start funding along with a requirement for Head Start programmes to use CLASS indicators to monitor quality and inform improvements. Similarly, self-evaluation using ECERS is being encouraged and supported by local authorities working with providers in England. However, while these strategies may hold some promise, there are limits to what can be achieved without additional resources for materials, training and higher wages, as Deborah Brennan and Marianne Fenech point out.

Finally, given the use made of informal care by many disadvantaged families, the value of policies that improve the quality of informal care should not be forgotten. The Sure Start children's centre model in England has been successful at providing a hub for integrated services, including 'stay-and-play' sessions and other activities for children, and social opportunities and parenting support for parents and informal carers. Children's centres have inspired similar strategies elsewhere, including family centres in Germany and *multi-accueil* centres in France, as the chapters by Fagnani and Oberhuemer testify, while integrated child and family centres are also being established in Australia, specifically targeting indigenous families.

4. Delivery: what matters?

Under this heading, we discuss four issues about the way ECEC is delivered and the extent to which these issues matter from the perspective of disadvantaged children's access to high-quality provision. We consider two issues of governance – ECEC responsibility at ministerial level, and the question of decentralisation. We then consider which sectors are involved in delivery, and in particular, whether problems arise from having for-profit providers in the mix. Finally, we raise some issues regarding the workforce.

Ministerial responsibility

The integration of early education and childcare services under a single ministerial responsibility, preferably the education ministry, has long been a recommendation of both early childhood experts and international organisations such as the Organisation for Economic Co-operation and Development (OECD) (2006; Kaga et al, 2010). Most of the countries in our study have moved in this direction, but in France there is continuing division, with responsibility for *crèches* for under threes falling under social security and health and *écoles maternelles* under education. In the US, federal childcare policy is housed in the Department of Health and Human Services, although with recent links established with the Department of Education. In England, the Department for Education is the lead body, but the Department for Work and Pensions continues to have some responsibility. While formal responsibility may reveal social and political attitudes to the role of ECEC, our sense from our country case studies is that its practical significance for the nature, quality and equality of provision may today be overstated, and that a commitment to integrating, coordinating and improving services matters more than where responsibility is based.

Decentralisation

A repeated theme in the chapters is the trade-off between allowing lower levels of governance to be responsive to local needs and priorities, and ensuring overall equality across states/*Länder*/local authorities. In the federal states in our study – Germany, the US and Australia – it is notable that children experience very different services depending on where they live. On the other hand, local variation also provides opportunities for innovation and for learning from both good and bad practice. Local governments can also play an important role in supporting small providers to improve quality, a role centralised inspectorate systems are unlikely to cover, although funding from central government is needed to make this possible.

For a federal government, two roles seem important: first, to impose (or at least to encourage) minimum standards on all states or authorities; and second, to ensure that there is an effective method of open coordination, so that successful policies can be adopted (and adjusted) elsewhere. Australia's new National Quality Framework (NQF) aims to bring all states into a single quality assurance scheme, and imposes minimum standards on child-to-staff ratios and qualification requirements which will require significant changes in some states; the extent to which it will also facilitate policy learning across states is not yet clear. Germany's National Quality Initiative (2000–06) led to a non-binding Common Framework for Early Education which was agreed by ministers in all 16 *Länder*.

Decentralisation also raises issues with respect to funding. First, there are questions about how far funding from central to local governments should be ring-fenced or earmarked rather than fungible to other spending areas. The message here seems to be that until services are really established, earmarked funding is important, and that a shift away from earmarking is in any case risky without strong quality regulations. Norway has recently made the move from earmarked to general-purpose block grant funding, but in the context of a guaranteed right to a kindergarten place for all children and a structure of provision that already covers very high numbers. To date, the shift has not led to changes in municipal behaviour, but a government-appointed expert commission has called for additional quality regulations and controls to ensure that quality does not fall as a result of the change. Where services are less well established, the absence of earmarked funding could be problematic for access as well as quality, even where there is a formal entitlement to a place. In Germany, the entitlement that came into force from August 2013 does not seem to have been sufficient to force *Länder* to provide more places.

A second issue concerns the way in which central funding to local authorities responds to quality improvements at local level. The English experience shows that if funding from central to local government is unrelated to quality, it is difficult to create such incentives at a lower level: local governments rarely use their right to give providers quality supplements because it would mean other providers (often weaker providers in need of support) suffering. Likewise, in Germany, the amount of federal money *Länder* receive is not related to quality measures. In the US, on the other hand, Waldfogel and Magnuson describe how the Obama administration has sought to promote quality by providing states with additional funding, provided that they operate certain quality improvement initiatives.

The 'mixed economy' and the role of the private sector

By design, all the countries in the study have a mix of providers, and many of them have a growing number of for-profit providers. In France, provision of childcare services has been open to for-profit providers since 2002 with the explicit objective of increasing the availability of childcare places. In Norway, half of kindergartens are private; many are owned by parents, but for-profit actors are increasingly involved. In New Zealand the number of private sector providers grew by 47% between 2007 and 2011, compared to 3% for community services. In the Netherlands, publicly provided day-care disappeared after the funding reform of 2005, and only private for-profits (60%) and not-for-profits (40%) remain. Germany remains an exception, in which two-thirds of settings are run by non-governmental organisations (NGOs); but there are virtually no for-profit settings.

Concerns have been raised that making profits from the provision of early education is unethical in itself, and that the involvement of for-profit providers is damaging to quality because resources are siphoned off for shareholders rather than invested in staff wages and other quality inputs (see, for example, Penn, 2012; Sumison, 2012). For-profit providers also have a motive to focus attention on higher-income families, which might not be conducive to equity of access. On the other hand, market logic predicts that a for-profit sector should drive up quality as providers compete to draw parents in – assuming parents know what quality is and value it.

The few studies that specifically investigate this issue are from North America, and find that quality is often worse in the for-profit sector (Blau and Currie, 2006; Sosinsky et al, 2007; Cleveland and Krashinsky, 2009). In several countries, including Australia and the UK, research is hampered by the fact that publicly available data do not distinguish between for-profit and non-profit settings, but in England, state-maintained settings have been found to have the highest process quality, while those in the voluntary sector have made the fastest quality improvements in recent years (Mathers et al, 2007). In New Zealand, there is concern that private centres have been slower in moving towards qualified teacher targets and have poorer staff conditions. In Norway, municipal kindergartens have been found to be strongest at planning and providing training and education.

On the other hand, the contrasting situations of Norway and Germany show that high-quality provision can operate with a for-profit sector, while having not-for-profit providers is no guarantee of high quality. In Norway, the set-up appears to work because of strong quality requirements (staff qualifications) alongside limits on both prices (a price cap) and profits: profits are only allowed if they are 'reasonable' – and they are not considered reasonable if personnel costs are significantly lower than in municipal kindergartens. These tight regulations are particularly important in Norway because of the high levels of state subsidy to the sector; constraints are needed to ensure that government money is spent on the service and does not leak out into profits.

It should be noted, however, that the for-profit sector is still small in Norway. A more substantial for-profit sector, and one which includes large corporations, may be more difficult to manage as its size gives it greater power to resist regulatory reforms. This is one of the lessons of the Australian experience, in which a single chain, ABC, gained 25% of the childcare market before going into receivership in 2008. Brennan and Fenech argue that the private sector in Australia has acted as a brake on campaigns to improve regulatory standards in that country.

Furthermore, there is no evidence in our study that the presence of a for-profit sector will itself drive quality improvements. The experience of the Netherlands after its shift to a competitive childcare market was the opposite, with a measured decline in the quality of provision. This seems to be because quality is not well observed by parents, giving providers no incentive to invest in quality improvements. The message is that quality can be high in the private sector, but this comes about through regulation and tighter standards (which are likely to reduce profitability), not through pressure of competition, which is likely to be dominated by price.

One last issue worth highlighting under this heading is that the mixed economy may be an important factor contributing to the fragmentation of provision, and to less continuity for children as they grow. Norway stands out as the only one of our eight countries in which, while different providers are involved, there is one type of setting that covers the full age spectrum, and continuity of care from age one to age six is the norm. Perhaps choice and fragmentation are two sides of the same coin, and the price Norwegian parents pay for continuity is having fewer options. But as Hirschman (1970) argued, 'voice' can be as effective as choice in improving public services, and parental involvement on kindergarten boards in Norway appears to ensure that kindergartens respond to local needs.

Workforce issues

The workforce is clearly a central factor in the delivery of ECEC. The issue of staff educational requirements was touched on earlier in the chapter, but a second recurrent theme in the country studies is that of pay. Perhaps surprisingly, a problem of low pay emerges as a common theme in all the countries in our study and not only where minimal training requirements are likely to contribute to a 'low educated, low paid' workforce.

Highly qualified staff in the sector are found to command relatively low pay for their level of qualification, unless their wage is set at a par with that of teachers in compulsory education. Such parity exists in France and England, where écoles maternelles and nursery classes are an integral part of the school system and where preschool teachers belong to the same occupational group as primary school teachers. But when ECEC is delivered outside schools, pay is invariably lower. In Norway, where the presence of graduate staff is fairly large, kindergarten teachers have low wages, not only in comparison to other groups with higher education, but also relative to other teachers. In New Zealand, parity of pay between kindergarten teachers and primary and secondary school teachers was the outcome of a trade union struggle (May, 2005), but the same agreement did not cover teachers in care and education centres. As qualification requirements increase, the question of pay parity with other occupational groups – and with teachers in particular – will inevitably become more pressing.

A second question regards pay differentials among ECEC workers with different qualifications. In both the UK and Australia, wages are fairly flat, and workers are not rewarded financially if they upgrade their qualifications. In these contexts, quality initiatives centred on the promotion of new qualifications alone are likely to be short-lived unless they are underpinned by funding able to cover higher salaries.

More generally, adequate pay levels appear necessary simply to recruit and retain sufficient numbers of staff, irrespective of their qualifications. In France, Jeanne Fagnani explains how minimum pay requirements for childminders were introduced with the aim of making childminding more attractive and thus expanding supply. In the US, Waldfogel and Magnuson report how a positive trend in childcare workers' pay since the 1990s has been matched by a reduction in turnover rates.

5. Spending more or spending smarter?

An unavoidable truth that emerges from this study is that putting more public resources into ECEC helps to ensure both that quality is high and that all children are able to access it. The countries that perform best on the combination of access and quality, France and Norway, are those that we identified in Chapter One as pushing the boat out on the third corner of the 'childcare triangle', with the highest level of spending as a share of GDP. That providing high-quality ECEC in a fair and accessible way is expensive may be an unwelcome conclusion in an era of recession and retrenchment, but the wide differences reported in Table 1.4 remind us that countries do have choices, whatever the fiscal circumstances. As Jeanne Fagnani points out in her chapter, France has continued to increase investment in ECEC even in recent years, despite fiscal constraints.

Table 1.4 also illustrated the extent to which spending on under fives is concentrated on the older children in that age group, largely reflecting much higher enrolment rates for three-, four- and five-year-olds. Yet, as all chapters have testified, enrolment is rising for younger children. Unless resources are to be redistributed away from three- and four-year-olds, additional funding will have to be found from other government budgets: if spending on ECEC does *not* increase in coming years, it is likely to indicate that quality is falling. At the same time, the pressure of rising demand makes it particularly important to think about how resources can be spent most effectively to promote both quality and equity. We draw together potential lessons here.

A first general question is, does it matter to the effectiveness of the system whether public resources are organised as demand-side funding (that is, following the individual child) or supply-side (direct to the provider)? Demand-side subsidies appear to work well as a tool for encouraging the expansion of places where they are needed, but not necessarily as a tool for improving quality, for reasons discussed earlier in the chapter. Nor are they obviously superior to supply-side funding in promoting parental choice: choice rests on the availability of a range of options, but demand-side funding can, in practice, lead to similar prices and a mediocre level of quality across the board, as the case of the Netherlands illustrates. Demand-side funding may also rule out upfront, income-related fees, and this may be considered a drawback for reasons discussed below. Furthermore, some supply-side support is likely to be essential to making services sustainable in disadvantaged areas, where parental ability to pay fees is lower.

Overall, our findings lead us towards agreement with the OECD (2006, p 114), which argues that 'direct public funding of services brings, in the majority of countries reviewed, more effective control, advantages of scale, better national quality, more effective training for educators and a higher degree of equity in access and participation than consumer subsidy models'. On the other hand, existing demand-side funding systems could be made more sophisticated and effective by incorporating quality supplements of the kind suggested below.

This brings us to the second clear lesson, which is the importance of better integration between funding and regulation mechanisms. There is currently a tendency for governments to use funding mechanisms to improve affordability and regulation to affect quality. But if funding is not linked to the quality of provision, whether on the supply-side or on the demand-side, it limits the incentives (and opportunities) for providers to raise quality, while also risking pricing out lower-income families. Quality supplements that ensure that settings receive higher levels of funding if they employ more qualified staff (for example) are surprisingly rare and seem worthy of much greater policy attention. Such supplements would improve incentives to providers to invest in quality, while enabling parents with less ability to top up state support to opt for higher-quality care.

Third, the cross-country evidence makes a strong case for transparent income-related fees where universal free provision is not possible. In both Norway and France (for under threes), income-related fees operate to facilitate access without making it free to all. If fees reduce to zero for families without income, this also promotes social integration, and may be an effective way to ensure that parents can use early education settings as childcare when they are ready for this. The Norwegian example shows how universal access can be achieved through a system of income-related fees ranging from zero to a nationally enforced maximum cap. Income-related fees are much easier to implement in publicly provided systems, such as France, but the experiences of Norway and Germany suggest that they can also work where private providers are involved. However, as noted, combining transparent income-related fees with demand-side subsidies will at best be complicated and may simply be impossible. Where income-related fees are considered unworkable, countries should consider the Australian example, in which subsidies follow the child but can be paid directly to the provider, rather than as a reimbursement to the parent.

Fourth, there *may* be the potential to keep costs down by trading off different aspects of quality. Depending on a country's starting point, allowing child-to-staff ratios to rise slightly to pay for more highly qualified and better paid staff may be preferable to a system with large numbers of staff with low qualifications. However, any shift should be gradual, conditional on having high-qualified staff in post, and should pay careful attention to the nature of the education that settings are expected to deliver. An optimal service is likely to combine low ratios with a strong graduate presence, as in Norway.

Fifth, where for-profit providers are involved in ECEC delivery, mechanisms are needed to ensure that public resources do not simply boost shareholder profits. In Norway, where half of providers are private but the government pays 85% of childcare costs, fee-capping, combined with tight regulations with regard to staffing, appears to work well. In addition, strong incentives for providers to ensure access for disadvantaged children may be important in order to protect against social segregation, and discourage for-profits from seeking out higher-income parents, particularly in countries with greater social inequality than Norway. These might include higher state subsidies for disadvantaged children; these are used in England, but are currently too small in size to have much effect.

Finally, however, we return to the inescapable point that improving access and raising quality is expensive, and someone has to pay. Most parents are unable to cover anything close to the full cost of high-quality provision, just as they would struggle to afford private schooling at compulsory level. In the Netherlands, employers make a substantial contribution to making childcare affordable, but this may be difficult to implement more widely, and it may also be hard to get Dutch employers to fund improvements in the *quality* of provision on offer. The French system, in which employers pay a general national insurance-type contribution rather than a direct part of employees' individual childcare costs, may be worth pursuing, although this is really just another way of raising taxation. The bottom line is that in nearly all the countries in this study, more public resources are needed to ensure that ECEC provision is both high quality and accessible to all children. This requires political leadership and long-term vision.

Notes

[1] As discussed in Chapter Two, in Northern Ireland provision for three-year-olds is a policy aim but not a guarantee as in other parts of the UK.

[2] As discussed in Chapter Two, policies vary within the UK. Here and throughout this concluding chapter, when we refer to England, we mean that a statement applies to England only, rather than to the whole of the UK.

[3] 'Should pre-school be compulsory?', *The New Zealand Herald*, Friday 21 September 2012.

[4] The possibility of allowing child-to-staff ratios to rise if settings employed more highly qualified staff was put forward by the Coalition government in the UK in 2013, although it was unclear which level of qualification would trigger the higher ratio, and whether the ultimate goal was to improve quality or to reduce the cost of provision and therefore prices for parents (DfE, 2013). The proposal was controversial and had been shelved at the time of writing.

References

Blau, D. and Currie, J. (2006) 'Preschool, day care, and afterschool care: Who's minding the kids?', in E.A. Hanushek and F. Welch (eds) *Handbook of the Economics of Education, Volume 2*, Amsterdam: North Holland, pp 1163–278.

Blau, D. and Mocan, N. (2002) 'The supply of quality in child care centers', *The Review of Economics and Statistics*, vol 84, no 2, pp 483–96.

Cleveland, G. and Krashinsky, M. (2009) 'The nonprofit advantage: Producing quality in thick and thin child care markets', *Journal of Policy Analysis & Management*, vol 28, no 3, pp 440–62.

DfE (Department for Education) (2013) *More Great Childcare – Raising Quality and Giving Parents More Choice*, London: DfE.

Ellingsæter, A.L. and Gulbrandsen, L. (2007) 'Closing the childcare gap: The interaction of childcare provision and mothers' agency in Norway', *Journal of Social Policy*, vol 36, no 4, pp 649–69.

Hirschman, A. (1970) *Exit, Voice, and Loyalty: Responses to Decline in Firms, Organizations, and States*, Cambridge, MA: Harvard University Press.

Kaga, Y., Bennett, J. and Moss, P. (2010) *Caring and Learning Together*, Paris: UNESCO.

Kremer, M. (2007) *How Welfare States Care: Culture, Gender and Parenting in Europe. Changing Welfare States*, Amsterdam: Amsterdam University Press.

Lewis, J., Campbell, M. and Huerta, C. (2008) 'Patterns of paid and unpaid work in Western Europe: Gender, commodification, preferences and the implications for policy', *Journal of European Social Policy*, vol 18, no 1, pp 21–37.

Mahon, R. (2006) 'The OECD and the work/family reconciliation agenda: Competing frames', in J. Lewis (ed) *Children, Changing Families and Welfare States*, Cheltenham and Northampton, MA: Edward Elgar, pp 173–97.

Mathers, S., Sylva, K. and Joshi, H. (2007) *Quality of Childcare Settings in the Millenium Cohort Study*, Research Report SSU/2007/FR/025, Nottingham: Department of Education and Skills.

Mocan, N. (2007) 'Can consumers detect lemons? An empirical investigation of information asymmetry in the market for child care', *Journal of Population Economics*, vol 20, no 4, pp 743–80.

OECD (Organisation for Economic Co-operation and Development) (2006) *Starting Strong II: Early Childhood Education and Care*, Paris: OECD.

Penn, H. (2012) 'Childcare markets: do they work?', in E. Lloyd, and H. Penn (eds) *Childcare Markets*, Bristol: Policy Press, pp 19–42.

Propper, C. (1996) 'Market structure and prices: The responses of hospitals in the UK National Health Service to competition', *Journal of Public Economics*, vol 61, no 3, pp 307-35.

Propper, C., Wilson, D. and Burgess, S. (2006) 'Extending choice in english health care: The implications of the economic evidence', *Journal of Social Policy*, vol 35, pp 537-57.

Saraceno, C. (2011) 'Childcare needs and childcare policies: A multidimensional issue', *Current Sociology*, vol 59, no 1, pp 78–96.

Shager, H.M. (2012) 'What role do peer effects play in early childhood education? Evidence from the 2003 Head Start Family and Child Experiences Survey (Faces), Doctoral dissertation, University of Wisconsin-Madison.

Sosinsky, L.S., Lord, H. and Zigler, E. (2007) 'For-profit/nonprofit differences in center-based child care quality: Results from the National Institute of Child Health and Human Development Study of Early Child Care and Youth Development', *Journal of Applied Developmental Psychology*, vol 28, no 5, pp 390–411.

Sumison, J. (2012) 'ABC Learning and Australian early childhood education and care: a retrospective audit of a radical experiment', in E. Lloyd, and H. Penn (eds) *Childcare Markets*, Bristol: Policy Press, pp 209–26.

Index

Page references for figures, tables and appendices are in *italics*; those for notes are followed by n